A Century of Celebrating Christ

The Diocese of Birmingham, 1905-2005

The statue of Charles Gore, first Bishop of Birmingham, Jubilee 2000 demonstration, 16 May 1998.

A CENTURY OF CELEBRATING CHRIST

The Diocese of Birmingham, 1905-2005

Terry Slater

Phillimore

2005

Published by
PHILLIMORE & CO. LTD
Shopwyke Manor Barn, Chichester, West Sussex, England

© Terry Slater, 2005

ISBN 1 86077 341 9

Printed and bound in Great Britain by
THE CROMWELL PRESS
Trowbridge, Wiltshire

For Primrose, my Mother,
and to the memory of
Richard, my Father.

Contents

List of Illustrations

List of Tables

FOREWORD

by the Bishop of Birmingham
(Archbishop of York Designate)

When I was appointed Bishop for Birmingham in 2002, I realised very quickly that I was moving to the most vibrant and exciting area of the country. The Diocese of Birmingham has a population of nearly 1.5 million people in 292 square miles of the West Midlands region. This year the diocese celebrates its centenary. The Act establishing the diocese was given Royal Assent on 12 January 1905 and its first bishop, Dr Charles Gore, was enthroned on 2 March 1905. The story of the last hundred years is fascinating and important and I realised that it was vital that a book should be written to chart the history of our diocese.

The foundations of the diocese were laid in the 19th century when the West Midlands' economy expanded rapidly. New jobs were being created in the 'City of a Thousand Trades' and new self-confidence manifested itself in commerce, industry and learning. Birmingham and its surrounding towns were centres of religious Nonconformity and Roman Catholicism, as well as Anglicanism but, with the new growth in civic pride in the 1870s, there was a recognition of the importance of Birmingham's independent identity. First, Birmingham became a city in 1889, then there was a desire that there should be a Bishop of Birmingham. Thus, the story of the Diocese of Birmingham begins. However, this book goes back further and gives us glimpses of how the Church came to be established in this region once St Chad had built his cathedral church in Lichfield in the seventh century.

In this excellent history of the diocese, Terry Slater provides a very readable and informative account of the growth of our Christian life together. I cannot think of a better person to have written the book. Terry is Reader in Historical Geography at the University of Birmingham where he has taught for over thirty years. After outstanding service in the diocese, including serving as Chair of the House of Laity for Birmingham Diocesan Synod, he is now a Lay Canon of Birmingham Cathedral, the Church of St Philip, and a lay member of General Synod. Terry has a unique understanding of the diocese and tells a fascinating story. Reading this book helps us all to sense our historical roots and have a stronger sense of identity in the present and hope for the future.

There is also a story here for the wider Church. The Diocese of Birmingham has been in the forefront of showing how the Church can develop the sort of exciting and worthwhile community projects that were encouraged by 'Faith in the City' and the Church Urban Fund; many of our parishes are now demonstrating how we become a more effective multi-ethnic Church; there are exciting developments in youth and children's work, including my own Bishop's Youth Council which enables young people to have a voice at the heart of Church decision-making; and most critically for the future of the wider society in which we live, we have established effective dialogue with other faith communities in the West Midlands. All of us who live in 'Middle Earth' have much to give thanks for. We can now also have greater confidence as we are called to build God's Kingdom of love and justice.

Preface and Acknowledgements

This has been a difficult book to write and compile. An Anglican diocese is a complex entity. At heart it is a collection of parishes with parish priests and congregations (and their church buildings) under the overall leadership of a bishop, trying to work out what being individual Christians, and the People of God collectively, means for them in those places, at those times. Ideally, the history of a diocese should be written from the bottom up; from those individual stories; and the stories of those parish communities. Such a time-consuming enterprise is beyond the capacity of most authors and like most published diocesan histories this one is rather more from the top down, than from the bottom up. It is the story of bishops, archdeacons, fund-raising, buildings and all the other paraphernalia that is required for a modern diocese to operate effectively. I have tried to weave in individual stories where I can, but I am more than aware of gaping holes, missing parishes, saintly individuals even from my own 35 years in the diocese. I can only apologise, but the book is already twice as long as was planned and the centenary celebrations have begun!

One of the things that I have learnt is that the Diocese of Birmingham has forgotten quite a lot of its story. Since it is an interesting and, at times, inspiring story, that is a pity and I hope that this history brings some of our past back in to view. We had the great good fortune to have one of the greatest theologians and most holy men of the early 20th century as our first bishop. He got Birmingham noticed and his successors have been almost equally notable personalities. A lot of things have been, and are being, worked out in the melting pot of this city, its suburbs and the surrounding countryside: evangelists; great missions; building communities; training the laity; renewal; new church structures; building a Black, White and Asian Church; meeting with other faith communities; giving responsibility to young people – all these themes and more find a place in the pages which follow.

I must say straight away that probably half of the book is compilation as much as writing. I am enormously indebted to a large number of people for writing so eloquently, and often at very short notice, about some of the things about which I knew very little. Some of them have made me laugh out loud, and some of them have moved me to tears with their stories. It has been a privilege to act as editor for these contributions. There is much more than I could use, and on some matters I was sworn to secrecy, so the writer of the bi-centenary history will need to consult my archives!

Acknowledgements are necessarily lengthy. First and foremost I must thank historian Roy Peacock. On hearing of the centenary history volume he immediately placed his article on the complex schemes and negotiations leading up to the formation of the diocese at my disposal; an act of great generosity. Chapter Five is almost entirely his work, whilst more of his material is found in the education chapter. Secondly, I have been able to draw on the work of biographers of no fewer than four bishops of Birmingham (Gore, Barnes, Wilson and Montefiore) as well as Hugh Montefiore's autobiographical volume. Thirdly, I am extremely grateful for the time and trouble taken by a whole bench of bishops to reply to my enquiries. ☦Mark Green, ☦Michael Whinney, ☦Colin Buchanan, ☦Mark Santer, and ☦John Austin have all written extensively on their time in office in Birmingham. ☦Christopher Hill (Guildford), ☦Stephen Platten (Wakefield) and RC Archbishop Kevin McDonald all replied courteously to requests for information on ARCIC. Lord Hunt of Kings Heath, David Ritchie, ☦John Austin, Canon Marlene Parsons, Canon John Wesson, Ven. John Duncan, Ven. John Barton, and Revd David Newsome all provided information which enabled a rounded picture of ☦Mark Santer's episcopacy to be drawn.

I am indebted to Jean Jepson for providing from her extensive archives and long memory material on the history of St Martin's-in-the-Bullring and Canon Brian Green. Yvonne Hadley provided material on Smethwick Old Church, Canon Michael Blood on Cotteridge church, Revd Keith Claringbull on Hampton-in-Arden, and J.B. Hall on St Michael's, Gospel Lane. Anthony Collins, Canon David McInnes, ☦Michael Whinney, George Tuck, Sue Rawlings, Revd Sally Davies and Graham Hopkinson provided material which enabled the story of renewal and evangelism since the 1960s to be pieced together. Ven. John Duncan provided valuable information on the university chaplaincy and Ven. John Barton and Canon Michael Blood on diocesan communications.

The Dean, the Very Revd Gordon Mursell, has been a tower of strength in Chairing the Centenary Committee, of which I was privileged to be a member, as well as providing information and publications on the cathedral. Michael Delany, the cathedral Administrator, showed me round the hidden corners of the building and dug out the few documents and photographs that are not in the archives. Revd Andrew Gorham, Bishop's Chaplain, has similarly offered much support and information and enabled access to Bishop's Croft to photograph the episcopal portraits. Canon John Wilkinson provided me with the electronic text of his 1993 book *Church in Black and White*, and has allowed me to quote extensively from it, whilst Canon David Collyer sent me a copy of his book *Double Zero*, again with permission to quote extensively, two more acts of great generosity. Dr Mukti Barton shared with me some of the written and verbal responses in workshops she led with Black and Asian Anglicans in the diocese and which will form part of her book on this theme, *Rejection, Resistance and Resurrection*, to be published later this year by Darton, Longman & Todd. I am especially grateful to Revd Elsada Watson for taking the time to share some of her experiences as a Black minister with me whilst she was seriously ill.

Dr Roy Massey, Beresford King-Smith, Marcus Huxley, and Professor Colin Timms contributed to the chapter on organs and choirs, the first-named very substantively. Blair Kessler provided information on St Basil's and Revd Les Milner whilst ☦John Austin has allowed me to quote from his funeral oration on the life of Canon Roger Hooker. Claire Laland, Jennifer Owen and Valerie Hamley provided illustrations and history on the Mothers' Union and other topics, and Canon Marlene Parsons provided information on women's ministry. Revd Chris Feak, Robin Rolls, Juli Wills, Marjorie Carnelley (née Freeman), Revd Nora Sanders, Muriel Graveley and Jeanne Shaw all contributed to the chapter on children's and youth work, whilst Rachel Jepson allowed me to use material in her MA thesis on 19th-century Sunday Schools. Canon Dr Brian Russell helped to coordinate these responses as well as providing a paper on Birmingham's multi-ethnic church, from which he allowed me to draw material. His secretary, Pam Rhodes, has worked in the diocesan office longer than almost anyone and has been a mine of information.

The Ven. Dr David Lee provided me with a copy of his lecture on Dale and Dawson and has allowed me to quote from it; Hugh Carslake, the Diocesan Registrar provided material from his archives. I am grateful to Professor Hugh McLeod for providing bibliographical leads on the social history of religion, a topic that is much more his than mine. Dr Michael Gilman's PhD thesis was invaluable in tracing the development of church building in the 20th century. Dr Ian Gregory of Queen's University, Belfast provided help with the medieval base maps; Tim Clayton provided assistance above and beyond the call of duty with the diocesan GIS and his electronic archive of church photographs. The illustrations in the book would have been much thinner if Jessica Foster had not allowed me free access to her filing cabinets in the Diocesan Communications Office. I am grateful to Ann Ankcorn for drafting the maps for publication; and to Geoff Dowling ARPS for photographic work, again above and beyond the call of duty. I am especially grateful to Jenny Harris in the Birmingham Diocesan Office for distributing vast numbers of letters to possible contributors. Edwin Green has generously allowed me to use the atmospheric drawings of churches by his late father, W.A. Green, in the early part of this book, and I am most grateful to Alastair Carew-Cox for allowing us to use his photograph of the Burne-Jones 'Last Judgement' window in the cathedral for the cover of the book. My most sincere apologies if I have left anyone out – because I probably have! As always, Noel Osborne and the staff at Phillimore & Co Ltd have been unfailingly helpful and have been a pleasure to work with in making this book happen. They did not even shout at me when it turned out to be twice as long as contracted for! It seems appropriate to finish on the day the diocese really began one hundred years ago.

TERRY R. SLATER

The Feast of St Chad, 2005

Illustration Acknowledgements

The author and publishers are grateful to the following for the use of illustrative material. John Barnes and William Collins Sons & Co.: 47; Yvonne Bell: 80; Jackie Dewsbury: 135, 141; Geoffrey Dowling: 19, 40-2, 44-5, 49, 52, 61; Nick Gerrard: 139; Dr Michael Gilman: 97; Edwin W. Green: 7, 9, 11-2, 15-7, 101-2; Kevin Gulliver and Brewin Books: 115-7; Graham Hopkinson: 140; Jean Jepson: 91-2, 130-4; Rachel Jepson: 126-7; The Revd Rob Johnson: 98, 112, 157; Claire Laland: 118-20, 122, 124; The Ven David Lee: 142; Roy McKay and Hodder & Stoughton: 51; John Peart-Binns and Anthony Blond publishers: 54, 58, 6-, 79; Anthony Slater: 48, 81-3; Canon John Wilkinson: 153-4; Paul Wrobel and the Sparkhill Project: 149; Birmingham & Warwickshire Archaeological Society: 13-4, 18, 32; Birmingham Cathedral: 37, 39, 71-2, 74-8; 80; CBSO: 84; Diocese of Birmingham: 50-1, 53, 55-9, 62-7, 69, 89, 93, 95, 106-8, 110-1, 113-4, 121, 123, 125, 128-9, 136-8, 146-48; 155, 158; St Agnes, Moseley PCC: 46, 68, 85, 109; St Mary's, Hampton-in-Arden PCC: 33, 43, 104; School of Geography, Earth, & Environmental Sciences, University of Birmingham: 20-3, 25, 27-8, 34, 70, 73, The Hub, Hazelwell: 150; The Ordnance Survey via Dotted Eyes (Licence no. 100002215) for data in 1, 2, 88, 94, 105. The author: 3-5, 24, 26, 35, 36, 103, 115, 143-5, 151.

The Diocese of Birmingham in 2005

I The Secular City and Region

The West Midlands is one of the most strategic and exciting regions in Europe. It is the heart of Britain's manufacturing economy and at the centre of its transport infrastructure. Its rapidly changing employment patterns and dynamic social and cultural mix provide early pointers to wider changes in Britain generally. As Britain's second city, Birmingham has led the way in positioning itself as a key node in the European cities network and works closely with the leaders of its many city-twinning partnerships.

The Diocese is primarily urban. It encompasses the whole of the City of Birmingham and the urban parts of the Metropolitan Borough of Solihull; the majority of the Borough of North Warwickshire (which is mostly rural and contains former coal-mining communities); the Warley district of the Metropolitan Borough of Sandwell; and a small number of rural West Midlands' Green Belt parishes to the south, within the administrative areas of Stratford-on-Avon, Warwick, and Bromsgrove District Councils.

The West Midlands economy has largely recovered from the traumas of the 1980s and the economic collapse of the motor-car industry on which so much of the regional economy once depended. Unemployment rates are now close to the national average in the majority of the region, though not in inner-city and outer-estate Birmingham, Chelmsley Wood in Solihull, or in Warley. The region remains the manufacturing heartland of the UK economy. Motor-car production remains a significant sector, with factories in Castle Bromwich and Solihull. The recent closure of Rover's Longbridge factory has, however, revived memories of the dark days of the 1980s. To this has now been added a strong professional services sector, to the extent that Birmingham is now the second strongest location for financial service industries outside London. The National Exhibition Centre and International Convention Centre mean that the region is easily the most important exhibition and convention location in Britain, and is the third largest centre in Europe. Business tourism is consequently a major sector of the local economy. Birmingham is home to three universities and a number of FE Colleges so that education is another major 'industry', which brings large numbers of young people to the region from elsewhere in Britain, and from overseas.

Birmingham city centre has been subject to 15 years of redevelopment, which is still continuing, and which has transformed the physical environment. This includes the civic spaces of Centenary and Victoria Squares; the mixed use (office, retail, hotel and residential) 'Brindleyplace', and the redevelopment of Broad Street for the entertainment industry, which brings thousands of young people into the city centre

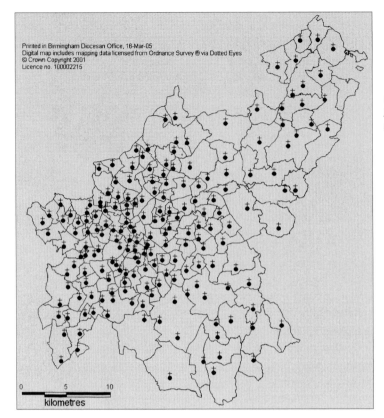

Printed in Birmingham Diocesan Office, 18-Mar-05
Digital map includes mapping data licensed from Ordnance Survey ® via Dotted Eyes
© Crown Copyright 2001
Licence no. 100002215

0   5   10
kilometres

1   *The Diocese of Birmingham: Parishes, churches and worship centres.*

every evening. The huge new Bullring shopping centre, with its iconic Selfridges store, opened in 2003, and the exclusive 'Mailbox', have transformed the retail sector of the city. The 'Millennium Point' museum/educational/cinema complex is planned to be the focus for the transformation of the east side of the city centre with creative industries and new education and library facilities. Retail development has also been a recent feature of the town centre of Solihull such that it has become an important sub-regional shopping destination.

The West Midlands is a major hub in the national motorway and rail networks. 'Spaghetti Junction' is one of the less desirable, but nonetheless effective, symbols of the region. In the past Birmingham was also the centre of the canal network and a decade of refurbishment has given Britain's most inland city a prize-winning waterfront! Birmingham International Airport is growing rapidly and has daily flights to European business cities, holiday destinations, to Newark in the USA, and the Middle East. The first Metro tram line (Birmingham-Wolverhampton) opened in 2000 and plans are in place for further lines, including one across the city centre.

Housing, Inner City and Outer Estates

A majority of current city-centre developments have high-status apartment housing as a major focus. However, the glitz of the city centre of Birmingham must not be allowed to obscure the grinding poverty and deprivation of Birmingham's inner city. The inner ring of slum housing was redeveloped with system-built high-rise developments in the late 1950s and '60s. Some of these tower blocks have already

Printed in Birmingham Diocesan Office, 16-Mar-05
Digital map includes mapping data licensed from Ordnance Survey ® via Dotted Eyes
© Crown Copyright 2001
Licence no. 100002215

2　*The Diocese of Birmingham:*
Deaneries and Archdeaconries.
The shading shows the built-up
areas of the diocese.

been demolished and replaced, and there are plans for more to be so. These areas (Newtown, Highgate, Sparkbrook, and the like) are amongst the top five per cent most-deprived urban districts anywhere in Britain. Beyond them is a broad belt of late 19th-century terraced houses, which are privately owned, or privately rented. These areas have high minority ethnic populations and many of them also have well above average deprivation levels. On the outer fringes of the city, and in the Chelmsley Wood district of Solihull, very large estates of local-authority housing were built in the 1960s and '70s, again with tower blocks. These estates are also often marked by high unemployment, long-term sickness, skills deficits, and other markers of deprivation. Warley, in Sandwell MB, is also failing to attract new investment or additional resources and many communities are increasingly disheartened. Mention must also be made of the former coal-mining villages of North Warwickshire where there are also pockets of deprivation.

Mid-20th-century housing in Birmingham is almost equally divided between very large low-density local authority housing estates and privately-owned, speculatively-built housing zones of semi-detached dwellings. Birmingham's economy was prosperous in the inter-war period and many people could afford to purchase their own homes. Experimental concrete houses in the local authority estates have required total rebuilding in the past decade, as in Pype Hayes, whilst on other estates a high proportion of houses were transferred to private ownership in the 1980s. Beyond Birmingham's then borders, Sutton Coldfield, Shirley and Solihull were expanding rapidly as the professional classes used commuter rail services and good road networks

3 *One of the most distinctive 'temples of commerce' in Birmingham city centre is the Selfridges store in the Bullring development opened in 2003.*

to escape the city. Municipal parks, linear natural zones along the local rivers and the huge country parks at Sutton and Lickey, ensure that the conurbation remains 'green' in most of its parts and Birmingham supposedly has more trees than any other city in Europe!

Minority Ethnic Population

Birmingham has the greatest variety of minority ethnic communities of any city outside London. Minority ethnic populations also characterise the eastern portion of Sandwell. Irish and West Indian migrants to the city predominated in the 1950s, south Asians from Pakistan, Kashmir, India and Bangladesh in the 1960s and '70s, together with a large number of the Asians expelled from Uganda. There are significant Yemeni, Somali and Chinese communities as well, together with numerous smaller ethnic groups. Most of these communities were geographically concentrated at first into particular parts of the 19th-century terrace housing ring. Subsequently, they have begun to disperse outwards into better housing areas. Most ethnic communities are now well into their second generation of British-born family members, and some into their third. There is also a significant mixed-race population in the region. In total, the minority ethnic communities constituted 29.6 per cent of Birmingham's population in 2001 and 10.3 per cent of Sandwell's. The largest groups in Birmingham are those of Pakistani (10.6 per cent), Indian (5.7 per cent) and Caribbean (4.9 per cent) descent. In Sandwell those of Indian descent dominate the Asian fraction of the population (9.1 per cent). They are overwhelmingly young people and in some inner-city districts 50 per cent of the population are under 25 years old. Some schools, including some Anglican schools, have rolls where up to 90 per cent of children are from the minority ethnic communities. Solihull and North Warwickshire are overwhelmingly White with only 5.4 per cent and 1.4 per cent respectively of their total population from minority ethnic groups.

Other Faiths

Islam is easily the largest of the other faith communities in the region and large mosques now mark almost all of the main radial roads in Birmingham. There are large numbers of smaller house mosques and madrassas in the inner-ring housing areas. Some 14.3 per cent of Birmingham's residents declared themselves to be Muslim in 2001 and 4.6 per cent of Sandwell's population. There are sizeable Hindu

4 *The municipal Castle Vale estate was built on a former airfield in the 1960s. It was marked by a group of high-rise towers. They have now all been demolished and the whole estate significantly remodelled.*

communities in these two areas and one of Europe's foremost Sikh communities, especially in Smethwick, many occupying former churches and chapels as gurdwaras and temples (6.9 per cent of Sandwell's population were Sikh in 2001 and 2.9 per cent of Birmingham's population). The spectacular new gurdwara prominently located beside the Soho Road in Handsworth is the largest in Europe. There are a number of Buddhist groups in Birmingham with two temples of national significance, and there are long-established Jewish communities of both Orthodox and Reformed persuasions.

II THE DIOCESE OF BIRMINGHAM: FACTS AND FIGURES

The Diocese of Birmingham is the second smallest in area (294 sq ml), twelfth most populous (1,386,997), and third most densely populated (4,903 persons per sq ml) of the 43 dioceses of the Church of England (excluding the Diocese of Europe).

Parishes and Clergy

The diocese has 155 benefices, 163 parishes, and 195 churches and multi-use worship centres. There are some 177 full-time stipendiary parochial clergy when all are in post giving a ratio of 1.11 per parish (the fifth highest diocesan ratio), and 0.13 clergy per 1000 of population (the lowest ratio of any diocese). There are 65 women clergy in the diocese, of whom 12 are of incumbent status; nearly half of the assistant curates (15 out of 36) are women. There are 183 active Readers in the diocese and a further 41 over 70 years of age with permission to officiate. There are seven parishes which have petitioned the bishop for Extended Episcopal Oversight, and a further 13 parishes who have signed Resolutions A and/or B with regard to women's ministry. There are five Team Ministries (Erdington, Hodge Hill, Kings Norton, Shirley, and Solihull) and two Groups (Handsworth and Smethwick) with many more (15) under consideration. The diocesan report *Together in Ministry and Mission* (1996) (TIMM) recommended that team working should become the norm in the diocese. To this end parishes were 'clustered' with neighbours and new Groups and Teams have begun to form from some of these clusters. There are some 18,200 people on the Electoral Rolls of the parishes in the Diocese and a 'usual Sunday attendance' of some 14,000 adults and 3000 children and young people. The most recent statistics suggest that continuing decline in these statistics has ended and some modest growth has characterised the last three years.

Dignitaries, Cathedral and Offices

The diocese has a Suffragan Bishop of Aston (Rt Revd John Austin); two Archdeaconries (Birmingham and Aston); and 13 Deaneries. The parish church Cathedral of St Philip is a small, 18th-century, Grade I listed building of considerable art-historical importance as it contains the Pre-Raphaelite stained-glass masterpieces designed by Burne-Jones and produced by William Morris. It stands at the very heart of Birmingham where the retail, office and administrative quarters of the city meet. Its recently-renovated churchyard is an important city-centre open space.

The late 18th-century See house (Bishop's Croft) is in the western Birmingham suburb of Harborne and contains the bishop's staff offices and domestic chaplain's flat, as well as the bishop's domestic quarters. It is adjacent to the modern (1960s) Diocesan Office building, which is owned by the Diocesan Board of Finance, and which houses the Diocesan Secretary, his staff, and the offices of the Diocesan Boards and Forums of Education, Mission, Ministries and Social Responsibility, and of the suffragan bishop and archdeacons.

Education and Theological Resources

The diocese has 51 church schools spread across four local education authorities, of which 27 are Aided and 24 are Controlled. All but two are junior/infant schools. The Diocesan Education Department was also responsible for launching an innovative 'Post-16 Centre' in inner-city Newtown which occupies the premises of a former church secondary school. In partnership with FE and other providers, the Centre enables 'Curriculum 2000' courses, vocational courses, and Adult Education to be provided in a deprived area and provides a valuable local community resource. The city's three universities have full- or part-time chaplains resourced by the diocese.

The University of Birmingham has a theology department of international excellence with library resources to match. The nearby United Selly Oak Colleges of the mission societies recently merged their operations with the University of Birmingham. The Queen's Foundation for Ecumenical Theological Education (Queen's College) is close to the University of Birmingham campus in Edgbaston and provides ministerial training for Anglicans, Methodists and the URC as well as the part-time 'West Midlands Ministerial Training Course'.

Ecumenical Relations

There are ten Local Ecumenical Projects or Sharing Agreements in the diocese, and three Covenants. Nine are Anglican-Methodist, two Anglican-URC, one Anglican-

Methodist-URC, and one Anglican-Baptist-Roman Catholic. 'Birmingham Churches Together' works effectively across the Christian Churches in the region. It employs a Secretary and issues a bi-monthly newsletter. Industrial chaplaincy is also organised on an ecumenical basis. Relationships with the Roman Catholic Church are important since Birmingham is the centre of a Catholic Archdiocese. The present Archbishop (Most Revd Vincent Nicholls) has established a more vigorous ecumenical dialogue than we have had in the past. There is a large, long-established Irish Catholic population in Birmingham, now widely dispersed across the city.

Finances

Birmingham congregations are amongst the poorest in the country with average incomes of only a little over £10,000. It is all the more remarkable that the weekly average tax-efficient planned-giving by congregations is £8.50, a figure exceeded in only five other dioceses. Similarly, the average direct giving per week per Electoral Roll member (£5.03) is exceeded only by London, Southwell, and Guildford (the latter by a single penny!).

5　*The Diocesan Office, Harborne.*

The diocesan report *Financing Ministry and Mission* (1998) laid the foundations of the current 'parish share' formula and made other important financial recommendations which have all been implemented. Parochial Common Fund allocations have had an average of 97 per cent payment each year for the past five years.

The 2003 diocesan accounts showed a total income of £7.246 million. £5.303 million of this is generated from parochial Common Fund contributions and fees. Glebe and investment income accounts for only £599,000 of income. Church Commissioners contributions have been critical in keeping Common Fund contribution increases within reasonable bounds over the past five years. Expenditure in 2003 was £7.282 million, of which £5.810 million was accounted by clergy stipends, housing and pension contributions. £582,000 was spent on the work of diocesan boards and committees, and only £282,000 on administration.

Administrative Structures

The administrative structures of the diocese are streamlined and centralised since Birmingham has, of financial necessity, the slimmest administrative team of all dioceses. The Diocesan Synod meets three times a year and the Bishop's Council five or six times a year, often including one residential meeting. The Bishop's Council is also the Diocesan Board of Finance and the Diocesan Pastoral Committee. This enables it to understand the financial and pastoral effects of its decision-making. The Board of Finance is a charitable company limited by guarantee, and the Bishop's Council is its board of directors. Agendas of Bishop's Council meetings are necessarily carefully divided into its three constituent modes of operation. Detailed discussions and the devising of reports for decision-making are devolved to a Finance, Investment and Property Subcommittee (FIPS), a Pastoral Subcommittee, and a Grants, Loans, & Review Subcommittee. There are also the statutory Diocesan Advisory Committee, Board for Education, and the Diocesan Trustees. There are newly-constituted Forums for Ministries, Mission, and Social Responsibility.

Part One

BEFORE THE DIOCESE

2

Faith and Churches
in the Medieval Period

This section of the book explores the churches, parishes and people of the area before the diocese of Birmingham was formed. It is about rural communities rather than urban, and being at the edge of things rather than the centre. The area that was eventually to become the diocese of Birmingham was a poor land. It consisted of two flat-topped upland areas. One, the Birmingham Plateau made up of clayey mudstones and sandstone topped with glacially deposited sands and gravels; the other, the East Warwickshire Plateau, a narrower ridge formed from Coal Measures sandstones and the narrow band of coal itself. Neither plateau had good agricultural soils so these were areas of plentiful woodland, open heaths, and pastureland for raising animals rather than growing corn. Farmers who settled here could make a living, but it was never a very good living and opportunities for alternative income were always welcome, one of which was digging the coal. The plateaux were dissected by the valleys of five or six small fast-flowing streams – the Rea, Tame, Cole, Blythe and Anker in particular, that all flow north to join the River Trent beyond Tamworth.

The poverty of the region meant that this was not only marginal land economically, but also politically. The region emerged in the early medieval period divided between two kingdoms, and therefore two dioceses, and then subsequently, in the 11th century, it was divided between three counties. But perhaps we should start briefly with later Roman times and note that two great Roman highways passed through the western and eastern margins of our area: Watling Street (still the A5 road today) crosses north Warwickshire, south of Tamworth, and Ryknield Street crosses the present northern suburbs of Birmingham (a section remains visible in Sutton Park). There was an early Roman fortress at Edgbaston (under the University medical school), a pagan temple on the hilltop at Coleshill, and there were small towns on Watling Street just beyond the later diocese at Mancetter, and at Wall, a few miles south of Lichfield. The latter was important because we know that there was a late-Roman Christian community there. Some of that community's successors lost their lives in a great battle with incoming Anglo-Saxons in the Dark Ages of the sixth century. But there were survivors who kept the faith alive and almost certainly that was why St Chad, in the year 664, decided to establish his church at Lichfield as he came to evangelise the Anglo-Saxon kingdom of Mercia. It may be that the church of St Michael, in the southern suburbs of Lichfield, still stands on the site of the church of that early Christian community. However, there were also pagan communities a few miles to the south at Wednesbury and Weoley where the place-names suggest that Woden, the Saxon god of war, was being worshipped.

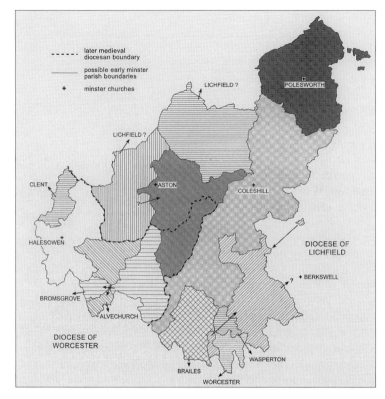

6 *The early minster parishes of the diocesan region. Much of the region looked to minsters beyond the area in the seventh to ninth centuries but Aston, Coleshill, Halesowen and Polesworth had been established by this period.*

In the same way as around Lichfield, to the south-west, in the Severn valley, another kingdom, that of the Hwiccan people, also gained a seventh-century bishop who established his seat at St Peter's cathedral minster at Worcester, where there had been another late-Roman group of Christians. We think that the little church of St Helen's, just to the north of the cathedral, was established on the site of their church. So, by the later seventh century there were bishops, cathedrals and dioceses centred on Lichfield and Worcester. The majority of the later Birmingham diocese looked to Lichfield, only a few Worcestershire parishes to the south-west of Birmingham looked to Worcester, and so it was to remain for the next thousand years.

Early medieval minsters

When sees had been established for the Anglo-Saxon kingdoms the next task for the bishops was to send out missionary priests to convert the pagan people of those kingdoms. Once a Christian community had been established, a church was built and a small group of priests living in community used it as the base for further missionary effort. These early medieval churches are usually called minster churches, *monasteria*, in Latin documents of the time. Minster churches can be recognised today because they had, and often still have, much larger than average parishes; they often have numbers of subsidiary chapels which only became independent parishes much later on; they have priests recorded in Domesday Book; and the churches have distinct dedications and plan forms. The favoured dedications for early minsters were to SS Peter and Paul (reflecting the primary missionary efforts of these apostles in founding the early Church), to St Peter alone (especially in the Hwiccan kingdom) or to St Mary, but others acquired dedications to Anglo-Saxon saints, especially those connected to the royal household of Mercia. Many of these churches had a cruciform plan when they came to be rebuilt in stone after the Conquest.

Examples of early medieval minster churches that were to be encompassed within Birmingham diocese include SS Peter and Paul, Aston, and SS Peter and Paul Coleshill. Aston retained the characteristics of a minster until the 19th century. It had a large parish that encompassed Bordesley, Erdington, Ward End, Castle Bromwich and Water Orton. Chapels were erected in most of these places to provide the local population with Sunday services (licence to rebuild the chapel at Water Orton is documented in 1346) but they remained dependent on Aston. Yardley was also originally part of Aston's minster parish, though it was later in a different county (Skipp 1970). The minster parish of Coleshill included Lea Marston and Over and Nether Whitacre chapelries and possibly the later proprietary parish churches of Maxstoke and Shustoke and the latter's chapel at Bentley. There was an even larger minster parish in the Worcestershire part of Birmingham where the whole district of north Worcestershire

7 *SS Peter and Paul, Coleshill minster church (E.W. Green). It was largely rebuilt in the 14th century and heavily restored in 1859 but it contains a fine Norman font.*

looked to St John the Baptist, Bromsgrove. Bromsgrove's huge parish reached as far towards Birmingham as Balsall Heath. As in Aston, other churches were built to serve settlements including the fine church at Kings Norton and another at Moseley (where the chapel was built in 1405), but Kings Norton chapel did not become a separate parish until 1848 and Moseley not until 1853.

To the north-west the picture is more complicated (i.e. there is less evidence!). This group of parishes, formerly in Staffordshire, was possibly centred on St Peter's Harborne. Harborne had chapels at Smethwick, West Bromwich and Edgbaston but the church is oddly sited at the edge of this territory (Bassett 2002). An alternative is that this whole area was originally served from the cathedral minster at Lichfield and that Harborne and St Mary's, Handsworth represent a second phase of missionary activity. Beyond Harborne was the Worcestershire minster parish of Halesowen stretching up to Oldbury, whilst Rowley Regis was a chapel of the minster at Clent. Birmingham may once have belonged either to the Harborne grouping, or to Aston but, when first documented, it was already an independent parish with burial rights. It has recently been suggested that the circular churchyard of St Martin's is reminiscent of those of early Celtic churches in the South West and along the Welsh Marches (Hodder 2004), so it may be that Birmingham's parish church was always independent of the Anglo-Saxon minsters. Two other possible minster churches are St Mary's Hampton-in-Arden, where there was a priest at Domesday and a large parish with later chapels

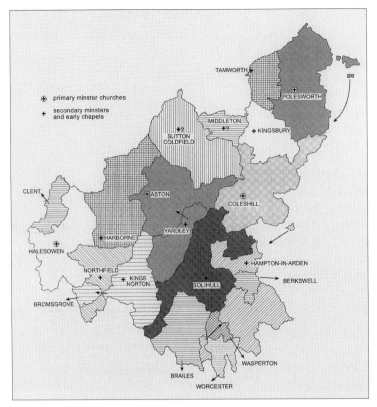

8 *The later-Saxon minster parishes of the diocesan region. By the 10th or 11th centuries more minsters and chapels had been founded.*

at Temple Balsall, Knowle and Nuthurst, and SS Peter & Paul Kingsbury which also had a large parish and a suggestive dedication. However, this church may have been founded on the royal manor of Kingsbury as an early daughter church of Coleshill, sharing its dedication.

Polesworth, Solihull and Yardley are of interest for their Anglo-Saxon dedications. Yardley is one of those churches dedicated to an Anglo-Saxon royal saint, Eadburga, the daughter of King Edward the Elder. She spent her life as a nun serving in the minsters of Winchester and Pershore in the 10th century, and it was to Pershore that Yardley church belonged by the 11th century. This is why Yardley was in Worcestershire and part of Worcester diocese, despite the fact that it had been part of Aston's minster parish. It took 70 years of lawsuits in the 14th century to sort out the various jurisdictions and confirm Yardley as a separate parish (Skipp 1970). Our other Anglo-Saxon royal saint is Eadburga's older sister, Editha. She had been married off to Sithric, the Danish king of Northumbria, who had promised to become a Christian. It seems he quickly tired of both his new wife and his new faith and she returned to Mercia and the ancient nunnery at Polesworth where the miracles that took place at her tomb led to the rededication of the church in her name. Tradition says that Polesworth nunnery had been founded by the Irish Celtic saint, Modwenna, in the seventh century, from an earlier-founded Celtic church at Burton-on-Trent in Staffordshire. Polesworth might therefore be amongst the oldest Christian sites in the diocese. Editha's residence there in the 10th century probably represents its refoundation as a Benedictine nunnery after the troubled times of the Danish invasions in the ninth century, but it was almost certainly another of the early minsters since its parish was extensive. St Editha, in her turn, founded a church in Tamworth that bears her name and, much later, when Amington church was built in 1864 it, too, took name from its mother church at Tamworth. Why the parish church of Solihull should be dedicated to the martyred 11th-century Archbishop of Canterbury, Alphege, no-one has been able to determine. Solihull was a very large medieval parish, however, and at Domesday it was linked with Sheldon to the north. Bickenhill, its outlier at Olton, and Elmdon intermesh with these parishes and together may have formed another minster centred on Solihull, but there is no proof of this.

The pattern of church provision in this Arden area of Warwickshire is made more complex by the way in which the farming economy worked. This was a region of wood-pasture and many blocks of land were held by estates located far to the south in the arable Feldon district of south Warwickshire beyond the River Avon. Consequently, when parishes were being formed based on these estates the detached woodland or wood-pasture holdings were regarded as part of the central estate. The most spectacular example is Tanworth-in-Arden which was a chapelry of Brailes,

9 *SS Peter and Paul, Aston minster church (E.W. Green). Only the 15th-century tower and spire survive from the medieval period. The remainder of Aston church was rebuilt in 1879-90.*

20 miles to the south, whilst Packwood belonged to Wasperton in the Avon valley. On a more local scale, Bentley was the former woodland of, and therefore became a chapelry of, Shustoke, and Nuthurst belonged with Hampton-in-Arden for the same reason, though it had earlier belonged to the church at Worcester.

After the Norman Conquest many existing churches were rebuilt in fashionable Romanesque styles whilst large numbers of new churches were founded by Norman lords on their newly-acquired estates. These churches were proprietary, that is they belonged to the lord, who consequently had the right and obligation to provide a priest to serve the church. It was these new estate churches which filled in the parochial topography in the 12th and 13th centuries. St Matthew's, Shuttington with its nave of *c.*1150 is a good example, whilst at All Saints, Seckington the 13th-century stonework of the church is rather later than the impressive motte and bailey castle of the new Norman lord which stands beside it. These north Warwickshire parishes were all derived from Polesworth minster parish. St Laurence, Northfield is another church that was rebuilt by its lord in the 13th century. The manor, centred on Weoley Castle, belonged to the Earls of Dudley but the church was probably planted much earlier from the bishop of Worcester's minster at Alvechurch. Both Alvechurch and Northfield are dedicated to St Laurence, whilst Cofton Hackett, which was certainly part of Alvechurch's lands throughout the medieval period, was a chapelry of Northfield. Northfield church has a 12th-century Romanesque doorway but most

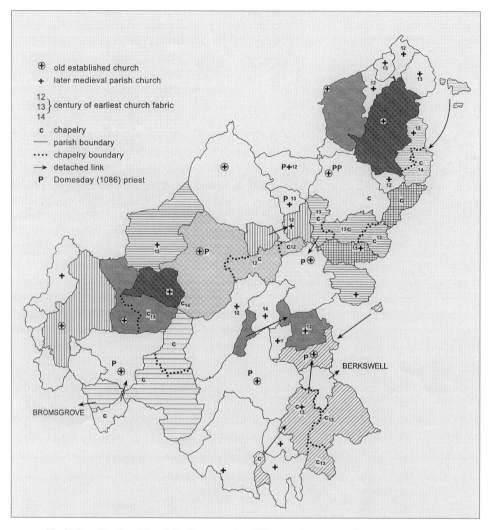

10 *The high medieval parishes of the diocesan region. This map gives some indication of how the medieval parishes were formed out of the earlier minsters, whilst the age of the building fabric suggests when this might have happened.*

of the church was re-built in the 13th century. The valuable rectorial rights of many of these churches, such as their tithes, were often granted away to monasteries by the next generation of lords and the monastery then provided a vicar or curate on a small stipend. In north Warwickshire, for example, the Norman lord of many of the manors there, Osbert de Arden, granted all his churches to the Priory of Markyate, in Bedfordshire.

Later medieval monasteries

There were very few monastic institutions in the area of the later diocese and, what there were, were all in what is now Polesworth Deanery. The only Benedictine monastery was the little priory of Alvecote in Seckington parish. It was founded by the lord of Seckington, William Burdet, in 1159, supposedly as an act of expiation for

11 *St Laurence's, Northfield parish church (E.W. Green). Northfield has the finest 13th-century chancel in Warwickshire and a Norman doorway.*

12 *St Matthew's, Seckington parish church (E.W. Green) is a typical manorial church in north Warwickshire. The tower and spire are early 13th-century.*

stabbing his wife to death on his return from the crusades, having wrongly believed that she had been unfaithful to him. The churches of Seckington and Shuttington were given to Great Malvern Priory on condition that they built a cell at Alvecote and staffed it with monks from Malvern. It remained a very small monastery until the Dissolution. Also Benedictine was the abbey for nuns at Polesworth whose antiquity has already been discussed. It was a much wealthier institution than Alvecote as it had many benefactors in the 12th and 13th centuries. It seems always to have been

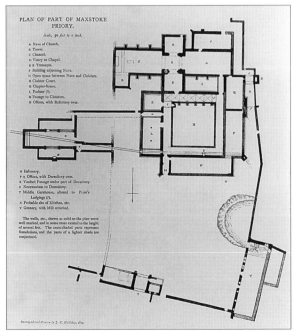

13 *Plan of Maxstoke Priory, surveyed in 1874.*

14 *Maxstoke Priory gatehouse.*

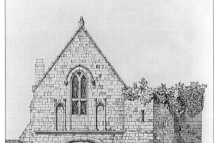

16 *St Nicholas, Kings Norton (E.W. Green) was founded as a Norman chapel of Bromsgrove. The beautiful 15th-century tower and spire and its setting amidst timber-framed buildings around a 'village green' makes it perhaps the most picturesque medieval church in the diocese.*

15 *The church of the Knights Templar, Temple Balsall (E.W. Green). The large chapel of the preceptory became the parish church of Temple Balsall. It was largely rebuilt in 1849 by Sir G. Gilbert Scott.*

17 *Knowle parish church and guildhall (E.W. Green). Knowle was rebuilt in 1397-99 and became a collegiate church in 1416. The 15th-century guild house was the headquarters of an important trade guild.*

held in high regard and there are none of the salacious stories associated with some other nunneries. It provided employment for lay people in the village, the nuns looked after the old and the sick, and they provided education for the daughters of neighbouring lords. There were a dozen nuns at the Dissolution of the abbey in 1539 under their abbess, Dame Alice Fitzherbert. The abbey at Merevale was Cistercian and was founded by Robert, Earl Ferrers. The monks came from Bordesley Abbey. The abbey held quite extensive lands in Leicestershire and Derbyshire, as well as in the vicinity of the abbey itself, including properties and the market in Atherstone, but it fell on hard times at the end of the 13th century. Nonetheless, at the Dissolution it was valued at £254 1s 8d, a considerable sum. Polesworth was worth only £87 16s 3d, for example. Finally there was the Austin Priory of Maxstoke founded by Sir William de Clinton in 1337. He originally intended to found a college but changed his mind and founded the priory for a prior and 12 canons. It was well-endowed and is very fully documented. When John Grene was prior (1432-50) more than £300 was spent on improving the buildings whilst several visits of 'minstrels, jesters and players' are recorded to entertain the canons and the workers on the estate. It was valued at £130 13s 7d at the Dissolution (Page 1908).

There were two other religious institutions in the south. First was the Preceptory of the Knights Templar at Temple Balsall, where the chapel still stands. The manor was granted to the Templars at the end of the 12th century by Roger Mowbray and was suppressed, with the rest of the Order, in 1308. The manor was returned to the Mowbrays by the king, but was then given to the Knights Hospitaller in 1322 in compliance with a papal ordinance. It was usually governed in conjunction with the Preceptory at Grafton, near Warwick, and there were rarely more than six or seven men in residence. The founding of the other institution, the Collegiate church at Knowle, is very fully recorded. We have seen that Knowle was merely a chapelry of Hampton-in-Arden and so it remained until the end of the 14th century. In 1397-99, Walter Cook, a canon of Lincoln cathedral and native of Knowle, rebuilt the church on a very grand scale, including a tower with bells. He also enclosed a churchyard, provided the endowment for a priest, and gained an episcopal licence for baptisms, marriages and burial to take place there, making it in effect an independent parish. In 1402, Walter, and his father Adam, established a chantry of two priests there and in 1413, Walter and a group of other men and their wives established a guild of St Anne. Finally, in November 1416, they gained royal permission to found a college of 10 chantry priests in honour of St John the Baptist, St Laurence and St Anne. Though 10 priests were specified, it seems that the college never had more than six at any one time. Nonetheless, it meant that in the 15th century Knowle was probably the best endowed church within the later area of Birmingham diocese and membership of the guild became extremely popular amongst ordinary trading folk in Warwickshire. The college was dissolved in the 1540s together with other institutions of this kind (Page 1908).

3

Reformation, Roman Catholics
and Dissenters

Henry VIII's Dissolution of the Monasteries probably had little effect on the church-going people of our area except in Polesworth. However, the dissolution of the guilds and chantries by Edward VI in the 1540s had much more direct consequences since the chantry priests normally assisted parish priests in their duties, which was especially important in the very large parishes of much of north Warwickshire. So we hear that the parson at Sheldon would have been unable to cope without the help of the chantry priest there in times of sickness in the parish. In Tanworth's large parish the commissioners responsible for dissolution were told by 'divers honest persons' that, if it were not for the two chantry priests there, 'many would perish in times of sickness without any ministration', whilst at Solihull they were told that the chantry had been founded 'to helpe the parson in ministering sacraments' to the 700 communicants. Birmingham was just beginning to develop new industries that was to see it begin its exponential growth and, in the town, the Holy Cross guild provided 'divers poor people with bread, drink and coals and buried them very honestly'. There was a population of 2,000 in the parish of St Martin's and even with the assistance of the two guild priests the rector found it hard to minister effectively. Across the River Rea, Aston provided a chaplain for Deritend chapel where there were a further 200 people living. One consequence of the suppression of the guild in Birmingham, as in many other towns, was the founding of King Edward's School. The Act of Suppression allowed that any school supported by a guild could continue in being supported by lands to the value of £20. The Holy Cross guild did not support a school but its lay members petitioned the king to be able to found one anew. Thanks to the support of the Earl of Northumberland, who was lord of the manor, the king agreed so, thanks to the quick-wittedness and opportunism of Birmingham's citizens, the town established its new grammar school from the wreckage of the guild whose building in New Street it occupied.

In pursuit of church wealth Edward also required inventories of all church goods and from these we discover that our churches were poorly endowed with valuable ornaments. Coleshill church had one of only two organs in Warwickshire and we learn that Shuttington church had had its chalice stolen. At Grendon, parishioners sold one of their bells for the practical purpose of building a new bridge on the highway. In Halesowen a new chapel was built at Oldbury in 1529 'because of the floods in winter' preventing attendance at the parish church (Page 1908).

Papists and Puritans

As Catholic Queen Mary succeeded Edward, and she in turn was succeeded by Protestant Queen Elizabeth, it was a dangerous time to be alive. Both bishops in Lichfield and Worcester were deprived of their bishoprics by Elizabeth and many clergy were ejected from their benefices, including those at Curdworth and Shustoke. Sometimes there were long vacancies (four years at Bickenhill, for example). However, north Warwickshire was to remain a major centre of people who refused to give up their Catholic faith, led by families such as the Throckmortons of Coughton and the Middletons of

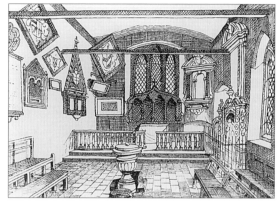

18   *Chancel of St Edburga, Yardley sketched by Allen Everitt in the 1860s before restoration showing its 17th- and 18th-century furnishings.*

Edgbaston. A list of recusants (people who did not attend Holy Communion in the parish church), made in 1592 because of the fear of Spanish invasion, shows that there were many ordinary people too who refused to give up their old faith. There were 23 in Solihull and Knowle, 24 in Tanworth and others in Sheldon and Birmingham. At Coleshill there was Humphrey Hawes, 'an old massing priest and obstinate papist', who was committed to Warwick gaol as a consequence.

Other clergy and lay people were heading in the other direction, towards Puritan beliefs. In 1609, Archbishop Bancroft held a metropolitan visitation in Lichfield diocese to enquire of churchwardens whether ministers made the sign of the cross at baptism, whether they wore the surplice when saying public prayers, and whether they 'duly observe all the Orders, Rites, and Ceremonies prescribed in the said Book of Common Prayer'. They also had to present all 'non-kneelers' at Holy Communion. It is interesting to see that the Church of England has always had problems with clergy discipline!

In 1641 Parliament abolished the office of bishop and made use of the Anglican Prayer Book, even in the home, punishable by imprisonment. Presbyterianism became the official state religion and clergy who refused to conform to the new rules were ejected from their livings. Thomas Baker, the rector of Baxterley, for example, was turned out of the rectory and his young child in its cradle was deposited 'on a dunghill'. The ministers of Birmingham and Solihull were amongst those who became 'Covenanters' a few years later,

19   *Job Marston's Chapel, in Yardley's large ancient parish, now The Ascension, Hall Green, is one of a number of new brick-built Georgian churches in the diocese.*

though the minister at St Martins-in-the-Bullring, Samuel Wills, was reported to be 'sedate, quiet, peaceable and able'. The minister at Moseley chapel in the later 1650s was a famous Nonconformist divine, Samuel Shaw. By the 1650s Anglicans, Roman Catholics, Unitarians and especially Quakers were being actively persecuted with fines and imprisonment, especially for refusing to swear oaths of allegiance. Poor John Ludford of Hurley was fined 10 shillings in 1659 for refusing to swear in the manor court of Kingsbury, and 40 shillings the following year for the same offence. Elsewhere poor ministers were given grants from the estates of the cathedrals, so the minister at Nether Whitacre got a grant of £50 in 1651 to supplement his meagre stipend of £20 a year.

Following the Restoration of the king in 1660, new bishops had to be appointed to the sees of Lichfield and Worcester since their previous occupants had both died during the Commonwealth. Clergy and people were then faced with new oaths of allegiance to the restored Church of England. Nonconformity was tolerated but licences had to be obtained for 'assemblies' and preaching by ministers so we know that Birmingham and north Warwickshire's later reputation for Nonconformity was already well established. There were Presbyterian ministers in Birmingham, Balsall Heath, Coleshill, Kingsbury, Merevale, Nether Whitacre and Sutton Coldfield, and Congregationalists in Birmingham, too. Indeed, in 1666-68 and again in 1672-74, Richard Moore, a Nonconformist minister, had licence to preach in the Anglican chapel at Wythall, and Oldbury chapel was served by Nonconformist ministers for a time. However, the 1676 religious census ordered by Henry Compton, Bishop of London, suggests that conforming Anglicans were very much in the majority. Within the later diocesan area there were 13,314 'conformists', 320 'papists', and 348 'nonconformists' (Table 3.1). It is interesting to note that the 'usual Sunday attendance' of adult Anglicans in the diocese in 2004 is almost the same as it was 300 years ago in 1670!

One of the most notable parish priests of the later 17th century was John Kettlewell. He was a tutor at Lincoln College, Oxford for five years before his ordination in 1677 and, after publishing the first of several books, was presented to be Vicar of Coleshill by Lord Digby in 1682. He preached regularly to his parishioners every Sunday and on feast days, celebrated Holy Communion regularly, fasted on Fridays and in Lent, supplied Bibles to the poor and 'was most assiduous in visiting the sick'. All things which the vast majority of country clergy did not do at this time. He was deprived of his living in 1690 for refusing the new oath of allegiance to William III and retired to London.

New churches

New churches were being added to the medieval stock in the 17th and early 18th centuries, some of them provided by the private patronage of the laity. Thus, Job Marston provided the money in his will to build a chapel at Hall Green in Yardley parish in 1703, which for long was known as Job Marston's chapel (it is now The Ascension, Hall Green). In 1719, Dorothy Parkes, who was the daughter and heir of Thomas Parkes, a gunsmith from Birmingham, settled lands in Smethwick and Halesowen on trustees who were to build and furnish a chapel on part of the Smethwick property within three years of her death. They were to provide bread and wine for communion, appoint the minister, who was to be a graduate and was not to hold any other ecclesiastical or teaching post, and his stipend was to be the residue of

Parish	Conformists	Papists	Nonconformists	Total
Ansley	214		3	217
Arley	50			50
Astley	147		2	149
Aston and hamlets	1446	13	45	1504
Austrey	238		9	247
Baddesley Ensor	45		8	53
Baxterley	57		5	62
Bickenhill	279	2	1	282
Birmingham	2582	11	30	2623
Cofton Hackett	38			38
Coleshill	253	1	14	268
Curdworth	216		13	229
Elmdon	56	1		57
Grendon	173		18	191
Halesowen	554	3	4	561
Hampton in Arden	1020	26	9	1055
Handsworth	500	101	1	602
Kings Norton	1058	19	5	1082
Kingsbury	236		6	242
Knowle	239	13		252
Lapworth	91	1	3	95
Lea Marston	63	2		65
Merevale	58		3	61
Middleton	407		3	410
Nether Whitacre	122	4	9	135
Northfield	300	6	3	309
Over Whitacre	54			54
Polesworth	500	7	22	529
Seckington	48			48
Sheldon	206		12	218
Shustoke and Bentley	107			107
Shuttington	66		12	78
Solihull	733	73	26	832
Sutton Coldfield	500	3	50	553
Tanworth in Arden	400	30	16	446
Wishaw	104		6	110
Yardley	154	4	10	168
Total	13,314	320	348	13982

Table 3.1 The Compton Census, 1676 for the parishes later in Birmingham Diocese

the income from the property after payment of £10 in charitable doles. Her will of 1723 confirmed the settlement and Smethwick Old Church was built in 1732 as a chapel of Harborne.

Other new churches of the early 18th century included St Swithin, Barston, built in 1721 as a chapel of Berkswell; the chapel at Castle Bromwich which was largely rebuilt in 1726-31; St Leonard's, Over Whitacre, built in 1766; St Bartholomew's, Edgbaston, which was rebuilt as a result of the extensive damage caused by Civil War

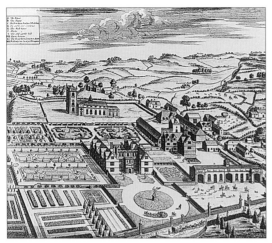

20 *Castle Bromwich Hall and church, 1733. The timber-framed chapel at Castle Bromwich was totally encased in brick in the early 18th century. It is a classic 'estate church' beside the intricate walled gardens of Castle Bromwich Hall.*

21 *St Martin's-in-the-Bullring, 1731. This composite engraving of map, plan and drawing accompanied J.T. Bunce's address to the first meeting of the Birmingham and Warwickshire Archaeological Society in 1870.*

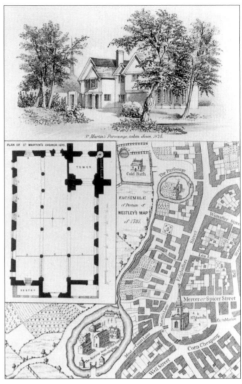

skirmishes that took place there; and St Martin's-in-the-Bullring, which was encased in brick in 1690 because the medieval stonework was in poor repair. It was also raised in height and filled with galleries to increase its capacity. The interior of St Michael's, Maxstoke is another church notable for its Georgian re-fitting which survived the Victorian mania for 'restoration'. However it was in Birmingham that the greatest number of new churches was built in the 18th century.

New churches were needed because the population of the town was increasing rapidly. In 1660 there were probably around 6,000 people living in Birmingham; by 1760 the population was around 35,000 people, and at the first census in 1801 it was nearly 70,000. Church building began with a new parish church, St Philip's, at the heart of the middle-class housing development on the northern edge of the developing town, built in 1709-15, of which more later (chapter 15). St John's chapel in Deritend was rebuilt in 1735 and a tower added thirty years later, whilst the new chapel of St Bartholomew's in the eastern part of St Martin's parish was built in 1749 on a plot of land gifted by the ironmaster John Jennens. St Mary's, in Whittall Street (with a distinctive octagonal plan) followed in 1774 thanks to generous donations of land and money from Mary Weaman, and St Paul's, at the heart of the Colmore estate, in 1777-79. These churches added new pew spaces (normally referred to as kneelings) for the growing population of the city, but only for those who could afford to pay; most of the free seats were reserved for children from charity schools at the main services. Christ Church, Colmore Row was built in 1805 specifically to provide free accommodation to all.

Bells also began to ring out over the town. A peal of eight bells was hung in the tower of St Philip's in 1727, but they had to be recast and increased to 12 in 1754.

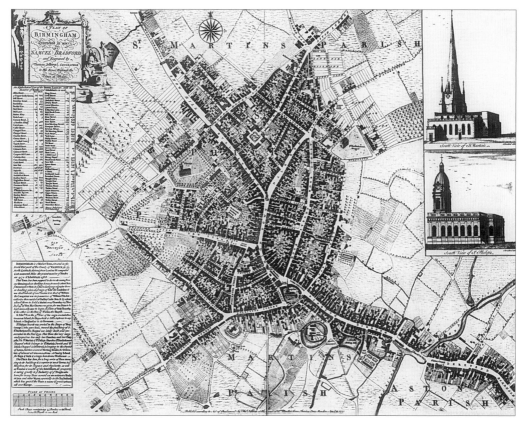

22 *Bradford's plan of Birmingham, 1750. The town was beginning to expand rapidly. There were four Anglican churches: St Martin's, its chapel of St Bartholomew's built the previous year, St Philip's, and St John's chapel, Deritend, in Aston parish.*

What the new church had the old church should have too, and so a peal of 12 bells was added to the venerable tower of St Martin's soon afterwards. There was also a peal of eight in St John's chapel, Deritend added in 1777 (Gill 1952). There were also less edifying consequences of the growth of population in 18th-century Birmingham, notably the problem of burying the dead in St Martin's tiny churchyard. As burial followed burial the ground rose and had to be contained by walls. William Hutton noted appositely, 'the dead are raised up, and instead of the church burying the dead, the dead would in time, have buried the church'! The opening of churchyards attached to St Philip's and the new chapels relieved the problem only for a short while and by the early 19th century containing walls were being built to contain these graveyards too (Buteaux 2003).

The challenge of Methodism

John Wesley visited Birmingham many times on his preaching circuits in the mid-18th century, beginning in 1743 when he had 'a small attentive congregation'. In the following years he found the town a 'barren, dry, uncomfortable place' but in 1761 he was still hoping that the Gospel would take root 'even in this barren soil'. The mid-1760s found his meetings being attacked by the mob, with stones and dirt being flung at congregations, but the rioters were contained by the magistrates. A

23 *St Martin's-in-the-Bullring encased in brick. This undated engraving shows St Martin's after a new brick skin had been added in 1690.*

24 *St Paul's, Birmingham. Built in 1777-79 to the designs of Roger Eykyns for the developing Newhall estate of the Colmore family, which was to become the heart of the Jewellery Quarter.*

visit in March 1772 was marked by snow 'mid-leg deep in all the streets' but the congregation still filled the meeting room at five in the morning! This was the normal mid-week time for his preaching so that people could then go on to work. By 1788, Wesley estimated his regular congregation at over 800 in Birmingham and the following year he was able to open a 'new house' or chapel in the town. These new Methodist nonconformists, together with older established groups and the Roman Catholics, were to become the hate-filled focus of three terrible days of rioting in Birmingham in 1791, the so-called 'Church and King' riots. Their cause was the tension between Anglicans and nonconformists over the latter group's attempts to repeal the Corporation and Test Laws so that they could play a fuller part in society. The laws prevented nonconformists participating in higher education, the law, and Parliament.

Discussions, sermons and pamphlets began to be produced in the late 1780s by the nonconformist leaders in Birmingham. They in turn produced sermons attacking the whole idea of repealing the Acts from the pulpits of St Martin's and St Philip's with George Croft, the lecturer at St Martin's, being especially virulent, warning that 'while their meeting-houses are open they are weakening and almost demolishing the whole fabric of Christianity' (Stephens 1964). The spark for the riots was a dinner to celebrate the French Revolution which enabled a mob to be whipped into a fury by

25 *Late 18th-century chapels and churches: A. 1. St Paul's (1777-9) 2. St Mary's (1774) 3. St Bartholomew's (1749); B. 1. Holy Trinity, Camp Hill (1820-22) 2. St John's, Deritend (1735) 3. St James's, Ashted (a converted house!).*

pamphlets and speeches. They destroyed the two Dissenting chapels in Birmingham and then went to Digbeth to attack the home of Joseph Priestley, Unitarian, scientist and Lunar Society member; the mansion houses of a number of prominent landowners to the south of the town were subsequently set on fire, before the military arrived from Nottingham to quell the rioters.

4

HIGH CHURCH AND LOW CHURCH
IN THE NINETEENTH CENTURY

Birmingham's religious history in the 19th century is usually couched in terms of Nonconformist and Evangelical zeal. Unitarian and Independent preaching of the 'Civic Gospel' in mid-century is the dominating theme, with an important substratum formed by the group of Quaker industrialists who played an important part in the town's economy and politics. Roman Catholicism also has an important story to tell through the second half of the 19th century as the town became one of the major centres for the revival of that denomination. One of the seven new churches provided after Catholic emancipation, St Chad's, became in 1848 the first Roman Catholic cathedral in Britain since the Reformation. Equally significant was St Mary's College at Oscott where John Henry Newman came soon after his conversion, before moving to St Philip's Oratory on the Hagley Road. It was also the place where the Gothic Revival architect, A.W.N. Pugin, amassed both an important library and a museum of Gothic artefacts. By contrast, it is easy to see the Anglican story as backward-looking and ineffective and the emergence of the new diocese in 1905 as really rather a surprise, but this would be unfair.

The 70,000 people that the 1801 census showed to be living in Birmingham were still largely crammed into the area of the medieval parish. This had been accomplished through the process of building tiny ramshackle cottages over the back gardens of the older properties of the early modern town, so that people were living cheek-by-jowl with their neighbours, and by building new houses on the fields surrounding the town at very high densities. These new houses were 10-12 feet square, three storeys high, and were built in terraces, back-to-back with others, in long narrow courtyards. The courtyards contained the 'brewhouse' for heating water and washing clothes and two

26 *Birmingham back-to-backs. These are typical three-storey, back-to-back 'front houses' built in the 1820-40 period in Birmingham's inner housing zone. The central wooden door on the right led into a courtyard with more back-to-backs around it.*

or three earth privies (toilets), which were shared by all the inhabitants of the court, who might number as many as 80-100 people. Water still came from the public wells that had supplied the medieval town, which became more and more polluted. For a large number of Birmingham's industrial population life was 'nasty, brutish and short' with a very high proportion of new-born babies failing to survive to their first birthday and an equally large number of children failing to reach their fifth birthday. The town was still governed by systems more suited to a country village, which is exactly what they had been designed for, and increasing numbers of those who were making money from the workshops of the town were moving to its ever-moving fringe; first to the Colmore estate to the north and, from the 1820s, to Edgbaston where Lord Calthorpe had begun leasing land for building superior houses (Slater 2002).

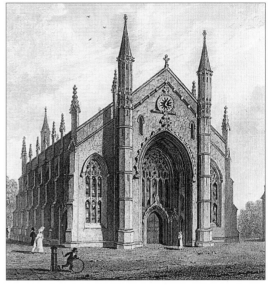

27   *Holy Trinity, Camp Hill was built in 1820-22 as a 'Commissioners' church' to the designs of Francis Goodwin. Though now redundant it still stands prominently beside the city ring road.*

More new churches

The Church of England added new churches to the outer edges of the rapidly growing town in the expectation that they would soon be surrounded by new housing; an expectation that always proved true. Nine churches were added before 1830 and a further dozen by 1867, whilst many more were enlarged or received additional gallery space. Some of these churches were provided through funds from the 'Commissioners for the Provision of New Churches', which followed the Church Building Act of 1818. Many of these early 19th-century churches have been subsequently demolished, of course, as Birmingham continued its remorseless outward expansion. One of the most notable to survive, though no longer as a faith community, is Holy Trinity, Camp Hill, a Commissioners' church built in 1820-2 to designs by Francis Goodwin and an early example of Regency Gothic architecture. After redundancy it became the Boot Night Shelter and still stands rather forlornly beside a busy traffic island. St Thomas's, Bath Row was another of the new churches, designed by Thomas Rickman in 1826-9, but it was destroyed by Second World War bombing, apart from its fine Neo-Classical façade, which now forms the background for the Peace Garden. The Lichfield Diocesan Church Extension Fund (founded by Bishop Ryder of Lichfield) provided another Birmingham church as its first project. It stood in Gem Street, and was consecrated in 1838 as Bishop Ryder Memorial Church, but was demolished in 1960. In 1838 the Birmingham Church Building Society was founded to provide ten new churches in the rural deanery of Birmingham. The first to be built was St Matthew's, Nechells in 1839-40. It has been able to survive as an active congregation thanks to an imaginative multi-use scheme for the building devised in the 1980s. The Society failed to raise sufficient money to undertake its plans in full and only another four churches were completed, using such poor materials that most had to

Registration District	% sittings	% attendances	% churches
Birmingham	43.8	46.0	25.7
Aston	58.7	50.4	35.3
Atherstone	59.1	57.0	44.1
Bromsgrove	60.6	59.9	36.6
Dudley	37.4	24.3	16.2
Kings Norton	62.3	61.9	35.3
Meriden	84.6	76.3	60.0
Solihull	87.6	88.0	72.0
Tamworth	73.2	74.5	56.8
West Brom.	42.5	37.0	26.0

Table 4.1 The Church of England in the 1851 Census of Religion: Percentage Share Measures

be subsequently rebuilt. St Luke's, Bristol Street, for example, was consecrated in 1842 but it was condemned as unsafe and demolished and rebuilt in 1899, whilst St Andrew's, Bordesley was seriously damaged in a storm in 1894 which saw the removal of its spire and considerable rebuilding over the next decade. St Mark's and St Stephen's, New Town, also had to be partly rebuilt at the turn of the century and have subsequently been demolished.

The Birmingham Church Extension Society, which operated from 1865-1905, was similarly hampered in its activities by lack of finance. Over 40 years it spent only £60,500. Most of this money was spent on grants to help purchase sites for new churches and to help with building costs, but it did not cover the whole cost of building. Some 32 churches were assisted in this way. The 1860s, when the Society was formed, was the peak decade in the 19th century for new Anglican church buildings in Birmingham, partly because, thereafter, mission chapels and mission rooms began to suffice. These were cheap, adaptable and could be abandoned if they lost their initial congregation. Some, of course, were successful and were replaced with permanent church buildings and were assigned parish districts. St Agnes, Moseley, for example, began life in such a mission hall in 1878, which was replaced by the first half of its present church building in 1884. The mission hall was then sold to St Bartholomew's Edgbaston for its mission to the Pershore Road area of the parish in 1886. It gained another successful congregation and was replaced by the church of SS Mary and Ambrose in 1897-8 whilst the 'tin tabernacle' mission hall still stands beside the church as its church hall. Rather good value from a structure that cost only £100 in 1878! (Slater 1984).

Beyond Birmingham itself, many new churches and new parishes were being created in the surrounding villages by the middle of the 19th century, especially where railway lines were aiding the development of suburban housing for the professional classes. Thus Holy Trinity, Lickey was formed from Bromsgrove in 1858; St Mary's Wythall from Kings Norton in 1853; All Saints, Kings Heath, again from Kings Norton in 1863, and Christ Church, Yardley Wood, from Yardley in 1849. In Sutton Coldfield new parishes were created at St John's, Walmley in 1846, St Michael's, Boldmere in 1857, and St James', Hill in 1853. There were seven new parishes formed from Halesowen in the 19th century, five of which were to become part of Birmingham diocese, including Christ Church, Quinton, created in 1841 (the church was built in that year too) and Langley, created in 1846 and divided again in 1890. Finally, new churches were needed in north Warwickshire as the coalfield was developed. Thus a church was provided for Hurley, in Kingsbury parish, in 1861; Warton (1849) and Dordon (1864) were created from Polesworth, and St Editha's, Amington was built in 1864.

The Religious Census of 1851 provides us with information about church and chapel attendance and church provision on Mothering Sunday that year. Within Birmingham's borough boundary there were some 54 chapels compared with 25 Anglican churches, which together provided seats for 61,554 people, just over 25 per cent of the population. Analysis of the attendance figures suggests that about 36 per cent

28 (right) Early 19th-century Birmingham churches. 1. St Peter's, Dale End (1825-27) 2. St George's, Newtown (1820-23) 3. Christ Church, New Street (1814) 4. St Thomas's, Bath Row (1826-29).

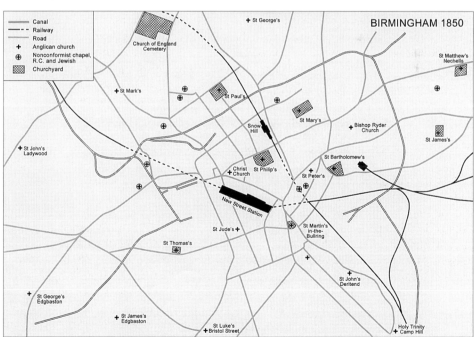

29 Birmingham's churches in 1850. Anglicans built many new churches in central Birmingham but they provided for only a fraction of the rapidly growing population.

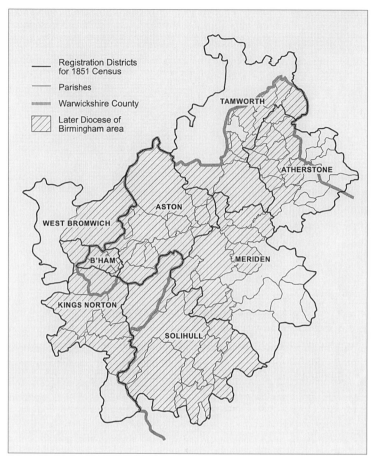

Registration Districts
for 1851 Census

Parishes

Warwickshire County

Later Diocese of
Birmingham area

TAMWORTH

ATHERSTONE

ASTON

WEST BROMWICH

B'HAM

MERIDEN

KINGS NORTON

SOLIHULL

30 *Census Registration Districts 1851. This map shows the allocation of parishes to Registration Districts used for the 1851 Religious Census (see Tables 4.1 and 4.2).*

of the population went to a service that day, rather better than in Manchester or Sheffield, but much worse than in Leeds and Liverpool. Despite their much larger number of buildings only 47 per cent of these attenders were Nonconformists, about one third of whom (some 10,700) were Methodists. Baptists and Congregationalists mustered between 6-7,000 worshippers each, Unitarians and Roman Catholics 3,000

Registration District	Av of Popln/ Anglican Ch.	Av Sittings/ Anglican Ch.	Sittings as % of population	Attendances as % of population
Birmingham	9,663.9	1,322	13.7	17.7
Aston	3,932.5	678	17.2	16.2
Atherstone	763.2	348	45.6	46.2
Bromsgrove	1654.8	450	27.2	35.1
Dudley	5918.3	1,026	17.3	16.3
Kings Norton	2,572.5	465	18.1	19.2
Meriden	751.1	359	47.8	23.5
Solihull	662.8	338	51.0	38.4
Tamworth	666.4	308	46.2	42.9
West Brom	3,873.8	723	18.7	18.9

Table 4.2 The Church of England in the 1851 Census of Religion: Church Size and Attendances

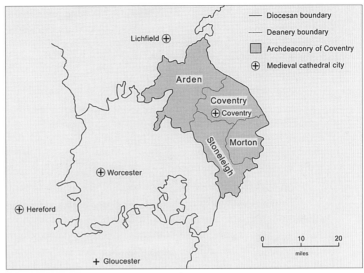

31 *Diocesan changes in 1836. The Archdeaconry of Coventry was transferred from Lichfield to Worcester in 1836.*

each, Quakers and Presbyterians some 700 each. The Church of England was by far the largest denomination with nearly 31,000 worshippers, representing nearly half of all churchgoers in the borough and, as such, was one of the few large industrial towns in which Anglicanism was numerically as strong as Dissent (Skipp 1983). Beyond Birmingham, suburban and country parishes came much closer to reflecting the national average pattern of church attendance with some 75 per cent being Anglican, though there were notable 'chapel' communities in the north Warwickshire coalfield and in Smethwick and Warley.

The first half of the 19th century also marks the point at which the Church of England began to reorganise itself administratively after the deliberations of a Royal Commission on the Established Church. In 1836 the archdeaconry of Coventry, part of the ancient diocese of Lichfield, was transferred to Worcester diocese so as to reduce the enormous size of Lichfield. This still left Lichfield nearly twice the size of Worcester in terms of administrative area and removed Birmingham itself from the edge of one diocese to the edge of another! However, for the first time, almost the whole area of the later diocese of Birmingham came under a single bishop. In 1853, the old Lichfield rural deanery of Arden was subdivided into four: Birmingham, Coleshill, Polesworth and Solihull, and in 1859 Sutton Coldfield was created as a fifth rural deanery. There was some debate about creating other new dioceses in the middle of the century, including a diocese for Warwickshire with its cathedral at Coventry, but no further action was taken (see chapter 5).

The Civic Gospel

The middle of the 19th century saw Birmingham being transformed into 'the best-governed city in the world' and Birmingham's church leaders played a significant part in that transformation. It also continued to grow rapidly in terms of its population from some 170,000 in 1841 to 522,000 in 1901. Change began to come after 1838 when the town was incorporated as a borough, slowly at first, whilst local politicians and the business classes found their feet. But in the 1850s the 'Civic Gospel' was born. This was a movement of thought and action *from* the pulpits *into* the civic arena:

politics was to become a part of the Christian mission. However, it was a group of four Nonconformist ministers, rather than Anglican clergy, who stood out in helping shape this vision for Birmingham:

- George Dawson, the theologically untrained prophet who blazed the trail, whose Birmingham ministry began in 1844
- Charles Vince, the minister who took over from Dawson at Mount Zion Baptist chapel, whose 26-year Birmingham ministry began in 1847 and who was described as the best-loved of all the ministers of the time
- Dr Robert Dale, minister at Carrs Lane Congregational church, whose Birmingham ministry began in 1854, and
- Dr Henry Crosskey, minister at the Unitarian Church of the Messiah, whose Birmingham ministry began 1869.

Though none of these men was Anglican, it is important to understand their influence on the faith community in Birmingham since many of the leading industrialists and politicians were members of their congregations. Unitarian families such as the Chamberlains, Kenricks, Martineaus and Nettlefolds held the mayoralty of the town almost continuously from 1840-1880. John Bright, Joseph Sturge and the Bakers, Cadburys, Lloyds and Taylors were Quakers who, besides running many of the leading commercial enterprises in the town, also involved themselves in social enterprises to improve the lot of the poor or oppressed, including the anti-slavery campaign, whilst the Dixons and the Rylands represented Anglicanism in this pantheon.

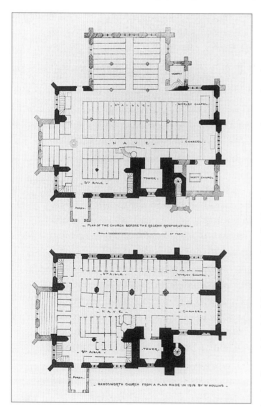

32 *Enlarging St Mary's, Handsworth. Like many village churches St Mary's was enlarged as it became suburban. In 1820 the number of pews was doubled and there were galleries as well. The Watt chapel was added to house Chantrey's celebrated statue of the engineer.*

George Dawson arrived in Birmingham in August 1844 and immediately threw himself into local affairs. You did not cross swords with Dawson lightly: he was pugnacious, articulate, and passionate. He was 'the greatest talker in England' (Dale 1909: 90) and 'his opinions provoked fierce prejudice and antagonism'. It is interesting that he was never ordained and was known as *Mr* Dawson throughout his life. In 1844, Dawson was invited to 'preach on trial' at Mount Zion Baptist Chapel in Graham Street (now demolished). Within two months, Dawson's preaching was so appreciated that he was invited to remain as pastor, and so he began his brief ministry in Birmingham as a Baptist preacher.

Dawson was a free-thinking rationalist who dismissed the Biblical portrait of Jesus the Son of God who died for us, and attacked the Evangelical tradition which looked back to the revivals of Wesley and Whitfield. Dawson satirised those whose devotion to the Saviour was marked by what that person did *not* do, rather than what a person *did*. Instead, Dawson pleaded that 'the day is coming when we must carry out the religion of Jesus Christ ... we must cease to hear about religion having nothing to do with politics ... Learn to trace [God] in the world's daily history ... watch the signs of the times, that ye may help on the cause of truth in the earth' (Dawson 1844:12). Not surprisingly, within 18 months he was asked to leave the Baptist church. A group of some 2,000 friends were so impressed with his ministry that they built a new chapel for him, the Church of the Saviour, Edmund Street, which opened in 1847 (now demolished). The church was based on three principles:

   (i)   no pledge should be required of minister or congregation
   (ii)   no form of theological belief should be implied by membership
   (iii)   difference of creed should be no bar to union in practical Christianity
           (Dale 1909: 81).

33 *Restoring St Mary's, Hampton-in-Arden 1878. An unusual photograph of a Victorian church 'restoration' in progress under the direction of architect Eden Nesfield who had just completed Hampton Manor House and its estate cottages.*

For 29 years (1847-76) Dawson ministered to a unique nonconformist congregation in Birmingham which drew on Christian vision and values in a freethinking and rationalist kind of way, but did not require people or minister publicly to believe any of them! This mix of freedom and passionate commitment influenced many Birmingham leaders, including Robert Dale and Joseph Chamberlain. Dawson firmly believed that he was one of a group introducing a new kind of Christian religion – 'practical Christianity' – which was a simple, universal religion which appealed to all good and clear thinking men, unfettered by creeds and doctrinal debates.

Robert Dale also played a significant part in the development of the 'Civic Gospel' in Birmingham, and as a formally-trained theologian he sought to keep more of the Christian tradition in play in his contribution. Dale was born in London but in 1847 he went to the Congregational Spring Hill College, in Moseley, to train for the ministry. Dale studied theology for six years, during which his preaching prowess grew, as did his interest in theology and politics. As a student, Dale 'helped out' at Carrs Lane and in 1853 he became the 'assistant preacher' at the prestigious Carrs Lane Church whose congregation had been built up by Revd John Angel James, the minister there since 1804. James's book, *The Anxious Enquirer*, had a readership in the 19th century that was only exceeded by the Bible and *Pilgrim's Progress*. When James died in 1859, Dale was welcomed as the sole pastor into a pulpit he would occupy until his death. Dale displayed 'eloquence and forceful massive presence'(James 1990: 16) as he preached Sunday by Sunday to 'throngs of shop assistants' and 'rows of gentle youth and maidens'(Driver 1948: 59). The congregation grew steadily until it was the largest in the town with over 1,000 members. Finally, H.W. Crosskey, the Unitarian minister, was especially influential in the passionate debates about education which dominated mid-century Birmingham (chapter 18).

Though the contributions of Anglicans to the religious, cultural, social and political progress of Birmingham as a town were not quite so spectacular as those of Nonconformists, Anglican clergy played their part. The Evangelical Dr J.C. Miller

34 *Christ Church, Birmingham stood where Victoria Square was later to be created. It was a chapel of St Philip's catering for the poorer classes since there were no pew rents. The engraving was published in 1829.*

was Rector of St Martin's for more than 30 years until his death in 1880 and his political liberalism allowed for an unfashionable ecumenical respect towards his Nonconformist neighbours. Good relationships with the Nonconformist churches seems to have been a feature of Birmingham through most of the 19th and into the 20th centuries. Both Miller and Grantham Yorke, the Rector of St Philip's, were concerned about contemporary society and anxious that it should be established on firm Christian principles. Miller began to revive the practice of open-air preaching as a way of reaching working people and wrote a number of pamphlets in the late 1850s. In one he noted that the Church must get alongside working men: 'We must go among them; we must improve their dwellings; we must provide them the means not only of mental self-improvement, but of physical recreation' (Miller 1854). Miller founded a Working Men's Association at St Martin's in 1854 and organised a group of men as missionaries to their neighbours (Mole 1975).

Yorke made his contributions especially to the educational debate. His interest ranged from the colleges at Queen's and Saltley and King Edward's to parochial elementary schools and the ragged schools for the poor (chapter 18); whilst Revd J.C. Barrett, who was minister at St Mary's for nearly half a century from 1837, drew large congregations to that church with his preaching. Barrett, and Revd G.S. Bull first at St Matthew's Duddeston (1840-47), and then at St Thomas's (1847-64), also led the way in providing large numbers of free seats so that the poor could attend Sunday worship (Mole 1975). Bull's predecessor at St Thomas's, William Marsh had founded The Provident Association for the working people of the parish in 1833. It included a dispensary, a medical club, life assurance, a savings club and a library. By 1837 it had over 1,000 members and expanded to other parishes in the town. It survived well into the 20th century as the City of Birmingham Friendly Society (Mole 1975).

35 *Mission hut of 1879, originally built for St Mary's, Moseley as the forerunner of St Agnes'. It was used for five years and then sold to St Bartholomew's, Edgbaston for their mission on the Pershore Road. It is now the church hall of SS Mary and Ambrose, Edgbaston.*

The Later 19th Century

Anglicans were hard at work in trying to improve the lot of the poor in the town. In 1858 Grantham Yorke claimed that home visits were made almost exclusively by Anglican clergy, that in emergencies the poor went first to Anglicans and that there was nowhere in England where priests were 'more respectfully treated than they are in Birmingham' (Stephens 1964). Yorke was also instrumental in an early example of 'civic improvement' when the churchyard of St Philip's was cleared of rubbish, gravestones repaired or laid flat, and new grass planted. In 1859 Dr Miller, the Rector of Birmingham, was largely responsible for introducing 'Hospital Sunday' into Birmingham's churches. This enabled very large sums to be raised, in small donations, from large numbers of people so as to finance the improvement and running of the many voluntary hospitals established through the century. 'Hospital Saturday' followed from 1869, with collections being taken amongst workers in factories and workshops. Miller, too, was committed to serving the poor whose houses pressed close to his churchyard railings: 'We must go among them, we must improve their dwellings, we must provide the means, not only of mental improvement but of physical recreation', he said in 1855 (Skipp 1983).

Under the ageing Bishop Philpott of Worcester (see chapter 5) there was little recognition that clergy who worked in industrial cities required different skills from their rural colleagues. There was no encouragement and little opportunity for clergy in Birmingham to examine problems together or to help each other. At one level there was the well run Evangelical parish, like St Paul's, Balsall Heath, which would have Day, Night and Sunday Schools, clubs for married men, young men, and young women, a temperance mission, a maternity club, and Bible classes, whilst others had Dorcas Societies, penny banks and libraries. In such parishes the emphasis was very much on working-class self-help. There are also examples of remarkably active and successful clergy like J.S. Pollock, at St Alban's, Highgate, and H. Foster Pegg, the Evangelical Vicar of St Mary's, Whittall Street. Both attracted large congregations in wholly working-class areas. But, equally, there were parishes where the clergy became isolated, demoralised and ill, as at St Stephen's, New Town Row, and St Andrew's, Bordesley, where the clergy were so depressed by their environment that they retreated into their vicarages and were hardly seen.

Church extension, the building of new churches and the enlarging of older ones together with the provision of clergy, proceeded unevenly under Philpott with no sense of the inequalities of work-load on clergy. In the diocese the divergence is

Denomination	Churches/ Missions	Adult Attendance	Sunday School Attendance	Total
Church of England	57/57	61,294	27,916	89,210
Wesleyan Methodists	28/3	22,304	8,398	30,702
Primitive Methodists	10	1,505	2,227	3,732
New Connexion Methodists		2,959	1,159	4,118
United Methodists		1,766	1,478	3,244
Welsh Methodists		398	71	469
Baptists	24/16	13,324	9,454	22,778
Congregationalists	17/10	12,121	8,954	21,075
Society of Friends	10	4,033	2,954	6,987
Unitarians	5	2,937	1,052	3,989
Presbyterians		1,891	1,275	3,166
Roman Catholics	12	11,528	905	12,433
Salvation Army	1/7	4,050	304	4,354
Other Small Denominations		3,516	1,689	5,205
Non-denominational		5,951	2,087	8,038
Various		11,670	0	11,670
Totals		161,247	69,923	231,170

Table 4.3: The Birmingham News Religious Census, 1892

shown in an extreme manner by comparing Worcester with Aston-juxta-Birmingham. In 1891 the city of Worcester had 12 churches and 25 clergy, as well as the cathedral and its staff, for a population of 36,000, while the parish of Aston had the vicar and his curate in one and a half churches for 42,000 people (the nave of a new church had yet to be completed since the congregation had run out of money). In the second half of the 19th century, Birmingham had grown rapidly beyond its packed central districts thanks to the development of tramways and horse-drawn bus routes. Areas like Bordesley Green, Balsall Heath, Winson Green and Aston were rapidly covered with tunnel-back housing but there were comparatively few new churches. Edgbaston gained new churches thanks to the munificence of Lord Calthorpe, but heavily working-class areas depended on the very limited efforts and partial grants of the Birmingham Church Extension Society. As a result, by 1890, there were 10 parishes in Birmingham with populations of over 15,000, while the four parishes of Edgbaston with ten clergy between them catered for a total population of only 25,000 (Owen 1894).

The 1892 religious census of Birmingham undertaken by the *Birmingham News* newspaper is an important record of the development of church life over the second half of the 19th century. It was carefully organised, took place on 30 November, the last Sunday of the Church's year, and required almost 500 people to do the counting of all worshippers at all churches and chapels that day. What it did not do was distinguish people who went to two or more services on the day. The population of Aston and Birmingham amounted to 547,822 in 1892 and the census recorded 231,170 attendances, 161,247 of which were by adults (Peacock 1975) (Table 4.3). 32.4 per cent of the population attended church that day and more than half of school-age children went to Sunday School. Looking back from 2005 this seems an unimaginably good state of affairs; in 1892 it was regarded as lamentable that two-thirds of the population did not attend a place of worship. Only four places were reported to be full on census Sunday: the men's afternoon service at All Saints, Hockley; the evening service at St Martin's-in-the-Bullring; at Aston parish church, and at the

36 *(a) St John the Evangelist, Sparkhill (b) St Agatha's, Sparkbrook. St John's was built in 1888 to designs by Martin & Chamberlain, Birmingham's foremost late-Victorian architectural partnership. It is a bastion of Evangelicalism. Half a mile away on the other side of the Stratford Road stands Anglo-Catholic St Agatha's, the masterpiece of Arts & Crafts architect W.H. Bidlake. It is a Grade I listed building. St John's tower contains the oldest bell in the diocese, from Ullenhall, c.1215.*

Salvation Army Citadel. What the census does confirm is the numerical strength of the Church of England and the Wesleyan Methodists, neither of whom played much part in the political leadership of the late-Victorian city (Peacock 1975).

The Church's administrative framework in Birmingham reflected a past age. In 1890 most of the city's population of half a million was contained in a single, ironically termed, Rural Deanery. It was one of 31 such deaneries in the diocese and contained some 50 parishes. At the same time, newly-developing areas like Aston were in other deaneries, whilst Handsworth and Harborne were in Lichfield diocese. The Rural Dean of Birmingham from 1875 to 1892 was the Rector of St Martin's, Canon W. Wilkinson, whose energies were expended in the near total rebuilding of St Martin's in the 1870s. This was a rewarding but exhausting enterprise. Providing proper management of a deanery the size of Birmingham would have been even more exhausting and certainly less rewarding. For Evangelical clergy such as Wilkinson the parish had always been the chief focus and, in any case, rural deans had very little authority.

The dominance of Evangelicalism was an important feature of Birmingham Anglican life in this period. This gave much vigour to parochial life, but its extremer form led Birmingham to become a stronghold of resistance to Anglo-Catholicism. The arrival of such ideas not only revealed the depth of local antagonism, but seriously weakened the influence of the Church of England. Holy Trinity, Bordesley, High

Church since its foundation, had been tolerated, but the proposal to found St Alban's, Coneybere Street in 1871, out of Holy Trinity, met stiff opposition. The massively magnificent church, designed by J.L. Pearson (the architect of Truro Cathedral) was opened in 1881, but not finally consecrated until 1899. Dr Oldknow, the Tractarian (Anglo-Catholic) Vicar of Holy Trinity, and a noted theologian, had invited the Revd James Pollock to start a mission amongst the industrial workers and the poor in 1865. He was assisted by his brother, Thomas. They started with a meeting house in 'Vaughton's Hole', an old quarry, and created a very successful mission in an entirely working-class district so that people had to be turned away from the mission hall services a few years later. They had to overcome all sorts of hostility, physical at first, then financial, but by 1890 their church with its 1,000 kneelings and its 25 services a week had become remarkably popular. There was considerable difficulty in forming the new parish because of the objections from the Evangelical Trustees of Aston parish. The Pollock brothers served as vicar and curate of St Alban's for some 30 years and largely financed the building of the church themselves, though James later bitterly regretted its vast scale.

The antagonism from Aston was reflective of the wider antagonism between Evangelicals and Anglo-Catholics in the later 19th century. In 1867 there were anti-Catholic riots in Birmingham stirred up by a notorious rabble-rouser. Not only were Roman Catholic churches attacked (though not badly damaged), but so were Anglo-Catholic churches such as St Alban's. Dr Oldknow's successor at Holy Trinity, R.W. Enraght, so enraged the Evangelicals with his practices that the Church Association set out to prosecute him under the 1874 Public Worship Regulation Act. Bishop Philpott, whose consent was needed, held out for some time, but eventually sanctioned the prosecution in 1881. Enraght was found guilty of various practices such as using wafers for Holy Communion and sent to Warwick Jail for two months (Enraght 1881). He was regarded by his congregation as a martyr and seen off at New Street railway station by a thousand cheering supporters. He was subsequently deprived of his living in 1883 because of his ritualistic practices. A similar fate nearly befell the vicar of Christ Church, Yardley Wood in 1903, but he was persuaded to resign his living by Bishop Gore. Harborne had a particularly dissident group of clergy in mid-century: first the Vicar of St Peter's, the Hon. W.T. Law seceded to the Roman Catholic Church in 1851 (as did the curate at Northfield), whilst in 1877, the Vicar of St John's, Harborne, T.H. Gregg, seceded to try to establish the Reformed Episcopal Church in England!

Part Two

BISHOPS AND DIOCESE

5

Four Bishops and a Diocese

THE CREATION OF THE BIRMINGHAM DIOCESE

What is surprising about the creation of the Birmingham diocese is how long it took. Manchester, Birmingham's rival in so many ways, acquired the status as early as 1847 but the process of taking Birmingham out of the historic diocese of Worcester took a whole generation. In 1877 Birmingham was included in a list of potential new dioceses but the chance was lost. In 1889, when Birmingham acquired city status by royal charter, Anglicans worked hard to create a diocese but, when the promoters could not raise the necessary funds, the scheme failed. It must be admitted that setting up a diocese was a complex matter, but the delay in establishing a diocese for the 'second city' was affected by some unusual considerations.

The first was (and still is) the importance of the diocesan bishops in national affairs. Once appointed, in practice by the Prime Minister, they held a dominant position, each controlling his diocese in his own way and subject to little control, either from below or above. The leadership of the bishops of Worcester, in whose diocese Birmingham was situated after 1836, was crucial. There were four significant bishops in the period before 1905. Three were the diocesan bishops: Henry Philpott (1861-90), John James Stuart Perowne (1891-1901) and Charles Gore (1902-5). To them must be added Edmund Knox, Suffragan Bishop of Coventry (1894-1903).

The next concerns the people who would form the heart of the new diocese. A necessary requirement was a well-motivated force of clergy and lay people with a clear identity and sufficient financial backing to provide for both the bishop and his administration. In Birmingham, however, the Church of England had for many years been perceived locally as taking second place to Nonconformity and, in the second half of the 19th century, appeared increasingly disunited as the dominance of the Evangelicals faced growing High Church influence.

The last consideration relates to the territorial area chosen to form the basis of the diocese. Existing dioceses were usually based on historic cities of natural importance and were the focus, both economically and socially, of counties or wider regions. The Birmingham diocese was not established for Warwickshire but specifically for a large city dominated by its trade and industries. Behind its prosperous façade, however, was the growing challenge of 'spiritual destitution' among sections of the lower classes. The realisation of this challenge emerged slowly in the late 19th century, and the outcome was a diocese which was widely different from almost every other and where the 'social gospel' came to acquire a distinctive importance for its people.

The Background

As early as the 1850s there were proposals for a new diocese. Under the continued pressure of rising population the Cathedrals' Commission suggested that Warwickshire should have its own diocese with its see in Coventry. In 1860 a report, *The Lay Memorial*, was sent to the Prime Minister under the signatures of Lords Calthorpe, Leigh, and Lyttelton, presenting a powerful case for a new diocese on these same grounds. Lord Lyttelton, in particular, was a great force behind the Church of England in the Midlands. He was a supporter of church building projects, of improving schools and he was a great benefactor of Worcester Cathedral. He tried three times in the 1860s to put a Bill through Parliament to increase the episcopate, but failed each time (Morrish 1980). One of the arguments against a see centred on Birmingham was that the Roman Catholics had a bishop in the town and it was therefore inappropriate that Anglicans should do likewise. If an influential layman like Lyttelton could get nowhere, the prospects were not encouraging. Whigs and Liberals dominated the political scene at this time and the Commons had more important issues to debate than the Church of England.

When the Conservatives were in power under Disraeli from 1874 to 1880, Richard Cross, the Anglican Home Secretary, took the initiative for subdividing large dioceses by Act of Parliament. It started with Truro, supported by a strong Cornish petition to be freed from Exeter. Then followed the Bishoprics Act of 1878, which created the dioceses of Liverpool, Newcastle, St Albans, Southwell and Wakefield. The original proposals from the 1877 Committee of Convocation also proposed Birmingham for a diocese, but the Bishop of Worcester chose not to support the proposal. Whereas the Bishops of Chester, Durham and Lichfield allowed their industrial towns of Liverpool, Newcastle and Nottingham respectively to develop into dioceses, in Birmingham the opportunity was lost. Archbishop Tait was also luke-warm towards the proposal and despite Worcester's population of over one million, there were larger dioceses left undivided, including London, Rochester and York.

Bishop Henry Philpott

Henry Philpott was appointed Bishop of Worcester in 1861, at the age of 53. He had had a successful career at Cambridge as Master of St Catherine's College and Vice-Chancellor of the University. Philpott had been recommended by both Prince Albert, who knew him as a royal chaplain, and by the Evangelical Earl of Shaftesbury. To begin with he was an active bishop, assiduous in his ministry and highly regarded in his diocese. Under his supervision Church life in the diocese at large thrived as the number of new churches increased, including many in Birmingham, as we have seen (chapter 4). Generous benefactors not only rebuilt old churches but were prepared to build new ones where they were needed. However, Philpott never came to grips with the prodigious expansion of Birmingham or with the consequences of industrial society for the Church's mission. He only visited Birmingham when necessary and had little sympathy for its industrial and commercial interests.

During the 30 years in which Philpott presided over the diocese, the Victorian Church changed a great deal but he would not relax his own strongly held views. He was in principle opposed to the creation of new dioceses and additional bishops. This meant not only an unwillingness to divide his heavily-populated diocese but also a refusal to appoint a suffragan bishop. (Lichfield at this time had an assistant as well as a suffragan bishop.) He also refused to increase the number of archdeacons and there remained just two in the diocese. The Archdeacons of Worcester and Coventry each represented a whole county, with the result that they were grossly overloaded in their duties.

Philpott was also unwilling to establish a Diocesan Conference and by 1890 Worcester was the only diocese without this means of involving clergy and laity in debate. The *Birmingham Daily Gazette* summed up his attitude, 'He does not hold that conferences and Congresses and much talking promote true piety or religion' (Worcester Diocesan Calendar, 1891: 432). He might well have been right, but the pressure for change was growing. He would not allow any clergy from Worcester to be members of Convocation, the Archbishops' increasingly important debating chamber. Lord Norton of Hams Hall and Saltley, M.P. for Staffordshire, for example, a government minister under Disraeli, and one of the Church's most prominent laymen, could only join the Canterbury House of Laity through nomination of the Archbishop. Philpott himself played little part in either Convocation or the House of Lords. His reasoning was that assemblies of any kind created faction within the Church. He would not even allow the influential Church Congress to meet in his diocese. In all these ways he was denying himself valuable support and inhibiting the natural evolution of the Church, while at large the diocese acquired the reputation of being 'the Dead See'! Owen Chadwick described him as the 'most old-fashioned bishop on the bench'(Chadwick 1970), but he was more than that; by 1890 he had become an anachronism.

In the broader religious scene in Birmingham the Church lacked self-confidence. It had been overshadowed by Dissent for half a century. In the period from 1865 Dale, Dawson and Crosskey maintained a high profile through the Civic Gospel while their supporters provided the inspiration for Birmingham's borough council. The outcome was that clergy and laity alike retreated to their parishes and even there it was significant that many parishes were prepared to give up their National School to the highly successful and Dissent-dominated Birmingham School Board (chapters 4 and 18).

All these difficulties were compounded by the fact that Philpott lasted too long. He refused to retire, even when he reached the age of 80. In 1890 he was still attempting to manage a diocese of 31 deaneries, 482 benefices, 685 clergy, and a population of over a million – all from Hartlebury. The Castle was not too far from a railway station but it was over 50 miles to the furthest outposts of the diocese in Rugby and Atherstone.

When the Local Government Act was passed in 1888, the ambitious Birmingham Council petitioned the Queen for city status. This was granted in January 1889 and sparked off an immediate demand for a Birmingham bishopric. Two years earlier yet another Church committee had recommended that a diocese was needed for Birmingham. Bishop Philpott had no alternative but to go along with the pressure. While still admitting himself out of sympathy with the hasty creation of new bishops, he said he had been convinced that Birmingham was a special case. His conversion was publicised in his Visitation Charge of June 1889 and he convened a meeting in Birmingham to sound out lay and clerical opinion. There was an enthusiastic response and at a public meeting held in September 1889 John Jaffray, a leading Churchman and editor of the *Birmingham Daily Gazette*, emphasised the need by asserting, 'what we want is a compact and coherent army' (29 September 1889). There was also much behind-the-scenes interest from Archbishop Benson, a Birmingham man educated at King Edward's School, though he was anxious to keep with convention and insisted that the initiative come from the local area (Morrish 1980).

There was plenty of early interest. Philpott made a generous offer to surrender £800 per annum of his diocesan income to help finance the new bishopric. This was a useful start to the raising of the £105,000 required, the figure representing the capital needed to produce an income of £3,000 per annum. Public enthusiasm was roused by a meeting in the Town Hall in January 1890, attended by the Archbishop of Canterbury and several other bishops. Subscriptions were offered on the spot: £1,000 each by Lord Calthorpe, Lord Norton and George Dixon, while Sir John Holder gave £1,500 and John Jaffray £3,000. At the end of the meeting the list reached £20,198. However, a whole year later the sum had grown only to £32,000, a long way short of the necessary sum. This was partly due to a suggestion that the substantial income of St Martins-in-the-Bullring be diverted to fund the bishopric, antagonising St Martin's and slowing further donations. *The Church Times* offered its usual explanation: 'Had Birmingham not for so long been under the spiritual tutelage of the Low Church School, it is impossible to believe that the city would not have poured forth of its wealth for the creation of its bishopric' (*Church Times* 18 December 1891).

Another reason was that Philpott's scheme did not meet with unqualified approval. His plan was to make the whole of the Archdeaconry of Coventry into the new diocese, arguing that a city diocese was not viable unless it possessed some adjacent rural areas. His point was that this enabled a bishop to reward overworked town clergy with country livings at the end of their careers. The chief drawback to this proposal was that it excited the hostility of Coventry, which had a previous episcopal history and was not prepared to accept the pretensions of Birmingham. *The Coventry Standard* emphasised that £38,000 had been spent recently on the restoration of St Michael's, leaving nothing for Birmingham's bishopric. It went as far as to accuse Birmingham of being a 'modern Jacob'. Coventry's resistance was supported by most of Warwickshire's towns. Leamington, Rugby, Warwick and Nuneaton had no wish to come under Birmingham's influence. Even distant Hartlebury was better for them, whilst the Lichfield parishes within the proposed boundaries were similarly antagonistic. The disaster was complete when Philpott resigned in August 1890 and the scheme was forced into abeyance. In many ways it was not a good scheme. The question of what the new diocese was for had been ignored and the alienation of Coventry was unnecessary. It could have been avoided by proposing a smaller area around the city.

Bishop J.J.S. Perowne

Bishop Perowne, who was appointed to Worcester in February 1891 from his previous post as Dean of Peterborough, could not prevent the demise of the scheme, which at the time had appeared to be so essential for the renewal of Anglican life in Birmingham. He could not afford to repeat the financial offer made by his predecessor since Philpott's pension, which came out of the bishop's income, was £2,000 per annum. It was suggested that the bishop give up Hartlebury to reduce costs. While Perowne was not averse to leaving Hartlebury, it was unthinkable to the diocese at large. His own suggestion was to finance the bishopric out of a union of the wealthy parishes of St Martin's and St Philip's. This idea found little favour, however, and only succeeded in alienating Archbishop Benson, himself a Birmingham man. There seemed little support in Parliament for the required Bill. Salisbury, the Prime Minister, was certainly not prepared to give the aid of his government to the project, as he had no wish to antagonise his vital political ally, Joseph Chamberlain. Faced with such practical difficulties, Perowne allowed the scheme to collapse in 1892. In the crucial and divided final meeting of the Bishopric Committee he was obliged to use his casting vote in favour of returning the subscriptions. Perowne became the villain of the piece (Morrish 1980).

The irony of the years after 1892 is that, although the scheme had failed, Perowne succeeded in giving the Church in Birmingham the quality of leadership that it had lacked for so many years. He was able to put new heart into the city's clergy and new vigour into fund raising. At the same time as the bishopric scheme was collapsing, Bishop Perowne had written to Lord Salisbury, the Prime Minister, telling him that the workload was too heavy for himself alone and requesting a suffragan assistant and a third archdeaconry. The new Archdeaconry of Birmingham, established in 1892 and comprising the deaneries of Aston, Coleshill, Northfield, Polesworth, Solihull and Sutton Coldfield, gave the Church of England in the city a chance to realise its corporate identity, and the appointment of Canon Bowlby, Rector of St Philip's, as the Suffragan Bishop of Coventry provided a man who knew the city and its needs (though his title antagonised Birmingham folk). Unfortunately he had to remain Rector of St Philip's as there was no income to support him. Bowlby was succeeded on his death in 1894 by Edmund Knox, a man Perowne knew would inspire it with drive and energy. Perowne was no self-advertiser and his work was consequently underestimated by many historians. His achievements were undervalued by Asa Briggs, for example, who dated the Church's revival in the city to the appointment of Gore to Worcester in 1902 (Briggs 1952). Perowne lacked the flamboyance of Gore, but his part in the recovery of the Church of England in Birmingham was fundamental.

Few, perhaps, expected much of Perowne when he arrived at Worcester at the age of 68. He had been Dean of Peterborough for 13 years, since he was out of favour with Gladstone. His academic worth was not in doubt. He had excelled at Cambridge, first as a Fellow of Trinity, and then as Hulsean Professor and Whitehall Preacher. As soon as he had arrived at Worcester, his strong Evangelicalism became apparent as the driving force behind his actions. He stood for the more conciliatory form of Evangelicalism, attempting to find common ground and heal the party splits within the Church of England. In Birmingham he soon came to see the worth of the Anglo-Catholics ministering in the central slum areas. Ultimately, it was his Evangelicalism that convinced him that the spiritual destitution of Birmingham was the most serious problem facing the diocese and that drove him to head a campaign of church extension. It was the same force, too, that led him to share the Anglo-Catholics' concern for the improvement of social conditions. He was not afraid to take a political stance on such matters if he felt this would improve the condition of the working classes. His willingness to lead a major campaign to improve the housing of the poor in 1900 and to challenge the city council is a clear indication of how far Church leaders had come since 1890.

There can be no doubt that he saw Birmingham as the fundamental priority of his ministry. His first public engagement as bishop was at Aston, just five days after his consecration and here he asserted his hope for Birmingham to be 'the centre of Church work throughout the diocese'. In June 1891 he presided at the Town Hall over a meeting of the Birmingham Church Building Society and emphasised the importance of the Church's mission in overcoming 'spiritual destitution' in the city. Fund-raising soared and in the next 11 years 10 churches were built and an additional 20 clergy were appointed.

Perowne's actions were also designed to encourage local Church leadership. He created the Archdeaconry of Birmingham as a focus for the Church in the city and appointed the much respected Canon H. Bowlby of St Philip's as Suffragan Bishop

37 *Bishop H.B. Bowlby, Rector of St Philip's from 1875 and Suffragan Bishop of Coventry from 1892. He died in 1894.*

of Coventry. This was an inexpensive appointment because St Philip's had an ample income for a suffragan and a fine parish church worthy of being the base for a bishop. It also paved the way for St Philip's to become the eventual cathedral for Birmingham. To harness the support of both clergy and laity he set up a Diocesan Conference and used this as the forum to debate changes in the diocese. Sometimes he had to listen to some 'home truths', as in 1894 when an Edgbaston incumbent commented, 'Birmingham with her gigantic spiritual needs suffers acutely ... As far as practical assistance is concerned, Birmingham might be quite as advantageously situated in the diocese of Honolulu, perhaps more so!' (Worcester Diocesan Magazine, November 1894). In August 1891, Perowne licensed laymen for the first time in the diocese as Readers to work in mission churches. Three of the first four parochial Readers in the diocese were at St Mary's, Saltley and Christ Church, Edgbaston.

In 1893 Perowne invited the Church Congress to Birmingham and they took as their main theme 'The Church and the working classes'. A year earlier the remarkably efficient *Birmingham News* census of church attendance had alerted all denominations to the potential loss of working-class support. The census showed that in an area of nearly 600,000 persons about 40 per cent of the adults and nearly 50 per cent of the children attended a form of worship on the census day. While this indicated just how much had to be done, there was some encouragement for the Church. In particular, it revealed that the appeal of the Nonconformists had in the main been restricted to the middle classes, while it was the Church of England that had continued to labour in the working-class and slum districts of the city (Peacock 1975).

In 1901 the condition of housing in some of the inner-ring areas of the city became a matter of public debate. T.J. Bass of St Laurence, Duddeston, had become so concerned about the effects of poor housing in his parish that he initiated a campaign through his pamphlet, *Every Day in Blackest Birmingham: Facts not Fiction* (Bass 1898). Perowne wrote a foreword for the publication and challenged the Church to demand action on 'slumland'. Although they failed in the end to impress the city council, the campaign had allowed the Church to discuss the severe shortcomings of the much vaunted 'civic gospel' and to emphasise the importance of the 'social gospel'.

The reaction of a few Birmingham clergy was to turn to Christian Socialism. Arnold Pinchard of St Jude's took up the cause of low-paid women workers and tried hard to attract the poorest groups in his parish. He became notorious for his ending of pew rents against the wishes of many of his worshippers. He lost one congregation but then filled the church with active working-class supporters. He set up clubs which were open every evening and had hundreds of members. Next door at St Martin's, the Evangelical A.J. Robinson tried to make contact with the 'Peaky Blinders', the young men he described as 'the problem, social, civic and Christian of our great city' (St Martin's Annual Record 1899-90).

Bishop Edmund Knox

When the first Bishop of Coventry died in 1894, Perowne appointed Edmund Knox, the Vicar of Aston, as his successor and gave control of the Church in the city to a man whose leadership would make full use of the new spirit of Evangelicalism. He was eventually translated to Manchester where he was a very successful bishop, but it was Birmingham that gave him the chance to show his potential. He had come to Aston in 1891 from a Fellowship at Merton College, Oxford, and an incumbency at Kibworth Beauchamp, Northamptonshire. When he arrived in Birmingham, he found, as he wrote, 'no team-work, no team spirit'(Knox 1924: 140). At Aston he discovered the urban church with all its frustration and tensions, but found this challenge much more to his liking. His energy and organisation were remarkable. He soon had seven curates, each with a mission hall, school room or 'tin tabernacle', and then appointed seven lady workers as their assistants. He also commissioned no fewer than 200 Sunday School teachers. After three years at Aston he had become the most influential Churchman in the city.

As with Perowne, a strong Evangelicalism motivated his actions, and led him to give the highest priority to work with the working classes. His leadership gave the Church a new coherence, conciliating the old party differences and bringing the best out of individual clergy. It was Knox who was behind most of the new initiatives of the late 1890s, giving new life to the Church Extension Society and proposing the 'Two Million Shilling Fund' for building new churches in 1900. He was chairman of the new 'Lay Work Committee', which was set up to engage the efforts of lay people, and was also the driving force behind the Commission to enquire into the resources of the Church in Birmingham. Its *Report*, published in 1898, vividly demonstrated the need for more clergy and churches. The most telling statistic was that a single Birmingham parish had a greater population than the combined population of 85 parishes elsewhere in the Worcester diocese, each with an incumbent. Controversially, he suggested redeployment of clergy. At root the new self-confidence of the Church owed much to his inspiration, with the result that by 1900 it is possible to say that the Church of England in Birmingham had genuinely emerged from the shadow of Nonconformity.

Bishop Charles Gore

On the retirement of Perowne in 1901 Knox was a favourite for appointment to Worcester. Curiously enough, this was a fearful prospect for Birmingham Anglicans. If he were promoted, this might jeopardise all their recent achievements and leave them leaderless. However, the vacancy at Worcester was given to Charles Gore, Canon of Westminster. At 49 he was the leading exponent of Christian Socialist ideas in the country and an eminent High Churchman (chapter 6). He was an astonishing choice for a diocese with a long Evangelical tradition and for a city with its Nonconformist background. 'Lord Salisbury's latest surprise' could well have led to a confrontation in Birmingham between the Evangelicals and the 'enfant terrible' of the High Church party. As a writer in the 'Review of Reviews' put it, 'Imagine John the Baptist, appointed by Pontius Pilate to be bishop over Galilee when Herod was in his glory, and we have some faint idea of the nature of the appointment by which Lord Salisbury sent Canon Gore to be Bishop of Birmingham' (Prestige 1935: 227).

The evangelical Church Association was bitterly opposed to Gore but Knox, the ardent Evangelical, could see beyond party slogans and perceived the advantage to Birmingham that Gore's approach could bring in terms of church extension and social policy. Only one year later Knox's turn came and he left Birmingham to become Bishop of Manchester. In practice, Gore himself got on well with the city's Evangelicals simply because he detested autocratic methods. Without losing his own passionately held beliefs, he made no attempt to interfere with the views of others. Even more surprisingly, Gore soon struck up an effective relationship with Joseph Chamberlain, the long-standing Unitarian opponent of the Church of England. On his many visits to Birmingham Gore often stayed at Highbury, Chamberlain's Moseley home.

It seems probable that Gore preferred Birmingham to Worcester and his eventual move to Birmingham as its first bishop was not a surprise to his friends. He liked its enterprise and vigour, but he was also conscious of the great challenge it offered to the Church. He, of course, had never been afraid of a challenge and saw Birmingham as his priority in the diocese. He was not enamoured of life in Worcester. Many disliked his abandonment of Hartlebury Castle for a more modest house in Worcester and he preferred the services of the local Co-op rather than the long-established city grocers. In the same way he stayed at the home of a bricklayer when performing a Confirmation in a working-class Birmingham parish rather than in Edgbaston.

Although it was Gore who achieved the creation of the Birmingham bishopric, at first he was not inclined in this direction. He inherited a more coherent body of Churchmen in the city, but the memories of 1890 remained. He needed convincing, and he did not intend to take up the bishopric plan too soon. Others saw the bishopric scheme as unfinished business. Gore's hand was soon forced by an anonymous letter to *The Times* in 1902, which offered £10,000 to fund a bishopric for Birmingham if it could be established within three years. The donor was later revealed to be Canon T.H. Freer, a former Archdeacon of Derby. Gore could not ignore such generosity but he proceeded cautiously. He began successful negotiations with Lichfield for the transfer of parishes between the two dioceses, including the problematic Harborne, Handsworth and Smethwick. He then organised a meeting in Birmingham in February 1903, where he repeated Philpott's offer of £800 per annum from the Bishop of Worcester's income and offered £10,000 of his own money, which he expected as an inheritance from his mother, Lady Kerry, who eventually died the following year. He concluded by offering himself as a possibility as first Bishop of Birmingham. Even the *Birmingham Daily Post* had to offer its support after this, praising the Church of England as 'one of the great civilising and morally elevating influences of the country' (25 February 1903). When the first subscription list closed just four months later prior to an official Appeal, nearly £95,000 had been promised. As might be expected, the larger contributions came from the very wealthy, but the revival of grass roots Anglicanism in Birmingham was demonstrated by the great number of small donations from parishes and congregations in all areas of the city. By November 1904 the Ecclesiastical Commissioners confirmed that sufficient stock had been purchased to yield the necessary £3,000 per annum for the creation of a new diocese.

The scheme itself was carefully planned to avoid past mistakes. Coventry, Warwick and most of Warwickshire were excluded from the proposed boundaries of the new diocese. St Philip's was designated as the cathedral. Nevertheless, the scheme still had to pass through Parliament where the climate was not particularly welcoming. A similar Bill to create a diocese of Southwark out of Rochester had actually failed in the Commons in May 1902. Anglo-Catholicism was strong in Southwark and for some years extreme evangelical and nonconformist groups had demanded that Ritualists be disciplined by the bishops. Defeating the Southwark Bill was a further reflection of their antagonism and they were confident of further successes. The new Prime Minister, Balfour, was anxious to assist Birmingham and introduced a Bill in the Lords as early as June 1903. However, this Bill dealt with Birmingham and Southwark together in an attempt to help both, and there was a real danger that the opposition would bring down both schemes. It passed in the Lords but, ominously, failed on its first reading in the Commons and, because of lack of time, it was not proceeded with. However Balfour agreed to reintroduce it in the following session of Parliament. He introduced it personally in March 1904.

When the Bill came up for its second reading in May, the attack from the anti-Ritualist group was as strong as ever. But a Liverpool MP made the mistake of attacking Gore by name in the Commons. The response of Chamberlain was immediate. In a remarkable speech he said, 'I am not only a Nonconformist but I am myself, and always have been, in favour of the policy of disestablishment. I have thought and said that the adoption of that policy would really be a relief to the Church of England, that it would increase its spiritual influence, and that it would save it from attacks which are now made upon it on the grounds of it holding an exceptional and privileged position' but, he went on, 'the Bishop of Worcester, of course, came among us practically as a stranger … Now that we do know the Bishop of Worcester, we know that he has won golden opinions from everybody, from Nonconformists quite as much as Churchmen, and his moderate, generous, broad and religious influence is exercising the best effect upon the people of the city. … I hope the House will not stand in the way of the philanthropic efforts of the Church people of Birmingham, who, out of their own pocket, have found all that is requisite to endow the Bishopric, and will not make their sacrifices in vain' (*Hansard 134,* 1904). Chamberlain had, in practice, endorsed the Bill, which went on to pass comfortably.

The precise bounds of the diocese were left to negotiation by the Ecclesiastical Commissioners. Clearly the core was the Archdeaconry of Birmingham and the deanery of Handsworth. The people of Atherstone and Nuneaton decided they preferred Worcester to Birmingham; Dudley decided it wanted to stay with Worcester not go to Lichfield, but Langley, Rowley Regis and Oldbury were added to Birmingham from the west, Lickey from the south-west and Lapworth and Temple Balsall from the south. Since there was no large former monastic church to serve as the cathedral, the choice was between St Philip's and St Martin's. The former was preferred since it was already the base for the previous suffragan bishop. Minor architectural alterations were effected to accommodate the bishop's cathedra and completed in time for the enthronement (chapter 15).

Meanwhile it had been announced that Gore was to be translated from Worcester to Birmingham and he was enthroned on 2 March 1905 (the Feast of St Chad) at St Philip's Cathedral as the first Bishop of Birmingham. He became an inspiring bishop and an outstanding leader of the new diocese, but his predecessors also deserve to be remembered for their part. Philpott certainly delayed the creation of the diocese, but it could be argued that the Church in Birmingham was not sufficiently prepared for diocesan status. Perowne understood the serious challenges offered by a great industrial city and accepted the importance of the 'social gospel'. Knox provided the vital energy to build up a coherent body of clergy and laity and to give them the necessary self-confidence. In the last stage Gore offered the inspired leadership which enabled the new diocese to be welcomed by the city at large and to become an important voice in its future.

6

CHARLES GORE

FIRST BISHOP, 1905-11

Birmingham's first bishop was probably one of the most influential Anglicans of the second half of the 19th and the early 20th centuries. His theological writing is still widely referenced today and his practical work continues to reverberate through to the present. It is difficult to know where to draw the boundaries of this chapter since he was bishop of Birmingham for only six years. However, if we are to appreciate why Birmingham became an important see very quickly after its formation it is important to follow Gore's career before he came to the new diocese.

Gore was born into an aristocratic family. His father was the Hon Charles Alexander Gore, a cadet branch of the Earl of Arran's family, and his mother, Augusta, was the daughter of the 4th Earl of Bessborough (the Lansdowne family). She was Countess of Kerry, having married the earl in her late teens and bore him a daughter before he died only two years after their marriage. She spent eight years in widowhood before falling in love with and marrying Charles A. Gore, who was secretary to the Prime Minister, Lord John Russell. His salary as the Commissioner of Woods and Forests (£1,200 per annum) enabled them to live comfortably in a villa, set in 40 acres of grounds, on the edge of Wimbledon Common. It was there that Bishop Gore was born on 22 January 1853, their fourth child and youngest son.

Childhood and Education

He seems to have felt called to the Church at an early age since it is recorded that he used to 'preach' sermons to the nursery when only eight or nine years old! He was also attracted by a book describing the conversion of a Catholic priest to Protestantism – but it was the Catholic elements that attracted him. He went to school in Malvern Wells, Worcestershire, and then followed his brothers to Harrow. There he was quickly marked out as a scholar of exceptional ability in the Classics. He had a group of close friends with whom he discussed Catholic religious ideas, rather than the prevailing Evangelicalism of the school, and Radical political ideas rather than the prevailing Liberalism of his class. One of his teachers was R.A. Westcott, later Bishop of Durham. In 1870 he gained by examination one of the two scholarships to Balliol College, Oxford and went up the following year with a fistful of school prizes. At Balliol, theology and philosophy dominated his studies; he joined the English Church Union; he visited the Cowley fathers, and he heard Moody preach in Oxford during the great Moody and Sankey Mission of 1873, which apparently reduced him to giggles! The great political event of his undergraduate years was the attempt by Joseph Arch to organise an agricultural workers' union. Gore was appalled by the attitudes of the country clergy who took the side of the landowners; 'We always seem to see the truth about things when it is too late', he said, an early indication of his political Radicalism which was not to be moderated as he got older. He graduated in 1875 with first class honours in 'Greats' (theology, philosophy, history) and a few days later gained a Fellowship at Trinity College.

Early Ministry

1875 was also the year in which he and a group of slightly older dons at Oxford formed what they called 'The Holy Party' whereby they took over a country parish whilst the incumbent went on holiday, saying the daily services and enjoying the countryside to talk and argue about their faith. Gore was ordained deacon at Advent 1876 and priested in 1878. Though clearly destined for academic advancement, he was advised to get some parish experience so in June 1879 he went as assistant curate to Christ Church, Bootle for three months, and then to St Margaret's, Liverpool when the incumbent was imprisoned under the Public Worship Regulation Act. Within the year he was back in Oxford because he was offered the Vice-Principalship of Cuddesdon Theological College. Within a year he was established as a brilliant theologian, an inspiring teacher and a deeply human man. He 'rapidly became the most potent religious force in Oxford. The pious waited on him; the ignorant sat at his feet; the agnostic sought his company to talk and play, but left, if not converted, at least with a deeper sense of the seriousness of life implanted in their souls' (Prestige, 1935: 76). In 1883 he moved to become the first Principal of Pusey House. Pusey had been one of the guiding lights of the Anglo-Catholic 'Oxford Movement'. Pusey House was funded by his memorial fund as a home for researchers, teachers, pastors and students to be housed with the Pusey Memorial Library. Between the two jobs he went to India to help at the Oxford Calcutta Mission. He travelled widely across the country and talked with Buddhist, Hindu and Muslim priests about the texts of their faiths.

The 1880s saw the birth of what has come to be called the 'Modern Movement' in the Church. Modernists repudiated the Creeds in the light of modern scientific knowledge. They claimed that faith needed to be brought into line with other fields of knowledge and, though clergy might recite the Creeds as the mouthpiece of their congregation, they had personal reservations about the truth of miraculous events in the Bible as literal facts, including the Virgin birth and the physical resurrection of Jesus. Gore was the standard bearer for the revealed truths of the Church to the end of his long life and implacably opposed to the Modernists. The end of the decade saw Gore involved in three major new ventures.

First, the 'Society of the Resurrection' was founded in 1892 by his friends and colleagues at Pusey House and the earlier 'Holy Parties'. It was intended to support and encourage the fellowship of priests who intended to remain celibate so as to be better able to undertake mission work at home or overseas. It provided a Rule for prayer and simple living; though private capital was retained by individuals, income was held in a common fund; and books and possessions were also held in common. The vow of membership was annually renewable, though the intention was that men should join for life. The Superior was to be elected every three years and Gore was elected by the initial six members of the Order.

Secondly, following the Lambeth Conference's call in 1888 for church people to study and provide moral witness towards the solution of urgent social problems, the Christian Social Union was founded with Bishop Westcott as president and Gore and his dearest friend, Henry Scott-Holland, as vice-presidents. The two friends ensured that there were large branches in London and Oxford and within five years there was a membership of over 2,600. Its aims were to study how the moral truths and principles of Christianity should be applied to the social and economic conditions of modern times.

Thirdly, a book of essays was published in 1889 by the members of the 'Holy Party' called *Lux Mundi*. Gore's essay on 'The Holy Spirit and Inspiration' provoked widespread outrage. It brought the findings of Biblical criticism into a theological framework which said that Scripture (including some of Jesus' teachings) needed to be interpreted in the light of the knowledge and beliefs of the age in which they were written. Gore became 'that awful Mr Gore who doesn't believe the Bible', but the book went to 10 editions within two years! When he was asked to deliver the Bampton Lectures in 1891 at Great St Mary's church it was packed to the rafters for every lecture, but the vicar tried to bring heresy charges against him! However, to undergraduates he was an intellectual deliverer, providing a robust Catholic faith based on the living reality of the Church, not on the verbal inspiration of the Bible, undermined by science.

Westminster and Worcester

In 1895, Gore left Pusey House to be vicar of the rural village of Radley, five miles fom Oxford, to devote more time to thinking and writing, though the Community of the Resurrection came with him. Unfortunately his health broke down but the following year the Prime Minister, Lord Rosebery, offered him one of the Crown Canonries at Westminster Abbey. He accepted whilst retaining the vicarage of Radley as a base for the Community. It was eventually in 1897 to move to its present base at Mirfield in Yorkshire. The press congratulated 'by far the ablest of the younger clergy, ... the real leader of the liberal and philosophical wing of the High Church party' on his promotion (*Westminster Gazette*, 1895). At Westminster he had an immediate impact, instituting a daily Eucharist, organising the refurbishment of St Faith's chapel as a place for private prayer, and preaching to huge congregations. According to Dr W.R. Inge, a prominent Evangelical, 'no more stimulating Christian teaching has been given in our generation' (Prestige 1935: 198). He continued to write and speak for the Christian Social Union; he was interested in the activities of trade unions and cooperative societies; he campaigned for Armenian Christians suffering Turkish persecution; he lectured at both Oxford and Cambridge; he tried to help Anglo-Catholics who had fallen foul of their bishop; and he spent much time writing about Church discipline and working to amend unworkable Church courts.

Following the death of his father in 1897, Gore took time out to tour eastern America. However, this was no ordinary tourist venture since his fame preceded him and his travels included a reception at the White House to meet the President. In 1900 Gore was back in the political arena, writing letters to *The Times* opposing the Boer War, and particularly the concentration camps for Boer civilians where inhuman conditions were leading to the deaths of many children. This was a war being prosecuted by Joseph Chamberlain, of course, who was Foreign and Colonial Secretary. Nonetheless, two weeks after his letter, Lord Salisbury, the Prime Minister, nominated Gore as Bishop of Worcester. Worcester was absolutely not a Catholic diocese and its major centre of population was Chamberlain's city – Birmingham. A few extreme Evangelicals were outraged but most people seem to have welcomed his appointment and Suffragan

Bishop E.A. Knox preached from his St Philip's pulpit that 'God has sent the diocese as its chief pastor, in answer to its prayers, one of the most distinguished of the Church's sons' (Prestige 1935: 229). However, things did not go smoothly thanks to organised opposition to his consecration from the Church Association and other Protestant societies. Legal arguments were still being heard on the planned date of his consecration in Westminster Abbey and Gore refused to proceed. He was finally consecrated in the chapel of Lambeth Palace on 23 February and enthroned at Worcester Cathedral two days later.

He quickly decided to live in a modest house in Worcester, not at Hartlebury Castle. Despite his reforming convictions (and he set about reforming his diocese immediately) he was rapidly overwhelmed by the size of the diocese and the routine business that it engendered. When the opportunity arose to divide it and form a new diocese around Birmingham, he grasped it like a drowning man. That story is told in chapter 5. Gore was a man of the city, not the countryside (his unhappy time at Radley had shown him that) and so he quickly made an impact in Birmingham. In 1904 he led a great mission to east Birmingham; he had led missions before in the 1880s (including one in Walsall), but had been rather frightened by the power they unleashed so had concentrated on clergy retreats thereafter. He stayed in a city hotel for a week and celebrated and preached in east Birmingham churches morning and evening. He was impressed with the evidence he found for active Church life, and congregations were impressed with his preaching.

Organising Birmingham

38 *Charles Gore as Bishop of Worcester (Gore 1932).*

When he arrived in the new diocese of Birmingham as its first bishop his first act was to appoint a commission to enquire into the needs of every parish. Fund-raising for particular needs was instituted, new parishes formed, churches and mission halls and vicarages built, additional clergy attracted to the diocese, and lay workers, both men and women, were encouraged. He held regular meetings for his clergy and for churchwardens of the parishes and he aimed to preach in every parish every three years. He very quickly created a diocesan sense of itself and of belonging. It quickly became clear that Gore was not surrounding himself with High Church appointees and that he exercised his patronage fairly according to the traditions of parishes, so he was respected by Evangelical clergy.

There was no palace, so he rented a house in Edgbaston ('the ugliest house in Christendom') which he called 'Bishop's Croft'. There he lived simply. For example he kept no car or carriage but used public transport when he could and, when there were longer journeys to make, a 'guild of private owners' volunteered their vehicles and drivers to his use. The Archdeacon of Birmingham, Mansfield Owen, was Vicar of Edgbaston, so lived close by and the two men often used to breakfast together.

39 *Procession at the Installation of Charles Gore as Bishop of Birmingham, 2 March 1905.*

Gore set aside £1,000 from his income for charitable purposes. He gave practical help to poor priests and their families – paying for Christmas food, holidays, or sending a cheque when he felt it was needed. He played host to his diocesan ordination candidates during the week of the ordination and continued to instruct them regularly afterwards and he held regular retreats for his clergy to teach them the faith and urge them to action. Gore, himself, was very much a man for seizing the moment. He quickly got bored with meetings and hated the routine administration of being a diocesan bishop. He never thought that he was doing his best and he worked long hours in his study. Each Lent he delivered a course of weekly teaching sermons in the cathedral to large congregations and his preaching was always fully reported in the local press. His episcopacy was particularly noted for two diocesan synods of his clergy in 1907 and 1910 when such meetings of the bishop in council were extremely rare. The first was to discuss the findings of the 1905 Royal Commission (see p.58) and the second was to take counsel on the indiscriminate baptism of infants where there was little likelihood of them receiving a Christian education. In the autumn of 1908 he held a week-long diocesan convention in the Town Hall and so many clergy and laity attended that overflow meetings had to be held in the cathedral and St Martin's. This was followed by two three-day retreats for clergy which over two-thirds of the clergy attended. Finally, in 1909, a general mission was held across the diocese with huge attendances at the main gatherings. The diocese was inspired by these events and had no doubt about the inspiring leadership of its bishop.

His contributions to civic affairs were equally extensive and he goaded the city council into action on a broad range of social concerns. He chaired a meeting to discuss housing reform and ways in which the city could begin to build social housing. He was good friends with the Quaker Cadbury family and paid visits to Bournville to watch the progress of the Bournville building estate, and he was interested in Cadbury's schemes to ensure his workers' health and recreation. That led him to campaign for recreational spaces to be provided in other industrial areas for workers. He continued his support for trade unions and the process of collective bargaining, spoke vehemently for the concept of a 'living wage' for industrial workers, and he was several times called upon to mediate in industrial disputes in the area. He campaigned against child alcoholism, which was all too evident around the cathedral churchyard and slum courtyards, and against gambling. This brought him into conflict with brewers and club owners who organised noisy heckling in the public meetings which were held. His goading of local councils was always done within a more general framework of support for civic interests, however, and Birmingham City Council were happy to entrust him with the toast to 'our city' at Chamberlain's 70th-birthday celebrations.

He gave unstinting support to the new University of Birmingham and was already friends with Oliver Lodge, the principal, before he came to the city. In 1909, as part of the celebrations on the opening of the Edgbaston campus, the University conferred an honorary degree on Gore. In presenting him the orator said:

> The diocese of Birmingham is fortunate in having as its spiritual director one of the greatest of English bishops. As teacher, scholar, theologian and earnest student of the problems of modern society, he commands a respect that is universal. For he spares himself neither in body, nor estate in his devotion to the cause for which he stands. A man of dauntless courage, of utter umworldliness, of a simple piety and an excellent charity, he brings into our midst a lofty ideal that is an inspiration to many, and teaches us by his example to translate into our lives the cardinal doctrines of the Christian faith.

In 1905, he became the University of Oxford's nominee on the Governors of King Edward's School. He gave a great deal of time to the school and even served as Bailiff (Chairman of the Governors) for one year.

On the national stage he joined the national campaign by the Church against the 1906 Education Bill which would have seen the end of religious education in schools. He chaired a huge meeting in Birmingham and spoke no fewer than eight times in the House of Lords; the Bill did not become law. He supported the Liberal government's plans to raise the school leaving age to 14, to provide state-funded ante-natal care for mothers, Poor Law reform and contributory old-age pensions.

He had a particular enthusiasm for the Worker's Educational Association (WEA) founded in 1903, and he spoke out for the organisation, and to them. He believed strongly that education enabled people to lead a fuller life, whatever their social and economic circumstances, but he also had no doubts about, and spoke on the theme of, 'knowledge is power'. He continued to agitate in international affairs too, speaking on Turkish atrocities in Macedonia, Belgian actions in the Congo, and the evils of the opium trade forced onto China.

In national Anglican affairs he spoke on behalf of missionary societies, the Church Reform League and the Christian Social Union. In Convocation (the national meeting of bishops and elected clergy) he helped establish parochial church councils to give voice to the laity in parish affairs, and extended the franchise to women in parishes. In 1906 he chaired an enquiry on the moral witness which the church ought to bear on economic questions and largely drafted the report himself. As a consequence each diocese

40 *The official portrait of Charles Gore as Bishop of Birmingham in Bishop's Croft, Harborne.*

was recommended to have a standing social service committee to study these themes and strengthen enlightened public opinion. Most dioceses, and the national Church, continue to have such 'Social Responsibility' boards or committees today. He underwent an appendectomy in 1908, just before the Lambeth Conference of that year, but still managed to attend the final sessions.

Finally, he continued to be prominent in the debates about clergy discipline and got involved with a number of high-profile cases. He presented evidence to the Royal Commission on alleged Disorders in the Church in 1905 and they spent a whole day examining his contribution. He was adamant that Church law and its courts needed to be reformed, but equally adamant that if a bishop was to maintain good discipline then the law of the land had to be obeyed and where new practices were allowed they should

41   *Portrait of Charles Gore in the Diocesan Office, Harborne.*

be undertaken in moderation and obeying regulations set by the bishop. Some of these debates seem arcane today, but others are still very much with us. For example, he was appalled by some of the new hymns in *The English Hymnal* when it was published; there were problems with the use of incense in some Catholic parishes, and with reservation of the Sacrament – a debate that was to rumble on for several more decades.

Charles Gore believed that 'Christianity exists to make us uncomfortable', so he was very much aware of the dangers of settling down in Birmingham. In 1908 he was asked for his opinion on possible candidates for the vacant bishopric of Bombay; half jokingly he suggested himself, so naturally was offered the post but in the end he rejected it as he was in the midst of his fight with the Birmingham brewers over licensing. However, in the summer of 1911 Francis Paget, the Bishop of Oxford, died. Gore was offered the vacant see and after much hesitation decided to accept it. He was 58 and if he was to move it was the right time; he was also attracted by the schools and colleges of Oxford. Inevitably, his departure from Birmingham was marked by appreciative gatherings and written testimonials. There were two from the clergy; the first had been so exuberant that some clergy had felt unable to sign it! Gore understood. There was another from Nonconformists, who admired his fight for social justice, and there was a third from the civic community of the city. Gore's farewell sermon was on the theme 'Seek ye first the Kingdom of God'. The city decided to commemorate his work in Birmingham by commissioning the statue that continues to stand at the west door of the cathedral by Thomas Lee. Gore thought that 'I'm afraid it's horribly like me'! It was unveiled in 1914 in the presence of the Archbishop of Canterbury. It was thoroughly restored in 2003 by Eura Conservation Ltd. Gore was Bishop of Oxford for eight years before he retired. He died in 1932 and was buried at Mirfield at the Community of the Resurrection.

7

HENRY RUSSELL WAKEFIELD

SECOND BISHOP, 1911-24

Birmingham's second bishop, Henry Russell Wakefield, made few marks in the history books and that is a pity since he was an interesting man. He was born on 1 December 1854 at Mansfield, Nottinghamshire, the only son of an Irish gentleman, Francis Wakefield. Young Henry was sent to Tonbridge School, Kent, where he was good enough to make the football team. When he left school, rather than university it was determined that he should prepare for a career in the Diplomatic Service. He therefore went to the Lycée Bonaparte in Paris, and subsequently to the University of Bonn. He returned to England fluent in French and German and, spurning the civil service, he had determined on ordination. He trained at Cuddesdon College, Oxford for two years and was ordained deacon in 1877. He served his curacy in St Peter's, Vauxhall, in south London. He moved to the more salubrious pastures of Barnes for a second curacy between 1878-81, being priested in 1879. He married Frances Sophia Dallaway in 1878 and over the next decade they had four children, three sons and a daughter. They moved from Barnes to the rural Kent parish of All Saints, Swanscombe for the next two years (1881-83), before he became vicar of the outer suburban London parish of St Michael and All Angels, Lower Sydenham, in Rochester diocese, for the next five years.

In 1881 he began lecturing at the Crystal Palace School of Literature on philology and English literature, and published essays on *Life and Religion*, in 1890, and on two of Shakespeare's plays. In 1888 he left Sydenham to become Vicar of Sandgate on the Kent coast for six years. His relief work amongst his parishioners following the huge landslide along the Sandgate cliff face in 1893 brought him to the attention of Lord Rosebery, the Patron of the prestigious St Mary's Bryanston Square, in the Marylebone district of London. Lord Rosebery nominated him as the next rector of the parish in 1894.

Mayor of Marylebone to Dean of Norwich

In Marylebone he got involved in local politics. He was an elected member of the London School Board for its last three years, before it was succeeded by the London County Council, and was elected Liberal Mayor of Marylebone 1903-05, the first clerical mayor anywhere in the country. His public speeches gave 'persuasive expression to his views' according to his obituary. He was appointed a member of the Royal Commission on the Poor Law in 1905, strongly supporting its minority report, and was Chairman of the Central (Unemployed) Committee for London in the same year. He was also president of the Christian Counter-Communist Crusade. Whilst undertaking these public duties he ministered successfully to his large congregation, few of whom would have sympathised with his Liberal views, but he was a good preacher.

In 1905, Prime Minister Balfour offered him the post of Vicar of Leeds, usually a stepping-stone to episcopal preferment, but Wakefield refused. He was appointed a Prebendary of St Paul's Cathedral in 1908 but within a year had left Bryanston Square and St Paul's to become Dean of Norwich and Vicar of St Mary-in-the-Marsh, one of the city's many small medieval parishes, whose stipend supplemented that of the Dean. He was nominated by Prime Minister Asquith. He acquired a Doctor of Divinity degree from Lambeth Palace (in the gift of the Archbishop of Canterbury) on his appointment in 1909, but was clearly sensitive to his lack of a university degree. The move to Norwich put him within reach of Cambridge University, so he elected to become a Fellow Commoner at St Catherine's College in 1910. His preaching brought large congregations to the cathedral evening services and he and his wife quickly established generous hospitality to the clergy of the diocese and their families at the Deanery. He travelled widely across the Norwich diocese happily preaching in village churches at a time when dignitaries of the Church tended to confine their preaching to the pulpits of larger urban churches. At the same time he continued his political interests in social reform, which necessitated frequent visits to London. He was at Norwich Cathedral for only two years before he was recommended by the Prime Minister (Asquith once more), to become the second Bishop of Birmingham in succession to Gore. He was consecrated bishop in Southwark Cathedral on 28 October 1911.

Like his predecessor, Wakefield had a clear interest in social questions of the day and politically was a Liberal. He was less of an Anglo-Catholic than Gore and, though he was quite happy with Catholic ritual, he felt more at home in the centre ground of ecclesiastical politics and strove constantly to get the various factions of the Church to work together cooperatively and harmoniously. He seemed initially to most people to be an excellent person to carry on the short-lived traditions of the diocese established by Charles Gore.

Catholics and Discipline

In the first decades of the 20th century a second phase of Catholic revival was underway with a much greater emphasis on ritual in worship and the use of specifically Roman Catholic services, which were not part of the Prayer Book. One of the most contentious of these practices was the reservation of the consecrated bread and wine in churches so that people could pray before it at any time. This was also bound up with different theologies of what happened at the consecration. To Roman Catholics the dogma of Transubstantiation meant a belief that the bread and wine were transformed into the living body and blood of Christ. To Catholic Anglicans such as Bishop Gore, there was a belief in the 'Real Presence' of Christ at Holy Communion, to Prayer Book Anglicans the bread and wine *represented* the body and blood of Christ. Wakefield took a leading part in these debates and was one of those who presented a petition to the newly-appointed Archbishop Davidson in 1903 to try to ease Anglo-Catholic difficulties with the 'Ornaments Rubric' of the Prayer Book. In 1911 the bishops agreed that they would tolerate reservation of the sacrament for the communion of the sick, even though this was illegal, but not for any other purpose. Bishop Gore had insisted that reservation take place only in a secluded chapel with no public access, so that adoration of the sacrament could not take place. Bishop Wakefield took the view that 'not even locked chapels and brick walls would prevent people showing reverence and saying their prayers'. Wakefield thus did little to prevent the display of the reserved sacrament in Anglo-Catholic parish churches in his diocese, or the increasingly ostentatious Roman practices that accompanied it, policies which were to cause his successor untold difficulties.

Wakefield's attitude was that clergy and laity should be less concerned with the outward differences between factions than with the much more important matters on which they agreed. To this end he was president of the Free and Open Church Society. He took this attitude into his relationships with the Nonconformist elite in Birmingham and willingly consented to allow occasional corporate Holy Communion services between Anglicans and Nonconformists. Inevitably this too drew the ire of some of his clergy who protested strongly. Later, in 1920, he expressed the view that he had probably been too precipitate and that a union of outlook was preferable to a unity of method so 'to attempt to combine worship, except on special occasions, is to foster unreality'.

42   *The official portrait of Henry Russell Wakefield as Bishop of Birmingham in Bishop's Croft, Harborne.*

It was not only on Church unity that Wakefield held radical views. In 1916 he had proposed a drastic redistribution of ecclesiastical endowments between dioceses, a greater variety of permitted services, and a more definitive share in Church government for the laity. A year or two earlier he had advocated the institution of a permanent diaconate, 'the members of which would continue in their secular callings while devoting part of their time to the service of the Church'. They were also to be allowed to assist at the celebration of Holy Communion by administering the chalice (*The Times*, 10 January 1933).

The First World War

Wakefield's episcopacy, of course, coincided with the First World War. In 1915 he went on an official visit to the Western Front and contributed a long article to *The Times* detailing his experiences. The piece is uncritical of any aspects of policy or people and dwells only on the excellence of the morale and behaviour of British and French troops. He gives high praise to the chaplains he met, and to the French clergy to whom he was introduced. It is clear that he was taken to the front lines and he describes the burial mounds in the trenches of soldiers killed where they were then interred, but this was high summer so the mud and filth of trench warfare was less apparent (*The Times*, 14 September 1915). The article was later published as a pamphlet. In the first two years of the war he had considerable difficulty in preventing younger clergy from joining the services as combatants, which he thought completely wrong; but he encouraged them to become service chaplains.

The following year he undertook an official mission to Canada and the United States. He travelled some 18,000 miles from one end of the continent to the other. At each stop he eloquently put forward Britain's case for the conflict, dealing with moral issues and the need for subsequent social reform as well as physical reconstruction.

43 *Dedication of the 'Great War' memorial at Hampton-in-Arden by Bishop H.R. Wakefield.*

He met a huge range of people in the USA including 'film "stars" at Los Angeles', where the new film industry was developing rapidly. His tour was intended to bolster support for the war effort in the Dominion of Canada and, more important, encourage popular support for American entry in the conflict on the side of the Allies. He was created Commander of the Order of the British Empire (CBE) and Commander of the Belgian Order de Leopold in 1919 for his services to the war effort.

His other claim to popular fame during this period was his presidency of the 'National Council of Public Morals' from 1913 to 1922. This was a voluntary body which we might be tempted to see as the equivalent of Mary Whitehouse and her group in the 1970s. It worked through 'commissions' which produced reports on worrying social questions of the age. Thus there was one on the cinema, another on the birth rate in Britain, and a third on 'adolescence' as the perennial problem of young people and their activities came to the fore. Wakefield took these reports very seriously and we know that he consulted with Marie Stopes, for example, on questions of birth control. Later rumour, reported by Canon Douglas Maclean in the 1980s, was that the bishop was extremely fond of this *enfant terrible* of her day.

Wakefield was a genial man but, seemingly, he was unpopular with the city's commercial elite and some factions amongst his clergy. In 1919, the Prime Minister's advisers suggested he might be moved to Truro 'where his genial ways might commend him to the Cornish people', but nothing came of the idea. In 1922, his position as a leading Anglo-Catholic saw him chair the Anglo-Catholic Congress in Birmingham. During his episcopacy the ministers of more and more churches began openly to take up Ritualist practices and the services associated with them. These clergy were well organised in the diocese and were supported nationally by the English Church Union. As always in such circumstances, lay people found themselves forced out of their parish church if they disagreed with the new rituals because clergy drew to themselves, and to their Parochial Church Councils, sympathisers from without the parish. Former worshippers therefore had to look for the nearest acceptable services in a more congenial neighbouring church.

Sadly, in 1923, Wakefield suffered a severe stroke and his chaplain was forced to report to the Archbishop of Canterbury that the bishop would 'never be capable of another hour's work of a serious kind' (Barnes 1979: 155). On his resignation, which had to be forced from him by Archbishop Davidson, on the grounds that he was no longer capable of conducting his official business, he demanded a pension of £1,500 from the official episcopal funds of £4,250. The Prime Minister reduced this to £1,250, a sum which still made a substantial hole in Bishop Barnes's stipend whilst Wakefield lived, which he continued to do until 9 January 1933, when he died aged 79 at his home in Hove.

8

Ernest William Barnes

THIRD BISHOP, 1924-53

Ernest Barnes was the eldest of four boys born to a Baptist elementary school teacher, John Barnes, and his wife Jane. Ernest was born in Altrincham, Cheshire in 1874 but, because his father was appointed to a headship in Birmingham, he spent most of his boyhood in the city where he was eventually to be bishop. He went to King Edward's School in New Street and then to Trinity College, Cambridge. He was President of the Cambridge Union in 1897 and graduated with a 1st class degree in Mathematics. In 1898 he was the first recipient of the new Smith's Prize in Mathematics and was elected Fellow of Trinity College. This was the beginning of what seemed likely to be a glittering academic career. He was successively Assistant Lecturer (1902-06), Junior Dean (1906-08), and Tutor (1908-15) and in 1909, at the age of only 35, he was elected Fellow of the Royal Society (FRS). At Cambridge, Barnes was known as a generally shy man, but not one who suffered fools gladly. He did not shy away from declaring trenchant views, either in his academic world of mathematics or in his social situation and he followed in the footsteps of other academics in being considered arrogant by many of his opponents.

Barnes had gone to Cambridge an atheist but he experienced a conversion to Christianity whilst a student and quickly went forward for ordination training. He was ordained deacon in 1902, and priest the following year. As a don he was not required to undertake theological training. As a scientist of high ability, it is perhaps not surprising that he was antagonistic to the sacramentalism of the Anglo-Catholic wing of the Church and he was hostile to all forms of the doctrine of the real presence of Christ in the Eucharist. To him the essence of Christianity was found in the personal discipleship of the Jesus of the Gospels and the ethics of the Sermon on the Mount. He believed it to be his duty to preach a world outlook based on the natural sciences rather than the traditional scriptures and to this end preached what came to be known as his 'gorilla sermons'! These supported the Darwinian evolutionary theory of human descent from earlier ape-like creatures. His ethical stand led him to proclaim ardently for pacifism from the outbreak of the First World War in the face of fury from many of his fellow academics.

In 1915, whilst continuing to teach at Cambridge, he became Master of the Temple Church, in London, with its congregation of lawyers, and in 1918 was made Canon of Westminster. The lawyers, whom Barnes considered to be mostly 'wistful agnostics', seem to have appreciated the challenging incisiveness and intellectual honesty of his sermons and disagreed only with his pacifism. However, at Westminster his preaching gained a wider audience and he became a controversial figure. His attacks on the 'real presence' doctrine caused pain and distress to many and his 'gorilla' sermons were thought to be unnecessary as 'educated church people' had long accepted evolutionary theories.

Back to Birmingham

He was nominated to the see of Birmingham, aged 50, in 1924, by Prime Minister Ramsay MacDonald. He was enthroned in October 1924 and was to remain bishop for the next 30 years. There was to be no more controversial bishop in the Church of England. Despite the controversy he was much admired by most in Birmingham since he related well to the city's business community and he was a good pastor. It was, of course, a different world from that of today. Barnes only 'kept residence' in the diocese for the university terms that had previously ruled his life. He also had 10 servants to keep him in the manner expected of a lord bishop at Bishop's Croft, Harborne.

Unlike his predecessors he was a 'modernist'. He determined to improve the academic quality of the clergy of the diocese and would normally only appoint men with degrees. He also began to favour men who had been trained at Ripon Hall, one of the most liberal of the theological colleges. He apparently began his sermon at one institution with the words, 'I would have thought that the patrons of this living would have chosen a man with intellectual qualities equal to those of his parishioners, but apparently they thought otherwise' (Montefiore 1995: 191). Large parts of the diocese were 'high church' in character at this time and so it was not long before the new bishop came into conflict with the accustomed practices in many parishes. He thought his predecessor had not imposed sufficient discipline on the clergy and he was determined to bring to heel those he considered to be straying from the doctrines of the Church.

Battles with the Anglo-Catholics

His determination was fuelled by the national debate on the possible new Prayer Book that was being debated in these years. Barnes was a trenchant opponent of those who wanted to revise the Prayer Book to allow some of the Anglo-Catholic services and practices that had developed rapidly through the first two decades of the 20th century. The battlefield on which he chose to fight was the permanent reservation of the Sacrament. It was quite clear where the battle was to be since he had spoken in his enthronement sermon of the pagan sacramentalism of the adoration of the reserved Sacrament (Bishop 2001). The Anglo-Catholics were therefore ready for him. The first skirmish was an exchange of published letters with Revd G.D. Rosenthal, vicar of St Agatha's, Sparkbrook. Barnes then refused to allow the perpetual reservation of the Sacrament in any of the churches in the diocese. The incumbents of 15 parishes refused to accept his ruling and refused, too, to contribute to the Diocesan Board of Finance. They committed themselves to support one another and agreed not to resign their living whilst Barnes' ruling was in force. Barnes responded by not appointing assistant clergy to those parishes, or providing money from diocesan resources for assistant clergy. He refused to undertake confirmations and would make no official visits to those parishes. However, he continued to offer social invitations to their clergy, though they equally consistently refused them. Deadlock was quickly reached.

Exceeding his legal powers, he began demanding that men nominated to vacant benefices where the Sacrament was reserved promise to end the practice. In the first instance, in 1925, the incumbent designate of St Mark's, Washwood Heath, withdrew his nomination and a second candidate had to be selected. In St Aidan's, Small Heath, in 1929, where the Bishop of Truro was amongst the Patrons, the controversy over these promises left a vacancy for 18 months and the Patrons eventually resorted to a High Court writ directing the Archbishop of Canterbury to institute their nominee, which he did, to Barnes' disgust. As well as these intra-diocesan controversies, he remained a controversial national figure. In September 1927 there was a large-scale protest organised by a London priest and a group of his parishioners as Bishop Barnes was about to preach in St Paul's Cathedral. They demanded that the Bishop of London ban him from the cathedral and that the Archbishop of Canterbury try him for heresy. This resulted in another published series of open letters between Barnes and Archbishop Davidson as a means of discussing the relationship of science and religion.

44 *The official portrait of E. W. Barnes as Bishop of Birmingham in Bishop's Croft, Harborne.*

The new Prayer Book was finally published in 1927 and Barnes continued to speak out against it nationally and in his own diocese. At the Diocesan Conference that year both clergy and laity voted in favour of the new texts and this pattern was repeated nationally, leaving only the vote in Parliament to make it legal. In the same year Barnes preached another series of sermons in Westminster Abbey and in Birmingham on the compatibility of science, evolution and religion. The Birmingham sermon, in the presence of the Lord Mayor, at St Martin's drew particular ire, since Barnes challenged anyone to prove the changes to bread and wine after its consecration during the Eucharist. Whilst most of the press railed against him, Bishop Gore, who was still alive, called the text 'a plea that we should be free of obscurantism and this is wholesome counsel' (Barnes 1979: 193). He received more than 2,000 letters from everyone from bishops to ordinary lay people. He also published a book of his sermons with a lengthy preface, *Should such a Faith Offend?*, and within a year 12,000 copies had been printed. What really annoyed people was Barnes' refusal to put his arguments sympathetically. They were like buckets of cold water using extremely provocative analogies which were guaranteed to upset people. Much of his activity in 1927 was to try to persuade Parliament to reject the new Prayer Book and at the end of the year they did just that by 238 to 205 votes. Barnes was ecstatic claiming that the 'representatives of the English people have saved the doctrine of the English Church' (Barnes 1979: 210).

Preaching and Social Affairs

At the same time as all this was going on we should note that Bishop Barnes was working to advance the faith in his diocese. He worked particularly hard at ecumenical relations

45   *Bishop's Croft, Harborne. Formerly known as Harborne House, this lovely mansion was acquired in 1921. The chapel (now unused) was added in 1924. Barnes had six servants, a chauffeur, two gardeners and a children's nanny.*

with the nonconformists, and women as well as male ministers were welcomed to preach from Anglican pulpits. He also began the very necessary process of building new churches and halls on the growing outer estates of Birmingham by launching an appeal for £30,000. Almost the whole sum was raised in just over a year (chapter 17).

Bishop Barnes was, despite, or perhaps because of, his notoriety, in great demand as a preacher and writer at any event with scientific connotations. Thus he preached at services to mark the bicentenary of Newton's death and the centenary of Lister's birth; he gained honorary degrees from three of the Scottish universities, but none from English ones. Even Birmingham granted him an honorary degree only on his retirement. He found a new subject in his Galton lecture in 1926 by advocating sterilisation of the feeble-minded and used it in sermons in Birmingham. Bishop Montefiore recalls talking to an old lady who had been confirmed by Barnes and was subjected to a sermon on this topic. She 'was so angry that she went home and said "Daddy, I want to be confirmed again"'! His Gifford Lectures of 1927-29 were published as *Scientific Theory and Religion*, an enormous tome of 685 pages full of complex mathematical equations, which nonetheless received appreciative reviews. Barnes was also active in social affairs, especially over the disputes in the coal industry either side of the General Strike in 1926, whilst betting, drunkenness, bad housing and the lack of film censorship were other social evils that he repeatedly drew to people's attention, preaching moderation rather than absolutist remedies. He also advocated other liberal causes such as cremation rather than burial, and remarriage in church of innocent parties of divorce proceedings. Though he did not publicly advocate the use of contraceptives for birth control he was happy to advise couples to seek medical advice and use such resources as

46   *Barnes at the dedication of the new tower of St Agnes', Moseley in 1932.*

were advised, and he refused to condemn vivisection since he believed it to be a scientific necessity. However, he opposed abolition of the death penalty until after the Second World War.

In Birmingham the battle with the Anglo-Catholics continued to be fought as one of attrition. All Saints, Small Heath and St Anne's, Duddeston were 'recaptured' from the rebels in 1929, but then came a long battle at Stirchley, one of the most extreme rebel parishes, where two successive vicars had moved it to extreme Ritualist practices, alienating many of the congregation. The vicar died and the curate refused to give Barnes the assurances on reservation of the Sacrament that he required. Barnes warned him that his licence would be revoked and he resigned. A new vicar, Revd E.H. Parslew, was offered the living and made the necessary declarations to Barnes, but the PCC, at the instigation of the English Church Union, refused to remove the aumbry and holy water stoups that had been installed without faculty and appealed for help to Archbishop Lang, himself an Anglo-Catholic. He refused to intervene but the Chancellor of the diocese then joined the fray, complaining that the removal of fixtures from churches was within his jurisdiction not the bishop's. Parslew was eventually installed in 1930 and Stirchley was welcomed back into the fold, mainly because the English Church Union had moved their legal attacks on to St Aidan's, Small Heath.

St Aidan's was a perpetual curacy, founded in 1891 as a mission church from All Saints. In 1929 the curate resigned on the grounds of ill health and the trustees offered the living to Revd G.D. Simmonds. He refused to make the declarations that Barnes required over reservation and Barnes therefore refused to institute him. Both

Barnes and the English Church Union had determined to fight to the death on this case. Barnes proposed to force the ECU (in the shape of the trustees) to take action in the civil courts so that he would be sent to prison for contempt. Much legal and ecclesiastical opinion was expressed at great expense, all at the same time that the diocese was celebrating its 25th anniversary. As we have seen, the Archbishop eventually instituted Simmonds to the living, to Barnes' disgust. The final battle with the rebels was with St Jude's in 1941, where the Crown were the patrons. It was eventually agreed that a 'chaplain' would be appointed until the end of the war who would give Barnes his assurances. The last of the rebel clergy resigned his living in 1953 in the closing weeks of Barnes' episcopate.

Politics and the Second World War

In the 1930s he began to speak out on political matters. He spoke in favour of a United States of Europe; he held a Disarmament Sunday throughout the diocese in 1932; he was apprehensive for the future of Russia, and, in the spring of 1933, soon after the Nazis had come to power, he was publicly deploring the treatment of Jews. He helped to organise a united Christian meeting of protest in Birmingham, though he was careful to distinguish Nazism from the plight of the German people more generally in their post-Versailles Treaty state. He advocated self-government for India and the submission of all international disputes to the judgement of the League of Nations. His pacifism was no more popular with the government of the 1930s than it had been with his colleagues at Cambridge in 1914-18. He campaigned for unemployment pay in the desperate years of unemployment in the early 1930s, for free school milk for children, and for the compulsory purchase of land to aid town planning. In 1933 he entered the House of Lords.

He made only one official visit overseas, and that only as far as Armagh in Ireland for the 1,500th anniversary of St Patrick, but from the early 1930s he and his wife were inveterate travellers on their holidays. First to France, then Italy; the Holy Land in 1935; the Rhineland the following year and a Greek cruise after that, Barnes helping with the programme of lectures on board. In 1938 he and his wife bought what was to be their only home, other than official residences, on the cliff-top at Seaton, in Devon. He also learned to drive at the age of 60 and bought himself a number of antique cars, including a Rolls Royce. His two sons went to Winchester and Westminster schools respectively, and then both went to his old college at Trinity, Cambridge. His elderly mother lived nearby until her death in 1938, whilst his brother, Stanley, was Dean of the Birmingham Medical School and was responsible for the creation of the Queen Elizabeth hospital complex (Slater 2002).

By the late 1930s he was having to move on to a second tranche of senior appointments in the diocese. He had had a particularly loyal team but they were now old men. At the cathedral, Hamilton Baynes resigned as Provost in 1937, aged 83. He had come to Birmingham as Bishop of Natal, so was able to act as Assistant Bishop to Barnes. He was succeeded by the then Archdeacon of Aston, J.H. Richards who was already 68, whilst Archdeacon Hopton was 76 (chapter 14). As his new Assistant Bishop Barnes appointed bishop J.H. Linton, who had been rector of Handsworth since 1935. He had been a bishop in Persia for 16 years and though hard of hearing had impressed Barnes with his evangelistic flair. Other clergy who could have sought higher office were content to stay in Birmingham and offer Barnes their support. Most notably Guy Rogers, Rector of Birmingham, whose name was put forward for a number of episcopal posts. Barnes also launched another appeal for new churches and church halls. He was particularly concerned that existing parishes should play their part in the fund-raising and one clergyman who asked him to come and bless a new oak screen got the reply: 'Certainly not. At a time when the diocese is straining every nerve to build new churches, you have been raising money for a sheer luxury, the oak screen. It is scandalous!' (Barnes 1979: 337).

With the start of the Second World War he issued guidance to his clergy on early evening services, the blackout, dealing with casualties, and the legal aspects of their position. More important he was determined to try to advise against the nationalistic preaching of the Great War. He wrote: 'Preach as little as possible: pray as much as you can. Before beginning to prepare a sermon, put down your newspaper, turn off the wireless and for at least a quarter of an hour read slowly some passage of the

47 *Silver Wedding portrait, 1941, by Francis Dodd, RA.*

New Testament which reveals the mind of Christ. You are His minister.' (Barnes 1979: 354.) The advice found its way into the press and he received grateful letters from all over the country. He spoke up for conscientious objectors, both nationally and in Birmingham. With Bishop Bell of Chichester he opposed carpet bombing and night bombing raids 'on the little houses of Germany' and did his best to argue for famine relief to reach different parts of Europe. He was unsuccessful in both. He campaigned for the construction of deep concrete Haldane air-raid shelters accusing the cement industry of running a cartel. They responded by issuing a writ for slander and so Barnes found himself once more in the hands of the lawyers. Damages were awarded against him of £1,600 but Barnes responded with a motion in the House of Lords on air-raid shelters and a letter to the press; all this at a time when the air-raids of 1940-41 had cost 2,000 of Birmingham's citizens their lives. He was determined to pay the bill himself but the Diocesan conference collected some £1,100, nominally as a silver wedding gift to Bishop and Mrs Barnes.

The Rise of Christianity

During the war years Barnes also began work on a new book, *The Rise of Christianity*. He wanted to show how science could shape Christianity so that it was more palatable to the sceptical. It was published in 1947 to generally critical reviews. His science meant that the Virgin Birth, miracles and the Resurrection were dismissed and what was left was an early church characterised by socialism, pacifism and internationalism. One reviewer wrote to his editor: 'Honesty compels me to say that I think that *The Rise*

48 *Memorial in St Philip's Cathedral to Bishop Barnes.*

of Christianity is a very bad book indeed, amateurish and dogmatic'; another wrote: 'It is out of date, he has not kept up with contemporary work; it is arrogant and unscholarly' (Bishop 2001). His fellow bishops were appalled. Archbishop Fisher wrote to him that: 'Quite honestly, I think that the holding of your opinions and the holding of your office are incompatible, and I believe you ought in conscience to feel the same' (Barnes 1979: 405). Eventually Fisher publicly criticised Barnes at the Canterbury Convocation without allowing him the right to reply. Barnes was inundated with sympathetic letters from well-wishers and the sales of the book were boosted. It was also serialised for the six million readers of the *Sunday Pictorial* newspaper, and there was a debate on the BBC radio Third Programme in 1948 when it was generally agreed that Bishop Barnes wiped the floor with his opponent. Barnes eventually resigned on the grounds of ill-health on Ash Wednesday 1953 to the great relief of Fisher who clearly detested his recalcitrant bishop. His diocese thought otherwise. At his silver jubilee as Bishop of Birmingham in 1949, the *Birmingham Mail* wrote:

> The name of Birmingham is widely known in the world for many reasons, of which not the least honourable is that it is the See of Dr Barnes. Today after a quarter of a century the Bishop of Birmingham is unquestionably the outstanding figure in the Established Church. Since the death of William Temple, there is no one whose opinions and influence carry greater weight.

He died only six months after his retirement. His ashes lie in the cathedral, with those of his wife, below memorial doors bearing his likeness.

9

JOHN LEONARD WILSON

CONFESSOR FOR THE FAITH

FOURTH BISHOP, 1953-69

Leonard Wilson succeeded Bishop Barnes in 1953. He was to remain Bishop of Birmingham for 16 years. He was a man of national renown for two reasons: the story of his internment, arrest and torture by the Japanese military police whilst he was Bishop of Singapore during the Second World War had seared an enormous depth of faith into his soul which he succeeded in communicating to others; and, more tritely perhaps, because for many years he led the service at the annual televised British Legion Festival of Remembrance in the Albert Hall, where he always gave both dignity and fervour to the worship.

Youth, the Army, University and CMS

Wilson was born on 23 November 1897, the second son of the evangelical Anglican curate of Gateshead Fell, County Durham. His mother, Adelaide, ran a private school to help make ends meet. Three further sons followed Leonard's birth and his mother died soon after the birth of the last of these children. Wilson was educated at St John's School, Leatherhead, a school 'for the sons of poor clergy of the Church of England'. He went there aged ten and found himself unpopular and generally disliked by his fellows and by many of the masters. A contemporary has written that 'he was too clever; there was something about him that "got under your skin"'. (Mackay 1973: 53). When he was 18 he left to join the training battalion of the Durham Light Infantry. He later remarked how kind he found his sergeants who swore a lot but none clouted or beat him! He was soon promoted to sergeant himself and served in France towards the end of the First World War but, by 1919, he had decided to go to Oxford and seek ordination after taking a degree. His life course had been changed by spending time at the Knutsford Training School in Cheshire led by Mervyn Haigh as an experiment in equipping clergy for the post-war world. Leonard (immediately christened 'Tubby' by his fellow students because of his already stout build) determined that he wanted to be 'a new kind of parson'; he had an impatience with tradition that had outlived its usefulness and he had a 'modernist' theological outlook. This included an anti-literalist belief in study of the Scriptures and, long before the late 20th-century Bishop Jenkins of Durham, he refused to believe the literalism of the Virgin Birth of Jesus.

He went to Queen's College, Oxford and made many lifelong friends through the Student Christian Movement (SCM). Members of the SCM at that time were heavily influenced by the liberal theology promoted in the evening discussions held by Canon B.H. Streeter in his rooms. He provided the opportunity for Leonard to liberate his mind and spirit from the confines of his schooldays. Wilson graduated in

1922 and went to Isfahan, in modern Iran, to teach at a Church Missionary Society (CMS) school. However, he quickly fell out with the local clergy over his modernist theology and so returned to Wycliffe Hall, Oxford to prepare for ordination. He was sponsored by his native Durham diocese, but his first post as curate was at Coventry Cathedral, where a clergyman from CMS headquarters, Revd H.S.B. Holland, had been appointed sub-dean and vicar. Wilson was ordained priest in Coventry Cathedral in September 1924 and worked with great energy and success with the young people of the cathedral parish. Unfortunately, his radical views on the Virgin Birth brought criticism from his bishop and, by 1926, he was looking for a new post.

Oddly, he went back to the CMS, and to school-teaching, accepting the offer to become Principal of Old Cairo Boys School, in Egypt – once he had learnt to speak Arabic! He spent nearly two years in Cairo, keeping in contact with Coventry Cathedral as 'their' missionary, but he failed to learn Arabic sufficiently well, and failed to become Principal of the school once his radical theology became known to local clergy from sermons he preached in the cathedral there. Complaints to CMS followed. In the correspondence Wilson had to set out his views clearly. He said: 'I do "fervently acknowledge the Lord Jesus Christ to be my Lord and my God", but I do not accept the Virgin Birth. I do regard Holy Scripture as "a supreme authority", but the meaning of Holy Scripture has been and is being revealed to me by the mind of the Church and the guidance of scholars' (McKay 1973: 75). In the end CMS and the local bishop forbade him to continue his work in Egypt and so he wrote to Hensley Henson, the Bishop of Durham, asking to return to a post in his home diocese. Henson liked his outspoken young clergyman and found him a post as curate in charge of St John's, a daughter church of St Margaret's, Durham. Eight years of parish work in the North of England followed. He married Mary Phillips, whom he had met in Cairo, in 1930 and, in the same year, became vicar of Eighton Banks in Newcastle. Their first child, Christopher, died of meningitis just before his third birthday. A daughter, and three further sons were to follow in the next decade. In 1935 he moved to St Andrew's, at Roker in Sunderland and then, in 1938, a friend from his Newcastle days, R.O. Hall, who had become bishop of Hong Kong, invited him to become dean of the cathedral there. He was a great success and, in March 1941, accepted Archbishop Lang's offer to become Bishop of Singapore. He was consecrated bishop in Hong Kong Cathedral on 22 July and left for his new diocese a few days later with his wife and family. Four months later the Japanese invasion of south-east Asia began.

Singapore

Mary and the three children left for Australia only two weeks before the surrender of Singapore. Their youngest son was born a few months later. It was to be several years before father and son were to see one another for the first time. Bishop Wilson did his best to tend the sick and dying and offer hospitality to the homeless during the near continuous bombardment of the city. When the Japanese administration was installed, the bishop remained free from internment for the next 13 months and, thanks to the good offices of a Japanese Anglican, Lieutenant Ogawa, he was able to visit the prisoner-of-war and internment camps unsupervised, whilst churches and the cathedral were allowed to continue to hold services. His freedom meant that he was one of those engaged in smuggling money and foodstuffs into the internment camp. Adversity forced him to begin work towards another fervently held ideal – that of

Christian unity. A Federation of Christian Churches was formed, first to co-ordinate relief work, but secondly to work towards 'a Universal Church in Malaya' (McKay 1973: 23). At the end of March 1943, however, Wilson was interned in Changi prison camp.

Six months later, the feared military police (Kampetai) took charge of the camp and a large group of men and women, including Bishop Wilson were taken away to the appalling conditions of the police headquarters. The police suspected there was a spy ring in Changi, with radio communication with the town, where they were suspected of stirring up anti-Japanese feeling. The bishop was tortured for 36 hours and then spent some three weeks semi-conscious in an overcrowded cell trying to recover. The interrogations went on for several months thereafter and he lost four stone in weight. He did not dwell on the physical horror when he began

49 *The official portrait of Leonard Wilson as Bishop of Birmingham in Bishop's Croft, Harborne.*

recounting his experiences after the war; rather he pointed to the way in which his faith had been strengthened; to the way in which the strength God gave him passed to others in a whispered prayer fellowship in the cells; the conversion and baptism of a Chinese prisoner; Holy Communion celebrated with a few grains of rice and weak tea whilst constant watch was kept for the guards; and, after the war, the baptism and confirmation of many Japanese in prison for war crimes, including one of his own torturers.

Following the Japanese surrender, he immediately threw himself into organising relief measures for the local population and it was not until October 1945 that he left for Australia to be reunited with his family. Six months later they returned to England and Bishop Wilson was plunged into a maelstrom of speaking engagements, sermons and broadcasts in the midst of which he was invested as Companion of the Order of St Michael and St George (CMG) by the king, and he launched an appeal to raise £100,000 for work in his war-ravaged diocese. He returned to Singapore in November 1946 but found it difficult to inspire the necessary post-war reconstruction of his churches and their social action. By the time he returned to England for the 1948 Lambeth Conference of bishops, his friends were working actively to find him a position in this country and in September he was offered the deanery of Manchester. He returned to Singapore to attend to unfinished business and resigned his bishopric in March 1949.

His stay in Manchester was mercifully brief since the single-minded, reforming Dean, hoping for new projects to bring the Church alongside ordinary working people in the city, immediately clashed with a cathedral chapter wanting to get back to old familiar ways after the upheavals of war. However, he led the fund-raising necessary to complete the rebuilding of the cathedral after war-time damage and, in 1950, was asked to be an envoy for the Society for the Propagation of the Gospel (SPG) in their 250th anniversary celebrations by going to South Africa. On Queen Elizabeth II's Coronation day, Wilson received the Prime Minister's letter offering him the vacant post of Bishop of Birmingham.

To Birmingham

As successor to Bishop Barnes there was no great change in theological outlook. Both men were liberal-thinking Evangelicals who understood the necessity of reconciling science with faith, but who at the same time had deep personal faith in the saving power of Jesus and life after death which had been tested and not found wanting. Barnes had been an old man and had no stomach for the necessities of fund-raising for new churches and clergy in the difficult years after the war, though schemes were set in motion for new church halls on the vast council estates of the inter-war period (see chapter 17). Wilson was a man with an enormous breadth of experience raring to go after the disappointments of Manchester. It was not long before Birmingham Anglicans in particular, and Brummies in general, realised they had a bishop of singular gifts who was to serve them well.

His interests were not to be confined to Birmingham, however. He was in great demand as speaker and broadcaster and his experience of the world church was not to be diminished in his time as diocesan. He made official overseas visits during almost every year of his episcopate: to Canada, the USA, the West Indies (including a visit to Jamaica as representative of the Archbishop at Independence), West Africa (to see something of the horrors of Biafra when he was already 70 years old), the Holy Land, and many of the countries of Europe. Mary, his wife, usually accompanied him and between them they were excellent ambassadors for the Church, preaching the Word, speaking easily with people of other cultures, and sharing their experience of life and Faith.

Many of the practicalities of Leonard Wilson's time at Birmingham are to be found in later chapters. It was he who realised that there was a revolution going on in youth culture in the 1960s and that the Church needed to respond to it, so he appointed David Collyer as chaplain to the unattached (see chapter 19); it was he who saw the need to respond to the absence of faith in the secularised estates of the inter-war period and the equally large housing and slum clearance schemes that got underway in the mid-1950s, so he put his authority behind the major fund-raising efforts needed to finance new clergy, vicarages and churches on these estates (see chapter 17); it was he who saw that the diocese needed to respond to the inflow of migrants to Birmingham and Smethwick and so he again he appointed a chaplain to develop the work (see chapter 27), but most people get a feel for their bishop when he visits their church. In visiting the parishes of his diocese Bishop Wilson rarely failed to impress. He had a commanding physical presence, a magnificent speaking voice, prepared his sermons meticulously for each occasion, spoke authoritatively, and had a feel for liturgy to suit every occasion. He was a sacramentalist but could not tolerate fripperies in worship for which he could see no purpose; many stories are told in his biography of Anglo-Catholic vicars, churchwardens and others being left in no doubt of his displeasure at false pomp and ceremony. One unfortunate warden, trying to brief the bishop asked: 'You won't mind if I put you right on our procedure?' to which Wilson replied 'Not a bit, if you don't mind my telling you when I've had enough' (McKay 1973: 135).

Canon Maclean recalled that Wilson 'had a great sense of compassion for those who had made a mess of their lives, especially if they were young … he was a jolly, human bishop'. He was also instrumental in getting bishops out of their Victorian frock coats and gaiters through the simple medium of refusing to wear them himself; others quickly began to follow his lead. Indeed he was as often seen in collar and tie as with clerical collar and many recall the old raincoat and battered hat in which he appeared at church doors. However, for services he was perfectly aware that his magnificent cope transformed him into a figure of authority.

50 *Bishop Wilson at Butlins, Skegness with the diocesan youth in 1968 (McKay 1973).*

Bishop Wilson's biggest failing was in formal meetings; he did not relish the chair and was always fearful that others could think on their feet more quickly than himself. He reacted with flashes of anger and some people kept quiet rather than risk his wrath in these situations but, like many quick-tempered people, he did not bear a grudge. Canon Douglas Maclean recalled that 'he could fly into a sudden outburst of rage and one dodged behind the nearest piece of furniture and waited for the storm to pass, which it did instantly'. However, staff meetings, Bishop's Council, Convocation and the like depressed him and he rarely agreed to serve on commissions and committees. The major exception was a commission in the mid-1960s on the Police, the report being widely welcomed. He did have the knack of asking the question that everyone else was thinking but no-one wanted to voice. At a meeting of the bishops discussing whether Communion wine should be fermented or not, after several hours of debate Wilson suggested inserting 'good' before 'wine' and leaving it at that, at which everyone laughed and agreed! His presence and comments were valued by his fellow bishops for their practicality and common sense, and similarly his infrequent contributions to the House of Lords of which the most notable was certainly his comments on immigration in the 1960s (see chapter 27).

By contrast what he was very good at was individual relationships. His clergy quickly understood that here was a man who listened to them and did his best to help with whatever problems life threw into their path. He loved parties and social occasions where he could free himself of people's perceptions of his high office. The triennial meetings of diocesan clergy at Swanwick were regarded as going on holiday with them; there were garden parties on the lawns of Bishop's Croft, and there were visits to Twickenham, Lords and Edgbaston for cricket and rugby. He also enjoyed visits to the theatre and often went backstage to speak to the actors, and he was always happy to be asked to speak at Rotary and services clubs. He enjoyed relating that the number on his car SOB1 stood for 'Shepherd of Birmingham'; he enjoyed being 'Len the Bish' to the rockers of the Double Zero club; he enjoyed meeting people in the local pub as much as in church; he enjoyed the countryside, driving along country lanes, and staying in country hotels.

51 *Bishop Wilson greets Princess Margaret on her visit to Birmingham in 1960 (McKay 1973).*

Bishop Wilson was not a great theologian, he was a man of the people, partly because he had had to question his faith. He summed up his position splendidly in an interview for the BBC:

> I haven't got the kind of faith that is ready-made. I've had to fight for it. I've always been questioning. I've questioned the creeds; I've questioned the Bible; I've questioned the Establishment; I've questioned the way the Church works; and I'm going on questioning all my life, I hope, because I hope to find that the Holy Spirit will lead me to a deeper understanding of what God really wants in this world (McKay 1973: 147).

His questioning led him to support a more liberal stance on the way the Church treated divorced people; he had no truck with those clergy who wanted to prevent infant Baptisms of non-church members; and he was in favour of women's ordination; indeed, he was President of the Anglican Group for the Ordination of Women at a time when few bishops were willing to speak out on the matter. He was happy for it to be known that he could not 'see why women should not have their place in the ministry of Christ as deacons, priests or bishops ... I can't help thinking of the time when the early Church had to decide whether to let in the Gentiles' (McKay 1973: 184).

Leonard Wilson resigned the see in September 1969 when he was 72. That summer he had gone back to Singapore to make a film for the BBC about his experiences and was deeply moved by the reception he received from people who had known him from 25 years earlier; he said goodbye to his clergy at Swanwick in July, telling them about his experiences in Changi; he said goodbye to the city and laypeople of the diocese in the Town Hall in September and the Wilson's retired to a small house in Wensleydale. Sadly, he lived for only one more year. He had a minor stroke returning from taking a service at St Paul's Cathedral, and then a more serious one. He died at home on 18 August 1970. His simple memorial stone in Birmingham cathedral is set into the floor at the chancel step. It ends – 'Confessor for the Faith'.

Laurence Ambrose Brown

FIFTH BISHOP, 1969-77

Laurence Brown was born in 1907 in Bedfordshire. He came from a fairly lowly background and went to Luton Grammar School. He went on to Queens' College, Cambridge, where he read first history and then theology, graduating BA in 1931. He went immediately to Cuddesdon College, Oxford for theological training. It was there that he first displayed his gift for enthusiastic leadership that was to become his hallmark, and his commitment to the Boy Scout movement. He succeeded in enrolling almost all of his contemporaries at Cuddesdon into a Rover Scout Crew and sending them out to assist at local Scout Troops as leaders. This was not what was normally expected in a staid Anglican theological college! However, his fellow students were to thank him for it when they reached their first parishes and were expected to take an interest in the uniformed organisations meeting in their church halls. Their experiences with Laurie Brown's Rover Crew stood them in good stead.

Brown was ordained deacon in 1932 in the parish of St John the Divine, Kennington, south London, in the Diocese of Southwark. He was priested in 1933 and remained at St John's for three years until 1935. He certainly continued with his Scouting activities there, not only becoming Scoutmaster of the parish Troop, but apparently travelling all over south London visiting and encouraging other troops and speaking at Scout rallies, complete with his own ciné equipment. He undertook a second curacy at Christ Church, Luton (1935-40) in his home town, before spending the years of the Second World War as Vicar of Hatfield Hyde, Hertfordshire (1940-46).

Brown had considerable gifts of administration and, unusually, he moved into ecclesiastical administration as Assistant Secretary and, from 1952, as Secretary, to the South London Church Fund and Southwark Diocesan Board of Finance (1946-60). He combined this with a Residentiary Canonry at Southwark Cathedral where he was successively Precentor (1950-56) and Vice Provost (1956-60) as well as Archdeacon of Lewisham (1955-60).

To Warrington and Birmingham

In 1960 he was invited by Bishop Clifford Martin to leave London and the Home Counties and become Suffragan Bishop of Warrington in the Diocese of Liverpool. He was consecrated in York Minster in November and, since he was then aged 53, may well have thought that it would prove to be his last post. However, nine years later, in 1969, he was translated to Birmingham to succeed Bishop Wilson. Brown was a pastor and an administrator rather than a great theologian. He was very much a man of the people and was a popular and much-loved bishop amongst his laity. The grander citizens of Birmingham sometimes did not know what to make of him. He continued to serve the Scout Movement in Birmingham, becoming County Commissioner, and he once attended a Lord Mayor's function wearing Scout uniform, including shorts, not having had time to change between functions after a Scout rally.

Bishop Mark Green, his suffragan, suggests that he 'combined a Scout-master's jokinesss, a company director's perception that money talks, and a monk's understanding that life is prayer and prayer is life'.

One of Brown's accomplishments was to build on the work of his predecessor in developing ecumenical relationships. In 1972 the four leaders of the Birmingham Council of Christian Churches used the Week of Prayer for Christian Unity to issue a call to their church members to develop a 'New Initiative' to work together to proclaim the Gospel and to serve the community. This New Initiative ran for two years and culminated in 'March Together', a week of activities

52   *The official portrait of Laurence Brown as Bishop of Birmingham in Bishop's Croft, Birmingham.*

in March 1974. A large number of personalities were involved in the programme, including David Kossoff reading Bible stories in Solihull, Bishop Trevor Huddleston giving an address in Sutton Coldfield, and The Spinners performing at Birmingham Town Hall. The film of 'Jesus Christ Superstar' ran at the ABC cinema on Bristol Road, and Sunday Half Hour was broadcast from St Laurence's church, Northfield. There was a procession of witness in Warley to Lightwoods Park and Cliff Richard gave a concert in the Methodist Central Hall. Nothing quite like it was to happen again until the Millennium celebrations.

His *Times* obituarist commented: 'Bishop Brown's devotion to the Church of England was absolute. Moreover from the very beginnings of his ministry he had no doubt that the Church's work and influence depended, more than anything else, on the efficiency and pastoral sense of its parochial clergy. Even when he came to be a bishop, he still remained a parish priest at heart.' His pastoral sense began with his suffragan who

> found him invariably kind and understanding. No matter how busy he was always available to me. I could go into his office anytime. Often he would be dictating letters, but his secretary (a real terror to fools and time-wasters) taught me how to manage it. "Bring a book and sit down till he notices you" so I did. He would go on dictating and then suddenly throw a letter over to me. "Look at this one … another from old worryguts"!
>
> Laurie was most typically himself at the numerous public dinners we had to attend. His "Graces" for bankers, chemists, lawyers, Rotarians,

53 *Bishop Brown at the dedication of St Michael's, Gospel Lane Anglican-Methodist church centre in 1971.*

councillors, whatever, were skilfully crafted to convey thanks to God in amusing parody of the profession that had come together for this social occasion. They usually ended not with "Amen" but loud laughter and applause. Yet at the heart of the Grace there was often more than a comedian's wit. There was the touch of a surgeon's knife, or an Old Testament prophet's diagnosis.

Green thinks that 'Laurie was the ideal man for Birmingham: down to earth and relating easily to people of different religious denominations, different faiths, races, ages and social backgrounds; always being himself; a connexion between heaven and earth. You can't ask much more than that of any Christian minister, from cardinal to curate.' Brown was never a national figure like both his predecessor and successor and he reached the Episcopal bench of the House of Lords only in his last four years as bishop. His obituarist believes that he represented a 'distinct, if slightly old-fashioned strain within the Church of England. The phrase for it used to be "muscular Christianity"'. Bishop Montefiore's biographer (Peart-Binns 1990) says that Brown 'had the gifts of a Boy Scout and the temperament of a marriage guidance counsellor. He could be innovative but he was a reconciler at heart. The pint in his hand was natural, not affected. The cares of office hardly affected him. He was a focus of unity.' Brown retired from Birmingham in 1977 at the age of 70. He went to live in Salisbury and happily took up duty once more as a parish priest, taking charge of the village communities of Nunton and Odstock just outside the city, until 1984. He died in February 1994, aged 86. He and his wife, Florence, were blessed with three daughters.

Hugh William Montefiore

SIXTH BISHOP, 1978-87

Hugh Montefiore was born into one of the great Sephardic (Iberian) Jewish families of England. His great-great uncle, Sir Moses Haim Montefiore (1784-1884), was perhaps the most famous member of the family moving easily amongst the governing and business classes of mid-Victorian England. Sir Moses was childless, and in leaving much of his estate to his favourite nephew, Joseph Sebag, he asked him to add Montefiore to his name. Sir Joseph Sebag-Montefiore (1822-1903) had a son, Arthur (1853-1995). Arthur's son Charles was a prominent businessman in the City; he married Muriel de Pass in 1913, and they had three sons – Denzil (1914), Oliver (1915) and Hugh (1920). They lived in a palatial mansion, 2, Palace Green, Kensington, which had once belonged to William Makepeace Thackeray, and which is now the Israeli embassy. It was full of exquisite objects and works of art and there were a dozen servants, including a nanny for Hugh. There was also a summer holiday home in Aberdeenshire. The Sebag-Montefiores were observant, rather than strictly orthodox Jews, but synagogue, family prayers and the great Jewish feast days were potent and memorable parts of Hugh's childhood.

After a local preparatory school, he was sent to Beaudesert Park School at Minchinhampton (Glos) in 1929, and on to public school at Rugby in 1933 with an entrance scholarship. At Rugby he was in the classics group but never regarded himself as a scholar of great ability compared with many of his contemporaries. He spent much of his spare time in the art school, played rugby well and was an enthusiastic member of the school Scout troop.

Conversion and the Army

Aged 16, whilst sitting in his study at school, he saw a distant figure in white beckoning him, whom he instantly knew to be Jesus. The figure said 'follow me'. Later, he woke a friend in the dormitory to tell him, 'I have seen the Lord!', but was told to go back to bed and go to sleep. However, Montefiore knew that 'in the morning I was a Jew and by the evening I had become a Christian as well. I knew with absolute certainty that God had taken hold of my life, that Jesus was my Lord and that I must follow in his way … the next day I broke my Good News to my housemaster.' He then had to give the Bad News to his family, who were devastated.

It was decided at school that he should go to the Rector of Rugby, Richard Brook, and he was subsequently baptised in Rugby parish church and confirmed the following year in the school chapel. In 1938 he gained a scholarship to St John's College, Oxford and went up soon after war had been declared. He spent a year agonising over whether he should follow his pacifist leanings or join up. He was not enthused by the college chapel but the university church of St Mary and the Revd Dick Milford was more to his liking. He also joined the Student Christian Movement (SCM) and became intercollegiate secretary; there he met Elizabeth Paton, the daughter of a Presbyterian minister, with whom he quickly fell in love and proposed marriage.

He joined the army (doing his initial training with Gunner Denis Healey) and then went for officer training where he found that the commandant was the fearsome Colonel T.H. Sebag-Montefiore DSO, MC – his uncle, who was certainly not inclined to show him any favours. He was shipped to India in the Royal Bucks Yeomanry. He was a gunnery survey officer and in his own words it taught him about pastoral care and putting others before his own needs. He saw action in the fearsome Kohima campaign against the Japanese. He also became certain that God was calling him to ordination.

Hugh and Elizabeth were married in St Albans Cathedral in 1945 and he returned to his studies in Oxford taking a First in theology. He then went to Westcott House in Cambridge for his ordination training where he was regarded as the outstanding theologian of his year. Meanwhile Hugh and Elizabeth's two daughters, Teresa and Janet, had been born. The family were transported to Newcastle, to St George's, Jesmond, for his curacy and he was ordained deacon at Advent in 1949. Unfortunately, his parish priest left soon after to become Bishop of Jarrow and Hugh was left to care for the parish, supported only by visiting clergy and an equally new parish worker. He was certainly thrown in at the deep end but two years later he was invited to return to Westcott House as chaplain and tutor. The following year he became Vice Principal and was joined as chaplain by Robert Runcie (later Archbishop of Canterbury); between them they did all the teaching. This was not a happy time for Hugh as wives and families of both students and staff were not welcome at Westcott House; however, his first book, prompted by the formation of the Church of South India, was published. In 1954 he was glad of the opportunity to leave to be Fellow and Dean of Gonville and Caius College, Cambridge, and became university lecturer in theology the following year. He enjoyed teaching, caring for students, updating worship in the college chapel, and encouraging those of faith and those without. He did not enjoy the petty politics of college life.

Vicar of Great St Mary's

In 1963 he was offered the living of Great St Mary's, Cambridge in succession to Revd Joe Fison who had been elevated to be Bishop of Salisbury. He resigned his lectureship and took this new opportunity. He delighted in inviting the great, the famous, the good (and occasionally the bad) to use his pulpit during the university service, and the church was often packed to the rafters. He wrote critically of developments in the Church and in the town; he was a good publicist; and he allowed a quarterly 'beat' service, with pop music, to be organised by his curates. Another book, *Beyond Reasonable Doubt*, was published in 1963. As his biographer says, he was in the thick, but not at the centre, of theological thought and ecclesiastical ferment in the late 1950s and 1960s (Peart-Binns 1990). His succession of curates all speak of his care in training them and of the way in which everyone's nerves were on edge before major services as he prowled around ensuring everything was OK; something which was certainly familiar to Birmingham vicars and wardens too!

One of his friends at Cambridge was the Dean of King's College, Alexander (Alec) Vidler. Vidler had been Vicar at St Aidan's, Small Heath and had been banned

54 *Bishop Hugh and his wife Eliza in the garden of Bishop's Croft, Harborne.*

by Bishop Barnes for his Anglo-Catholic practices. It was he who stimulated an important edited book, *Soundings*. In 1967 came Hugh Montefiore's most notorious publication, a paper to the 50th Conference of Modern Churchmen, at Oxford. In it he speculated on the possibility of Jesus having a homosexual nature because of his unmarried state. There was a reporter present and before he knew what was happening he had become an international news event. Amongst other consequences, the Prime Minister's Appointments Secretary, John Hewitt, determined that, unlike his predecessors at Great St Mary's, he should not be recommended for a bishopric, and he was not, until after Hewitt's retirement. Hugh was deeply hurt. On the surface he was a self-possessed, dominating and extrovert person, but he was easily hurt by unkind words or printed criticisms.

His next intellectual endeavour was into the field of environmental matters, which stayed with him for the rest of his life. He was sometimes seen by the Church, and by himself, as a Jeremiah-like prophet who was certain of a coming environmental catastrophe and so called on people to repent and turn back. His early ideas were brought together in another book, *The Question Mark: the End of Homo Sapiens* (1969). This meant that if the media wanted a comment on environmental matters with a theological slant, it was to him that they turned. Books and articles poured from his pen, there were radio and TV appearances, Great St Mary's services, and he continued to teach in a number of colleges. To Margaret Baker, a student at Newnham College, he was 'conspicuously the best teacher in Cambridge'. All this work had its consequence in regular attacks of back pain from which he continued to suffer all his life. In 1969 he had a three-month sabbatical. It was during this time that he was approached indirectly by Bishop John Robinson, Dean of Trinity College, on behalf of Bishop Mervyn Stockwood of Southwark, to ask if he would like to be Area Bishop of Kingston.

From Kingston to Birmingham

The announcement of his appointment, in January 1970, when Montefiore was still only 49, generated immense national interest and some hysterical outpourings from both the Evangelical and Catholic extremities of the Church. He was consecrated in Southwark Cathedral by Archbishop Michael Ramsay. He and Elizabeth purchased a home on the south side of Wandsworth Common within the bounds of his episcopal area and to which they returned on his retirement. Kingston educated him on the issues of being a Black and White Church, since Brixton was within his area too; it also changed his views on Church schools since he was chairman of the Diocesan Board of Education. He began deeply prejudiced against them and ended as their champion. He also began to be drawn into the work of the national Church, first as Chair of the Central Readers' Board, and then as a member of the Board for Social Responsibility; he was elected to General Synod by the suffragans in 1976.

55 *Procession of the diocesan pilgrims at Canterbury.*

There was immense public interest in the appointment of the sixth Bishop of Birmingham in 1977 because it was the first to use the new Crown Appointments Commission established by General Synod the previous year. Montefiore's name came up frequently in the discussion and was eventually leaked from the Commission as a probable choice. The Birmingham *Evening Mail* was not keen, nor was a local Tory councillor, Anthony Beaumont-Dark (later MP for Selly Oak). Their fears were centred on Montefiore's supposed antagonism to the motor-car on which the whole regional economy was based. His appointment was announced in October 1977, and he was installed on 4 March 1978. His sermon set the priorities: 'The first priority of the Church is God'. It ended: 'The Gospel is not for the chosen few; it is for everyone, whether they hear or whether they don't; and I shall regard it as the first priority of my episcopate to take a lead by preaching, by public address and by informal discussions, in sharing the Good News about God with the people of this city'.

Bishop Mark Green had been Bishop of Aston for five years and had been one of the possibilities canvassed to replace Bishop Brown. He remembers: 'Hugh came in the middle of my ten-year stint; so for me it was like putting on a new shirt at half time. He came not without opposition. The Birmingham press carried a ten-day hate campaign against him. He came in like a tornado. I was surprised that with his razor-sharp mind and original thinking he began by scrapping the existing order of diocesan services and substituting those currently in use in Southwark. But it wasn't long before the real Hugh Montefiore was revealed. He was never in danger of being a mere photocopy of anybody else. I found it easy to get on with him. He never treated me other than as a brother in episcopal ministry, and in fact delegated rather more to me than Laurie Brown had done.'

In Birmingham Montefiore was in no-one else's shadow and he blossomed. He continued his teaching by founding a periodical for the diocese, *The Bishopric*, in which he could write about theological issues to his clergy and informed laity and stimulate people's thinking on ethical matters of the day such as human embryo research, divorce, and the ideas of people such as Don Cupitt. He grappled with the problems of balancing episcopal leadership and Synodical government at both national and diocesan level, determined that the Church should not become a sclerotic institution.

He had ideas and ideas led to action. In 1984 he thought that a diocesan pilgrimage to Canterbury would be a good idea; on 21 June 1986 it happened: 3,000 pilgrims travelled to Canterbury by chartered train and a fleet of coaches; one or two even walked. They had badges and brooches; Bible readings for the day; workbooks and pilgrimage pens for the children. In Canterbury there was a great procession from the cricket ground to the cathedral led by the mayor of Canterbury and Bishop Hugh, a Salvation Army band played, and banners and flags were waved; the destination was the 2.30pm service in the cathedral with the archbishop. There were so many pilgrims that the seats had been removed from the nave to allow everyone to crowd in. By midnight all were safely back in Birmingham. The previous year had seen another pilgrimage led by the bishop, this time to the Holy Land.

Another 'good idea' was 'Live, Learn, Share', a scheme to give more confidence and articulacy about their faith to lay Christians in the diocese. Canon Ian Bennett developed the idea into a practical course which ran in the 1984-86 period. He later recalled that everyone enjoyed the learning but people were more diffident of translating this into practical plans for living and sharing their faith. Bishop Michael Whinney recalls that 'Bishop's staff meetings were sometimes lively affairs with the then Archdeacon of Birmingham (an ex-rugby player!) ready to disagree strongly with Hugh whenever he thought it necessary. It produced energetic debates! All the more when Hugh would follow through some of his brainwaves, his "good ideas", when we were all on holiday in August – fait accompli! Bishop Hugh's leadership was as mercurial as his brain. He taught me so much and I enjoyed working with him greatly.'

Bishop Mark Green also recalls staff meetings:

> Patience was not his most prominent virtue. For example, at a staff meeting discussing some vacant parish which had been offered to a priest of another diocese, Hugh addressed his chaplain: "Chaplain, why haven't we heard from this man?" "Well, bishop", said Chris Boyle, his chaplain, "you only wrote to him yesterday"! But the impatience was a part of his far-ranging mind, seeing global warnings and global potentialities, as well as relating intimately to the needs of a great multi-racial city with its vitality, inventiveness and the desperate need of many of its citizens for help of various kinds, challenged the Church to a feet-washing ministry, combined with prophecy and proclamation of the gospel of God's universal love. There was thus a divine imperative about Hugh's impatience. It is badly needed today.

Montefiore also made it his business to get to know about the business that dominated the West Midlands economy, the motor car industry. In the 1980s it was going through a torrid time and British Leyland at Longbridge was being reorganised and streamlined by its management. It was subject to a series of damaging strikes and Bishop Hugh immersed himself in the problems by talking to management, trade unionists, workers and government and appealing for negotiation rather than confrontation. He was advised by one of his specialist chaplains, Canon Denis Claringbull, who usually accompanied him on his visits to factories and training establishments. He, too, recalls: 'It was rather like working for an unpredictable, yet lovable, whirlwind! … He would tour the factory at high speed, … dashing off into odd corners to talk to people who seemed to be tucked away out of sight. He was not afraid to ask searching questions on these occasions and recognized expert management when he saw it' (Peart-Binns 1990: 304). The City Council and its politicians were brought within his purview, too, and he enjoyed especially good relations with the leader of the council, Cllr Sir Dick Knowles.

56 *Canon Keith Withington, Vicar of St Francis, Bournville, preparing for the Holy Land pilgrimage.*

Increasingly, he was as active outside Birmingham as he was within it, especially during his final few years. By then he had reached the House of Lords as one of the 21 most senior bishops. He made an immediate impact, speaking on a wide range of issues, but especially on the environment, labour relations and in his last months sponsoring a Private Members Bill to cut the time available for abortion from 28 weeks to 24 weeks. In 1985-86 he made 22 speeches in total, three of them on the abortive Shops Bill designed to preserve the special character of Sunday. He was a powerful debater in General Synod, most memorably in the all-day televised debate on 'The Church and the Bomb' where his amended motion carried the day. He was a member of the Board for Social Responsibility from 1975, and its Chair from 1982. He always expected reports issuing from the Board to be thoroughly marked by serious theological reflection and reasoning, not simply discussing social problems *per se*. Though a surprise to some, he revealed in his autobiography that his name had been one of those considered when the Archbishopric of Canterbury became vacant; Robert Runcie was eventually appointed and Bishop Hugh doubted that he himself would have had sufficiently thick a skin to deal with the cares of that particular office.

Pastor and Friend

It is not every bishop who can be a great teacher, as Hugh was, as well as a prophet, a wise administrator, and a pastor who gave himself freely to others. He used to say that, if any of the clergy desperately needed to see him, then (providing he was not away from Birmingham) he would see them within 24 hours, as long as they didn't mind if it had to be 10pm or even later. What some of the clergy did not understand was that he made

57 *Bishop Hugh in the Bullring market.*

58   *Bishop Hugh at Dudley Road Hospital with a thriving premature baby who might legally have been aborted (Peart-Binns 1990).*

59   *Bishop Hugh Montefiore.*

this promise with absolute seriousness. He was that kind of person, and that kind of bishop. He himself records incidents of his dealings with priests who had got themselves into trouble and concludes: 'I can never understand why a clergyman should be ruined for life because of some foolish act, especially when he is inexperienced. Good heavens! I thought that Christianity is about forgiveness and a fresh start' (Montefiore 1995: 197).

One of Bishop Hugh's more significant gifts to the diocese, which has continued to stand it in good stead for a quarter century, was to appoint Sir William Dugdale as Chair of the Diocesan Board of Finance. Sir William was the descendant of Warwickshire's first historian, but he was an entrepreneur. He was chairman of Severn Trent Water and Bishop Hugh was firmly of the opinion that entrepreneurs were what the Church needed, not accountants. The large losses of 1981 were turned round; the Common Fund contributions of parishes reorganised to such good effect that some money was returned two years later; and money was invested in property to provide the diocese with long-term investments and regular income. Sir William's eccentricities, especially his careful mispronunciation of 'synod' at diocesan synod, were always relished by those present, but no-one was ever to regret his careful management of the financial resources of the diocese.

There can be little doubt that Hugh enlivened the diocese in so many ways and some of the funniest stories found their way into the 'retirement tribute' booklet edited by Colin Buchanan. Revd Adrian Hughes was able to recall being present when the bishop characteristically swept into a church hugging his bag containing his robes telling the anxious warden: 'Don't worry I know my way!' and proceeded to enter the capacious broom cupboard rather than the vestry! In the prestigious surroundings of St Alphege, Solihull he found that he had forgotten his crozier; looking round for a substitute he seized a churchwarden's stave topped with a Georgian silver crown, which he proceeded to try to wrestle off its mount. As a churchwarden myself during his

60   *NEC Arena at Bishop Hugh Montefiore's farewell Eucharist with a congregation of over 7,000 (Peart-Binns 1990).*

last years I, too, can remember him sweeping magisterially by me at a confirmation service, but our staves remained intact and he missed the broom cupboard!

Hugh decided to retire in 1987, when he was aged 67, because of the failing health of his wife Eliza. She had had recurrent falls and was beginning to suffer the early symptoms of Alzheimer's disease. He determined that they would retire to their former London home where he could look after her with some professional help. His retirement was deliberately announced on 1 April, which he thought was entirely appropriate. Bishop Colin Buchanan hired the Arena at the National Exhibition Centre and 7,000 people came to say goodbye. There was a huge choir, liturgical dance and, since Bishop Hugh had said he liked balloons, 3,000 gently floated down as he and Eliza left the hall after he had laid his cope, mitre and staff on the altar. It was a powerful and moving occasion for all privileged to have been there. The enormous regard in which he was held is well shown from the fact that the event featured on the BBC 9 o'clock TV News. There can be little doubt that as theologian, Churchman, prophet and pastor he was a worthy successor to the heritage that Gore had left in Birmingham.

Bishop Hugh died on 13 May 2005, the day after his 85th birthday, widely mourned and respected. Books had continued to pour from his pen in retirement: *So Near and Yet So Far* (1986) on the problems of reconciliation with Roman Catholics; *The Probability of God* (1985) on science and creation; *Credible Christianity* (1994) and *On Being a Jewish Christian* (1998), both on his views on faith, and finally a book on the New Testament miracles, published this year.

MARK SANTER

SEVENTH BISHOP, 1987-2001

Bishop Mark Santer was born in 1936, in Bedminster, Bristol. His mother and father were the first graduates in their respective families. His father was a parish priest in the diocese of Bristol for 40 years, retiring in 1975. Mark was sent away to school at an early age, and eventually went to Marlborough College where he received a solid classical education. In the Sixth Form he remembers particularly 'being taught by the remarkable Alan Whitehorn (father of the journalist Katharine) who had been a conscientious objector in the First World War and who instilled in us a questioning attitude towards all established authority'.

During his two years of National Service (1955-57) he found himself 'for the first time in a setting where the culture of the Church of England was not taken for granted as the background to everything else'. In retrospect two things of significance stood out: 'As a junior officer in a training camp I found myself dealing with the welfare problems of conscripts and their families; from time to time this entailed going to court when young soldiers were arraigned for various crimes.' Secondly, he decided to offer himself for ordination. Consequently, when he went up to Queens' College, Cambridge, he followed two years of classics with two more of theology. This gave him 'a solid theological foundation of a traditional kind – good on biblical languages and exegesis, and on early Christian history and doctrine, not so strong on philosophy and modern doctrine.'

For his ministerial training he remained in Cambridge, at Westcott House (1961-63). John Habgood was Vice-Principal, followed by Don Cupitt. This was at a time when, after the cultural retrenchment of the immediate post-war years, the questioning of received certainties in society at large was being mirrored by questioning within the Church, typified by John Robinson's *Honest to God*. However, there was also the steady example of Peter Walker, the Principal. During his first year at Westcott House Mark did a lot of reading in the Church Fathers. Most of his second year was spent as an ecumenical student in the Theological Faculty of the University of Utrecht, where he learned to speak Dutch. He says that 'the year opened my eyes both to continental Protestantism – very different from the English varieties (beer, schnapps, cigars and strong theology) – and also to continental Catholicism (different again). This was an exciting time, the first year of the Second Vatican Council. This year, together with my study of patristic theology, laid the foundation of my future ecumenical work. I also met a group of young Protestants who had long-standing links with friends in East Germany. This gave me my first encounters with the world and Christian life behind the Berlin Wall.' He also met his future wife Henriette, who was a clinical psychologist by profession. She came from a family that was in many ways typical of the thoughtful and morally serious Protestant bourgeoisie of the Netherlands, deeply committed to the expression of Christian faith in daily life. On Sundays they expected to hear and to discuss theological sermons of high quality.

Westcott House and Kensington

He was ordained curate in 1963, to the small village of Cuddesdon near Oxford, where he had also been appointed a tutor at the theological college. Robert Runcie, later Archbishop of Canterbury, was Vicar and Principal. Bishop Mark remembers his 'extraordinary gift for nurturing a community that was at ease with itself and the unselfconscious discipline of corporate daily prayer'. Mark was priested the following year and married Henriette, both within the space of a week. She, not surprisingly, found the move from a continental university hospital, where men and women worked together as colleagues, to an all-male theological college which was still run on Tractarian lines, very difficult. What saved her was finding work outside Cuddesdon in the NHS.

After four years of Cuddesdon, Mark Santer returned to Cambridge as Fellow and Dean of Clare College (1967-72). After a year he also became one of the college's Tutors and University Assistant Lecturer in Early Christian Doctrine (where at one time he had the young Rowan Williams, the present Archbishop, among his audience). At the end of 1972 he was asked to become Principal of Westcott House. He says that 'this faced me with a fundamental and irreversible choice: church or academia. I was clear where my primary vocation lay and accepted the appointment'. At Westcott House he was blessed with some remarkable colleagues and students. By this time ministerial education had become more theologically rigorous and many students combined their ministerial training with study for a theological degree in the university. Mark remembers that 'it was our purpose not so much to equip our ordinands with a set of up-to-date pastoral or missionary wheezes as to give them a theological and spiritual formation that would enable them to think for themselves, not to be blown about by fashion ancient or modern, and to handle change when it came – as come it surely would'. During this time, under Robert Runcie's chairmanship, he became a member of the Anglican-Orthodox International Doctrinal Commission. As well as using his patristic knowledge, this took him to places like rural Romania, Moscow and Athens, where he learned something of the depth and difficulty of the cultural and emotional gulf between western and eastern Christianity. He was appointed to an honorary Canonry of Winchester Cathedral in 1978.

By the end of 1980 he knew that it was time for a change; work with ordinands was intense and rewarding, but also narrow. Providence sent him change in the form of a letter (strictly personal and confidential – eat after reading) from Gerald Ellison, then Bishop of London, inviting him to be Area Bishop of Kensington. There he found himself responsible for about 100 parishes of astonishing social variety stretching from Kensington Palace to Staines. One of his Area Deans was John Barton who was later to join him in Birmingham as Archdeacon of Aston. It was Bishop Mark's first real experience of the Church of England as a multi-cultural, multi-ethnic church. Liturgical experiences varied from the Carnival Mass in Notting Hill (one year with a troupe of dancing banana trees!) to Morning Prayer with military band in the chapel of Chelsea Hospital. In this setting, partly because of its scale, and partly because financial and administrative matters were looked after at diocesan level, it was possible for an area bishop to know all his clergy and many of his congregations quite well. His six and a half years in London also introduced him to HIV/AIDS as a pastoral issue. Three things stand out: 'being called for the first time to a hospital chapel to confirm a man suffering from AIDS; a parish priest dying of AIDS; and the founding of the London Lighthouse', of which he was asked to be a patron.

The Anglican Roman Catholic Commission

Following the papal visit to England in 1982 and the establishment of the second Anglican Roman Catholic International Commission (ARCIC II), in 1983 Archbishop Robert Runcie asked Bishop Mark to become Anglican co-chairman. His partner was Bishop (now Cardinal Archbishop) Cormac Murphy-O'Connor. Because of the common cultural, intellectual and theological inheritance, this was a much less complicated project than dialogue with the Orthodox. Through meeting, eating, studying and praying together they 'became a band of close colleagues who found ourselves not negotiating over a chasm but exploring and trying to untangle what we knew to be shared problems'.

He remained co-chairman until 1998. ARCIC I had focused on the key issues in Anglican-Catholic relations: eucharist, ministry and authority. The brief of ARCIC II was much wider. As well as revisiting the agenda of ARCIC I, it worked on a variety of issues notably justification, ecclesiology, and moral theology.

The annual plenary meetings lasted eight days. Archbishop Kevin McDonald writes that 'it is hard to explain to someone who has never been part of such discussions the intensity of the experience both at the theological and personal level. The warm friendship between Bishop Mark and Bishop Murphy O'Connor was a key ingredient in the "chemistry" of the commission'. During his time on the commission it produced four major reports. These were *Salvation and the Church* (1987), *Church as Communion* (1991), *Life in Christ: Morals, Communion and the Church* (1994) and *The Gift of Authority* (1999). Also published in 1994 under Bishop Mark's co-chairmanship was a brief paper entitled *Clarifications* which sought to clear away some misunderstandings raised by the Vatican response to ARCIC I. This group of papers presented a significant advance in bi-lateral dialogues between two major world Christian communions.

Bishop Mark is remembered as an incisive, energetic and highly constructive chairman. He was always interested in what everyone had to say but could put his foot down if he felt the discussion was losing focus. His remarkable knowledge and memory for the writings of the Patristic period meant that he brought to the process a very substantial theological background. Bishop Stephen Platten of Wakefield writes that

> there were occasions when his contributions could be sharp and to the point but he and Bishop Murphy O'Connor were an outstanding duo. They brought different skills and background to the table but these skills were complementary and led to a very effective commission. Bishop Mark's encyclopaedic knowledge of the Fathers always made the sessions of the main commission and its sub-commissions very lively. Reflecting on a specific subject, in the middle of the session the bishop would leap up take a book from his own library and interject something like: 'it was Tertullian who said that'.

Bishop Mark was personally committed to the cause of Anglican-Catholic relations. He was very much his own man and kept up his reading to a remarkable degree for someone who had all the pastoral and administrative responsibilities of a bishop. As a result of his work on ARCIC he was also very good at enabling good ecumenical relations in Birmingham. He worked particularly closely with, and was very fond of, the Roman Catholic Archbishop, Maurice Couve de Murville, but he also very much enjoyed working with the other Church leaders in Birmingham.

Start of Episcopate

In 1987, Bishop Mark was unexpectedly translated to Birmingham. The very beginning of his episcopacy was surrounded in controversy. After the announcement of his appointment as Bishop of Birmingham, in April 1987, speculation began in the press that Mrs Thatcher had chosen his name in preference to the first name put forward by the Crown Appointments Commission, the then Bishop of Stepney, the Rt Revd Jim Thompson (subsequently Bishop of

61 *Official portrait of Mark Santer as Bishop of Birmingham in Bishop's Croft, Harborne.*

Bath and Wells). The *Church Times* (16 April 1987) stated that there were reports circulating that a group of Conservative MPs had lobbied her against the appointment of Bishop Thompson 'because he was too left wing for them'. Birmingham was expecting to welcome Bishop Thompson, whilst Bishop Mark must have been a little embarrassed since he was in print as saying that the Prime Minister ought not to have discretion to choose the second person on the Commission list, yet here he was, nominated in exactly that way.

His first chaplain, Revd David Newsome, suggests that the bishop's enthronement in Birmingham Cathedral on Saturday 3 October 1987 became a crucial statement not only of his theological vision but of his independence too. This, coupled with a sermon preached the following week to the Judges of the West Midlands, clearly indicated the priorities that were to mark the whole of his episcopate in Birmingham. At his enthronement he spoke of entering into an inheritance of faith that encompassed not only Charles Gore (first Bishop of Birmingham) but included, amongst others, the Congregationalist Robert Dale, pastor at Carrs Lane for more than 40 years, and Cardinal John Henry Newman.

> It is my prayer that in God's good time, and sooner rather than later, there will once again be only one Christian community here, presided over by one bishop – as it was in the days of St Chad … It will be the universal Church of Jesus Christ in this place. It won't be some bland monolith. Its life will be as richly diverse as the life of all the churches today – a living witness to the world that in the Lord diversity does not mean division, and difference does not mean better or worse.

Bishop Santer stated that it is human pride and pretension that keeps us apart from God and one another. He went on to argue how this had become institutionalised

62 *Bishop Mark Santer and his late wife, Henriette, at Bishop's Croft.*

within society with 'selfishness turned into a publicly acceptable principle of social and personal policy'. The editorial in *The Daily Telegraph* afterwards (15 October 1987) was headed 'Turbulent Priests' and suggested that the fire brigade in Birmingham should prepare for the bolts of lightning that followed Bishop David Jenkins' consecration in York Minster, for this thinly-veiled 'political' attack on Thatcherism!

The following week, with the judiciary of the West Midlands arrayed before him, he challenged them to use their power to press for judicial reform. It was a great exposition of judging, leading in to a detailed critique of sentencing policy, the use of imprisonment and (even more relevant today) the overcrowding of prisons. Afterwards the tabloid press fulminated against the 'do-gooding' bishop meddling in things he shouldn't. But the next day the then Home Secretary, Douglas Hurd, rang up to ask for a private meeting at Bishop's Croft in order to discuss the issues he had raised, recognising the seriousness and thoroughness of the Bishop's challenge. In the space of ten days Bishop Mark had firmly indicated the priorities for his whole ministry: the unity of the Church; the value and dignity of human beings created in the divine image; and for justice that reflects the mercy of God.

Looking backwards, Bishop Mark believes that two particular issues stood out as priorities. The first was already recognised in the diocese: the call to build a truly 'black and white Church'. He would now put that somewhat differently: it is a call to build a church of all peoples. Secondly, he became 'increasingly aware of the need to respond, theologically as well as politically, to Birmingham's character as a city of many faiths and cultures'. Significantly, he believes, the need to give due justice to the claims of other faith communities has created a new space in which the Christian community can witness without apology to its own identity. During his 15-year episcopate he showed himself to be sensitive to the changes in context and responded appropriately to those changes. He began to see, under the guidance of first Revd Roger Hooker and then Revd Chris Hewer, the growing importance of inter-faith relations in Birmingham. It meant that the relationships were in place when the attack on the World Trade Centre took place in 2001 for the other faith leaders of Birmingham to act in solidarity with their Muslim counterparts.

Working with Bishop Mark

The Ven. John Duncan, Archdeacon of Birmingham for much of Bishop Mark's episcopate, records that 'the focus of working with Bishop Mark as one of his central staff team was the monthly staff meeting, beginning with Holy Communion at 7.30am in the chapel at Bishops Croft. The clergy celebrated in turns, with the bishop as readily the server as the celebrant. It would have been unthinkable not to have begun at the altar; it was part of his catholic understanding of the Church; it was the place where prayers for the people and concerns of the diocese were offered to God; a task unfussed, undramatic and low key, but fundamental.' The bishop always made clear that the staff meeting had no authority, it was there to advise him in his decisions, but its spirit was collaborative. Tasks were allotted to individuals who were then trusted to get on with it in an orderly and timely way without interference. He had little patience with muddle, making it up as you go along, or late arrival.

Birmingham's staff meetings under Bishop Mark were never Barchester, they were not disabled by the tensions of competing egos, bad temper and back stabbing, more usually they were pleasurable, often entertaining, and occasionally inspiring. Bishop John Austin notes that 'when Mark was on form he was brilliant. He was fun to work with, a quick wit and a lovely sense of humour. He enjoyed stories illustrating human foibles and loved Birmingham people,

63 *Bishop Mark Santer at the opening of SS Mary and Margaret's Castle Bromwich nursery school.*

their humour and their accent.' Nonetheless, it is important to recall that there were some fallings out, most notably with the suffragan he had inherited, Bishop Colin Buchanan, in the aftermath of the mission led by Archbishop Desmond Tutu in 1989 (see chapters 14 and 24), and he seemed never to be able to have more than a superficially civil relationship with the Provost of the cathedral, the Very Revd Peter Berry.

Canon John Wesson, sometime Rector of St Martin's-in-the-Bullring, records that the quarterly meeting of the deans at the bishop's house was 'always run efficiently – and followed by an excellent buffet lunch! There was always a sense of positive leadership, but Mark unfailingly gave space to the deans for feedback on policy issues. His default mode was certainly decisiveness, so that at least things happened even if some in the discussion remained unconvinced.'

The collaborative working of his staff and deans' meetings was repeated in Bishop's Council, if on a rather more formal level, though he always seemed more comfortable with his fellow clergy than with lay people. He was a splendid Chair with the ability to see straight away the critical aspects of policies and proposals, and an impatience with those who insisted on providing paragraphs of argument where a sentence would do. He enjoyed the fellowship that was possible over dinner in the midst of Council meetings, and on the residential weekends that were a regular feature of each three-year electoral cycle. Bishop Mark was also a generous host at Bishop's Croft where his Epiphany parties provided his guests with good food, good wine, and good conversation.

Diocesan Synods seemed rather less to his taste, partly because they were so much more difficult to control! Dissident clergy, and laity lacking awareness, were always liable to ask questions which he would have preferred not to be asked. He was always punctilious in sharing the chairing of meetings with his lay and clerical Vice Presidents who were often the recipients of muttered comments on the debate from their bishop. For his last eight years I was Lay Chair and my own favourite was during an especially poor debate on nuclear disarmament where, to my amazement, he shared with me the fact that he had once been a sympathiser of CND. He was aware that presidential addresses at synod could be used to give wider messages to his diocese. These were often genuinely inspiring and such addresses met with generous applause. I remember especially one where he spoke movingly about how people could be trapped by the character of their upbringing. He used himself as the example, suggesting that his public school education was one of the factors which had inculcated a certain diffidence in his character and which prevented outward shows of emotion. Occasionally they hit the wrong note such as a hardline address on Christian marriage (with press and TV cameras present), which was met with a stony and uncomfortable silence from synod members.

Bishop Mark understood how institutions worked and was fully behind the reorganisation of the committees and boards of the diocese. This followed an independent report commissioned from the Ven. Stephen Lowe, and included the constitutional alterations by which the Bishop's Council became also the Diocesan Board of Finance. This ensured that the policy-making body and the body responsible for the finances of the diocese were held together. This proved its worth as Birmingham, like every other diocese, had to wrestle with the consequences of the meltdown of the national Church Commissioners' investments and new pension arrangements for its clergy. Unlike most other dioceses, Birmingham's financial situation has never got out of hand in the past decade. Likewise, at the national level, John Barton, his Archdeacon of Aston, recalls that Bishop Mark saw immediately that the Act of Synod which created the Provincial Episcopal Visitors for those who did not accept the ordination of women would be disastrous in the end because it would solidify the divisions within the Church. He was also very insightful about the reorganisation of the central institutions of the Church of England proposed by the then Bishop of Durham, known as the Turnbull Report. The original proposal was to call the central coordinating body the National Council. It was Mark who saw clearly that this was a caving-in to secularists' frame of reference and insisted that the national body should be called the Archbishops' Council, clearly indicating the episcopal nature of the Church.

Relations with the Clergy

Bishop Mark, himself, recalls that 'within the life of the diocese, demographic and economic factors meant that I spent much more time presiding over the closing and reorganisation of institutions than on the opening of new ones. This was hard. In this context I saw it as one of my chief priorities to nurture the morale and proper professionalism of the clergy'. Almost everyone contributing to this chapter recognises this aspect of Mark Santer's episcopate. John Wesson says that 'I valued his book recommendations and his encouragements to keep the clergy studying' whilst John Austin notes that 'he never lost his concern that the clergy should be properly equipped theologically to face the challenges of our changing society'. He actively encouraged two or three people to do research for a PhD, giving them the 'light duty' parish of Middleton and Wishaw from which to do this. He encouraged, too, the Director of Ministries to mount a series of study days when some of the best theological minds in the country were invited to share with the clergy current trends in scholarship of one kind or another.

Canon John Wesson writes: 'Despite his own limited parish experience, he seemed to understand something of the pressures and demands upon a city-centre church like St Martin's, and he articulated to us his concerns about our lack of resources. We felt supported. He could be brusque but he was straight. I never felt that having said something to me, he would change his tune for the next person.' Bishop John Austin remarks that, 'Mark was a very good and wise pastor, particularly for those clergy who got themselves into difficulty of one kind or another. Around Easter and Christmas he would thoroughly enjoy leaving all the paperwork on his desk and go out visiting the clergy who were sick, or suffering bereavement, or in any other kind of difficulties. It was then that the clergy, often for the first time, saw Mark's sensitivity and genuine warmth and affection for them.' It was also characteristic of his pastoral concern that in 1993 he undertook to visit all his clergy in their homes and, whilst this was a huge demand on his time, it left an indelible impression on him of just how blessed the diocese was in the quality, commitment, generosity and skill of so many clergy, who were often doing marvellous unsung work in very difficult conditions and with very few resources. He was absolutely clear that any institution that could command such loyalty was in fundamental good heart and had a future in spite of what the secular press might want us all to believe.

Involvement in Public Affairs

Throughout his period as Bishop of Birmingham, Bishop Mark played an important role in the life of the City of Birmingham and used his position to make major contributions at a national level to debates on matters of topical concern. He established good personal relations with civic leaders in Birmingham, Sandwell and Solihull, most notably with Councillor Sir Richard Knowles, for many years Leader of Birmingham City Council. Between them they recognised and helped develop the role which the Church could play in the regeneration of the poorest parts of the city. The Bishop was a strong protagonist for regeneration initiatives such as New Town/South Aston City Challenge, which was chaired by the Bishop of Aston.

When BMW sold the Rover Group, and for a time it looked as though the business would close, with widespread knock-on effects throughout the motor industry in the region, Bishop Mark was quick to establish his solidarity with the workforce and those looking to find a way forward for them and their families. The crisis coincided with a Diocesan Synod, and he turned over a substantial part of the debate to the concerns of local clergy and people about the motor industry (see chapter 1 for subsequent developments).

Though sensitive to other faith communities, he resisted encroachment by secular forces within the city which wished to marginalise Christianity and who, out of a mistaken fit of political correctness, felt that the city council should not be seen to support any festival with Christian links. His high profile campaign against the council's replacement of Christmas one year with a 'Winterval' festival won national support and made the council something of a laughing stock. The experiment was not repeated!

His membership of the Council of The National Association for the Care and Resettlement of Offenders (NACRO) and chairmanship of its Young Offenders Committee, reflected a long-term interest in prisons and prisoners dating back to his National Service years; many of his sermons were illuminated with his encounters with prisoners at Winson Green Prison (now Birmingham Prison) and elsewhere. Membership of the House of Lords gave him another stage on which to exert influence, and he took his responsibilities there very seriously. Lord Hunt of Kings Heath notes that 'he was a passionate advocate for Birmingham … and he contributed many a fine speech to debates there'. At the same time, it confirmed him in a more and more strongly held view that the current nature of Establishment was detrimental to the Church and its mission, and that the ending of current arrangements, including the automatic right of bishops to sit in the Upper House, would be liberating for the Church and its ability to proclaim the Kingdom of God.

When the Santers came to Birmingham in 1987 Mark's wife, Henriette, found a post as District Clinical Psychologist for Bromsgrove and Redditch. Bishop Mark, himself, became a member of the Queen Elizabeth Hospital Trust. Not surprisingly, therefore, he took a keen interest in developments within the National Health Service. He gave a powerful sermon at the Annual General Meeting of the British Medical Association in which he was strongly critical of quasi-market developments within the NHS, which he felt were contrary to the Gospel's imperatives. Lord Hunt knew him best for his work in the health service and recalls that

> his brave address to the BMA conference on the follies of a Thatcherite approach to the NHS was unforgettable! But he contributed much more. He served on my independent review of the future of Birmingham's health services and was an excellent member. No soft touch, he surprised a number of NHS leaders in the city by the robustness of his approach. We took evidence from many people and organisations and Mark proved to be a forensic questioner. To campaigners who seemed to oppose all change, his simple question …"well what would you do"… was devastating. And often answer came there none! The review was pivotal in breaking out of a log-jam of indecision lasting over 20 years. The result is a new University Hospital being planned and exciting developments throughout the city.

In the autumn of 1993 Bishop Mark went on sabbatical for three months. On his return, in the early months of 1994, Henriette was diagnosed with cancer and died in the August of the same year. It was a devastating blow. 'It became clear to him and actually to all of us who knew him well, that he was really not coping and in that year he took four months off to recover from the suppressed grief that the demands of the post had prevented him from dealing with', says his suffragan John Austin. It was at this time that his name was being mentioned for translation to Winchester but he realised that he was in no fit state to move to another diocese and requested that he not be considered further. In 1997, he married Sabine Bird, who was by profession a family court welfare officer, and who had been a close friend of Henriette since 1963. Mark and Henriette had three children. Their two daughters have continued their parents' commitment to the NHS, one as a human resources manager, the other as a GP and medical academic. Their son works for the BBC as a TV drama producer. Bishop Mark announced his retirement in 2001. He continues to live in Birmingham and to serve as an Honorary Assistant Bishop.

13

John Tucker Mugabi Sentamu

EIGHTH BISHOP, 2002-5

John Tucker Mugabi Sentamu was born in Uganda in 1949, the sixth of 13 children. His parents were both teachers. His father (who died recently aged 98) was a primary school headmaster and his mother taught home economics, so it is no surprise that the present Bishop of Birmingham loves cooking for guests in his newly-fitted kitchen in Bishop's Croft. He was baptised quickly by the missionary bishop of his homeland since he was a sickly baby and there were fears that he might not survive. He is still a tiny man, even when dressed in his episcopal regalia. His teachers, too, were missionaries and so he was perfectly conversant with English colonial culture. His schools were modelled on British ones; he took Cambridge examinations at both school and university, and he used products stamped 'Made in Britain'. Skills honed in childhood included music (the now-famous bongo drums amongst other things) and acting (always a useful attribute for churchmen in high office). His family were not rich so clothes tended to be passed from sibling to sibling, and food was sometimes in short supply. He tells the story of his father asking him to give thanks after a meal and his saying ' Dear God, thank you for the food, but we would have been more grateful if we had had more of it!'. Bishop Sentamu's characteristic bluntness, even to God, was well evidenced in his youth!

The parishes across central Africa are huge, so parish priests need all the help they can get from lay people to maintain regular services and pastoral care. John Sentamu was made a lay reader whilst he was still a teenager, so began preaching at an early age. At university he thought about doing medicine or engineering, but finally chose law. At aged 25 he found himself being made a judge, unfortunately just as Idi Amin came to power in Uganda. One of his cases involved convicting one of Amin's cousins of aggravated rape. Despite the personal intervention of the dictator, he was convicted and, since his own sentencing powers were limited, he sent the man to a higher court. A few months later Sentamu was suspected of helping a friend involved in student opposition to Amin to escape the country. Shortly after his marriage to Margaret he was arrested and thrown into one of Amin's notorious prisons. He was kicked and beaten by the guards and was aware of others being tortured to death in neighbouring cells. He feared he would be next, but the Chief Justice of Uganda had intervened on his behalf and he was released into house arrest. For months his home had an armoured personnel carrier outside.

Friends secretly organised a Cambridge scholarship for him to read theology at Selwyn College and he and his wife left their home in 1974 with one modest suitcase between them so as not to arouse suspicion as they went to the airport and the journey to England.

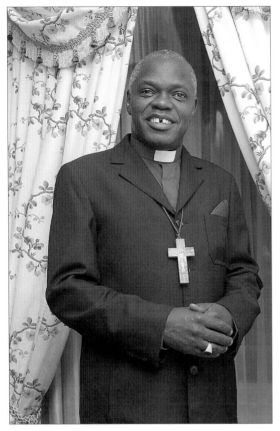

64   *Bishop John Sentamu.*

He was ordained, worked as a college chaplain then as a prison chaplain, became curate of a parish and then priest in charge of a large parish in Brixton, south London. In 1966 he was made Suffragan Bishop of Stepney. His legal training was put to further use in London as one of the assessors on the inquiry into the murder of Stephen Lawrence and the subsequent police investigations; whilst he himself headed the inquiry into the murder of Damilola Taylor. Both brought bags-full of hate-mail. His London friends commiserated when he announced that he was going to Birmingham.

He became the eighth Bishop of Birmingham (he prefers to be styled Bishop for Birmingham) in 2002, the first black diocesan bishop in the Church of England. He was enthroned in St Philip's cathedral on a wet and gloomy November day following a noisy procession from Snow Hill station (where he had arrived on a Metro tram) accompanied by bongo drums and whistles. Children took a prominent place in the welcome inside and outside the cathedral. The highlight of the service, for this observer at least, was the sight of assembled Anglican bishops and denominational and other-faith leaders being unable to resist the rhythm of 'We are marching in the light of Christ' (with drums!) and swaying in time, and with increasing gusto, in their pews.

By Christmas, following his first Diocesan Synod and Bishop's Council meetings, there could be no doubt that Bishop Sentamu was going to be very different from his predecessor. He had an infectious enthusiasm and moved easily amongst people in social gatherings. He also clearly had unbounded energy telling us proudly that he rose at 5am and, after morning prayers, repaired to the nearby university gym for an hour's exercise before breakfast and the day's engagements. We also knew that children and young people were going to be at the heart of his ministry: the announcement of his appointment took place in St John's Church of England School, Sparkhill; the Bishop's Youth Council was quickly established to give young people a voice in the diocese; and then two black teenagers, Letisha Shakespeare and Charlene Ellis, were shot dead as they were leaving a Christmas party in Aston. Bishop Sentamu leapt straight into the midst of the shocked response to the shootings – taking memorial services, talking with people on the streets of Aston, handing out leaflets, and publishing his home phone number for people to ring in confidence if they were too fearful to go to the police. Some 200 calls were received by the time six men were arrested for the crime. Those first three months were a true reflection of what was to follow. Dr Sentamu was announced as next Archbishop of York in June 2005.

14

SUFFRAGAN BISHOPS AND ARCHDEACONS

Clement George St Michael Parker, 1954-62

Bishop Parker went to Christ Church, Oxford, graduating BA in 1921. He went to Ely Theological College and was ordained deacon in 1923 and priest the following year. He came to Birmingham for his first curacy, to St Bartholomew's, Birmingham (1923-26). He moved to St Jude's, one of the city centre Anglo-Catholic churches, from 1926 to 1939. For much of the period he had only 'permission to officiate', since it was clear that the parish was under threat of closure from city redevelopment plans, but a substantive ministry was developed amongst city-centre workers during the working week. He went to be vicar of All Saints, Kings Heath from 1939 to 1957 and was rural dean of Kings Norton (1943-46) and Honorary Canon of Birmingham Cathedral (1944-46). He was made Archdeacon of Aston in 1946. Bishop Wilson requested funds for a suffragan bishop and Parker was consecrated the first Suffragan Bishop of Aston in Westminster Abbey on 18 October 1954. He remained vicar of Kings Heath until halfway through his period as suffragan bishop. Canon Douglas Maclean was later to recall an occasion when Bishop Parker 'left the pulpit in mid-sentence and shot into the choir stalls asking, "who is talking when I am talking?" And then returned to his sermon and completed the sentence'! He was translated to be Bishop of Bradford in 1961.

David Brownfield Porter, 1962-72

Bishop David Porter graduated BA from Hertford College, Oxford in 1927, and gained a Diploma in Theology in 1929. He went to Wycliffe Hall, Oxford for training and was ordained deacon in 1929 and priested in 1930. He served a curacy in St Augustine's, Wrangthorn, in the diocese of Ripon, 1929-31, and then returned to Wycliffe Hall as tutor and chaplain (1931-35); he was also chaplain to Wadham College, 1934-35. He moved to Durham diocese to be vicar of Highfield (1935-43) and Darlington (1943-47). Unusually, he moved to the Episcopal Church of Scotland to become rector of St John the Evangelist, Edinburgh (1947-61) and Dean of St Mary's Cathedral, Edinburgh (1954-61). He was consecrated Bishop of Aston in Westminster Abbey in February 1962 and spent ten years in the post. He lived at Park Mount, one of the early 19th-century villas on the Bristol Road that backs on to Edgbaston golf course.

Mark Green, 1972-82

Bishop Mark Green was born in 1917. He went up to Lincoln College, Oxford, graduating BA in 1940. He moved immediately to ordination training at Cuddesdon College and was ordained deacon in 1940 and was priested the following year. He was curate in

the parish of St Catherine's, Gloucester (1940-42) before becoming a chaplain in the
armed forces for the duration of the war and several years after. He left the services to
be Vicar of Newland, St John, in York (1948-53). Clearly he had enjoyed his time as a
chaplain since he returned to the forces for another three-year tour of duty (1953-56).
He returned to York for two years before becoming Rector of St Mary's, Cottingham,
sometimes characterised as the largest village in England, on the western fringe of
Hull (1958-64). He was made a Prebendary Canon of York in 1963 and moved from
Cottingham in 1964 to be Chaplain to the Archbishop of York and Vicar of the parishes
of Bishopthorpe and Acaster Malbis (1964-72), which provided his stipend. In 1972
Bishop Brown invited him to become Suffragan Bishop of Aston.

Bishop Mark Green provides us with an excellent summary of what the suffragan
bishop does in Birmingham. He says:

> In a one-suffragan diocese like Birmingham there cannot be a division
> into two or three areas, as in the larger dioceses. It is easy for the job
> to be dismissed as a sort of 'episcopal curacy'. In fact I found that
> being virtually 'senior curate' in a parish of one and a half million
> people was a wonderfully fulfilling role - providing of course that you
> got on well with 'the vicar'! It meant that I could be in and out of the
> parishes easily, not being tied down by the heavy administrative burdens
> carried by diocesans. If power without responsibility is a very horrid
> thing, responsibility without power is, or can be, a boon to the soul.
> Occasionally I had to take disciplinary or remedial action when some
> crisis happened in the absence of the diocesan, but by and large it was
> a matter of pastoral care, done with whatever patience, persuasion,
> encouragement, and 'alongsidedness' one could manage. I did of course
> have particular assignments of work; chairing the Diocesan Education and
> Social Responsibility Councils were two of them: and very important (and
> time-consuming) they were. But the most fulfilling of these particular
> assignments was to be in charge of post-ordination training.
>
> Every newly-ordained deacon does three years of this. With an average
> of ten new deacons a year there were always about 30 curates in the
> scheme. In Birmingham, being a compact diocese, it was possible for the
> whole group to meet every month. As to the quality of the curates, there
> is no doubt that Birmingham was drawing into the ordained ministry
> the brightest and best of not only 'the sons of the morning' but some
> very bright daughters too. We had in our ranks one who, years later,
> was to become one of the first woman deans of an English cathedral,
> the Very Revd June Osborne at Salisbury; not to mention one or two
> principals of theological colleges, archdeacons at two a penny, and the
> odd diocesan bishop! Thus the obvious thing for me to do was to form
> a few of these into a committee, and with me as chair, get *them* to run
> POT, which they did brilliantly. If a visiting lecturer failed to turn up (on
> one occasion it was Archbishop David Hope, in a previous existence),
> one of my committee could step in and do it instead. Apart from all
> this, I believe that there was a real value in one of the bishops being so
> closely in touch with the youngest and newest clergy. My role became
> intensely personal and pastoral, not least in trying to heal the rows that
> too often broke out between incumbents and these young rising stars.

Bishop Mark Green was a serious contender to succeed Bishop Brown on the latter's retirement. It is a mark of his pastoral skills that were so valued in the diocese, not just by the clergy, but by the laity too, that he was able to work with two diocesan bishops of such different character as Laurence Brown and Hugh Montefiore. As he himself says: 'no man can serve two masters – but I did! Hugh came in the middle of my ten years stint; so for me it was like putting on a new shirt at half time'. Bishop Mark certainly impressed his secretary since some years, and two suffragans, later Colin Buchanan was told that 'Bishop Mark, now he was a *real* bishop!'. Mark Green retired in 1982 and went to live in Hastings, where he served as an assistant bishop in the diocese of Chichester for another decade or more.

Michael Humphrey Dickens Whinney, 1982-85; 1989-95

Bishop Michael Whinney was born in 1930, a descendant of Charles Dickens. He went up to Pembroke College, Cambridge and graduated BA in 1955. He went immediately to Ridley Hall for theological training and was ordained deacon in 1957 and priest in the following year. He served his curacy at Rainham in the diocese of Chelmsford (1957-60). He was head of the Cambridge University Mission to Bermondsey, south London (1960-67) before becoming Vicar of St James with Christchurch, Bermondsey (1967-73) whilst continuing an association with the mission as their chaplain. He was made Archdeacon of Southwark (1973-82) and was invited by Hugh Montefiore to become Suffragan Bishop of Aston in September 1982.

Bishop Michael says that 'my roles were to chair the Pastoral Committee, Training Council, Communication Group and to be Director of post-ordination training (POT). The Training Council had the Provost, Basil Moss, and his wife, Rachel, on it and that ensured any loose thinking on my part was quickly addressed. It proved a remarkably effective body. POT was fascinating and I often look back and remember the high quality of our young clergy then; it was with that group that I was able to begin my ongoing research into the differing personality types of Anglican clergy.'

He followed his predecessor in building good relations with the University of Aston and the Vice Chancellor invited him to join the University Council. He was also widely involved in student affairs working closely with the chaplains, John Austin (not the later bishop) and David Fowles. He says, 'Happily I was rather fitter then than now and played squash regularly in their leagues in enjoyable partnership with the chaplains and the secretary of the Student Guild. The world was put to rights weekly in the student bar where they had made me a member. It was a vibrant place and there were many times when I was required to be an apologist for the Christian faith.' Another innovation was his 'media lunches' which helped the Church get 'good news' stories into the media, and which were continued by Colin Buchanan.

In December 1984, after just two and a quarter years in post, he was approached by Downing Street to become Bishop of Southwell. Despite his pleas that it was much too soon they persisted and so he moved to Nottinghamshire. Bishop Michael had been a popular suffragan and it was no surprise to Birmingham folk that he was translated to diocesan status.

Sadly, Bishop Michael suffered a breakdown in health and resigned the see of Southwell in March 1988. After a year's break to recover, Bishop Mark Santer, with Colin Buchanan's prompting, invited him to return to Birmingham as a full-time stipendiary assistant bishop with a pastoral role. Only four months later, Colin Buchanan resigned (see chapter 24) and Bishop Mark asked him to take on the duties of the Bishop of

65   *Michael Whinney as*
Suffragan Bishop of Aston.

Aston without receiving the title again. (There was some discussion as to whether he should become Bishop of Aston by title, but as he had been a diocesan bishop previously it was thought simpler that he continued as an assistant bishop.) This time he acquired an office at the diocesan headquarters in Harborne, rather than working from home as previously. As he says, 'It was so much better being based in the diocesan office. I saw my colleagues on a daily basis; communication and consultation was much better and we all got to know each other well. It was also much handier for Bishop's Croft.' As well as the administrative duties he inherited from his immediate predecessors, Bishop Michael looked after the 'Deliverance Group' (the clergy licensed by the bishop to undertake exorcisms and the like), and the hospital chaplains.

In 1992 Bishop Michael was asked to succeed Bruce Gillingham as Diocesan Missioner and to become a Canon Residentiary at the cathedral so as to release the Church Commissioners' funding for the appointment of John Austin as Bishop of Aston. The major feature of his last three years of episcopal ministry was associated with the national 'Decade of Evangelism'. There were plans to celebrate baptism and confirmation in the diocese with a large event in the National Indoor Arena but the fears of another financial disaster were too raw and eventually a scaled-down celebration for all those confirmed in the previous three years was held in the cathedral. It was a great success and has been repeated every three years since, including in this centenary year (see chapter 25). Bishop Michael retired at the end of 1995. He continues to live in Birmingham and to be an assistant bishop, and he continues to run his Myers-Briggs workshops for groups of people who want to explore their personality types in conjunction with others.

Colin Ogilvie Buchanan, 1985-89

Bishop Buchanan was born in 1934, the son of Professor R.O. Buchanan, a New Zealander who was professor of economic geography at the London School of Economics. He gained his degree in 'Mods and Greats' at Lincoln College, Oxford in 1959 and went to Tyndale Hall, Bristol for theological training. He was ordained deacon in 1961 and priested the following year. He was curate in the parish of Cheadle, Cheshire, 1961-64. He moved to become tutor of what was soon to become St John's Theological College, Nottingham in 1964, becoming successively Registrar (1969-74), Director of Studies (1974-75), Vice Principal (1975-78), and Principal (1979-85). In 1985 Hugh Montefiore asked him to become Bishop of Aston and he was consecrated on 25 July 1985 and installed on 9 October. Bishop Hugh 'made it clear when he invited me that he had his own retirement in view and would trust me to look after a vacancy in the see' said Bishop Colin, and in the event Hugh retired on 31 March 1987.

Bishop Colin was a high-profile appointment; not only was he Principal of one of the leading Evangelical training colleges, he had also been a member of General Synod (for Southwell Diocese) since its beginning in 1970, and had been a member of the Church of England Liturgical Commission from 1964 until 1986. Bishop Colin reflects that 'I went in head first, ... in many ways – particularly in terms of the care of the clergy – the job was in continuity with being principal of a theological college. But I was also involved in a reorientation of my life, because some elements that had been central to it (General Synod; Liturgical Commission; College Principal) were being removed.' His appointment was welcomed amongst

66 *Colin Buchanan as Suffragan Bishop of Aston.*

the Evangelical clergy of the diocese as providing leadership and support for their wider activities. His appointment also coincided with the so-called 'Handsworth riots' (in September 1985) and the publication of *Faith in the City* (in December 1985), so it would have been difficult not to go into the job 'head first', given his energy and larger-than-life personality!

A major watershed for the episcopate in Birmingham diocese was computerisation. Buchanan had supervised the transformation of St John's into the first computerised Theological College in the country in 1980-81. Just before he came to Birmingham the Diocesan Office had been computerised by Revd Jim Pendorf, the Diocesan Secretary. All that was left were the bishops themselves (Colin learnt quickly that September) and their secretaries. By his first Christmas in the diocese he had a new full-time secretary, Anne Graham, the wife of Revd Matthew Graham, who had just become vicar of Warley Woods. 'Anne was superb' says Colin, '– she had previous experience with both accountancy and legal firms, and ... I used to reckon I had twice the energy, and could cover twice as much ground as many, because of the backup I was getting from Anne. The computers she handled imaginatively from the start – but, if you want to glimpse how fast such things have come, she went on a 24-hour course for bishops' secretaries in April 1986, and on the course computers were not even mentioned. She and one or two others were horrified at this, but the great proportion of those on the course had no such reaction.'

As well as the defined administrative tasks of the suffragan, which included the important role of coordinating post-ordination training for the curates, chairing the West Midlands Training Course, and sharing in the pastoral care of the clergy, Bishop Colin's most memorable feat of organisation was Hugh Montefiore's farewell service in the 'Arena' of the National Exhibition Centre. No-one who was there will ever forget it; it was a liturgical triumph of the highest order. At the same time, in those first 18 months in office, he had already become sufficiently trusted, by clergy and laity alike, to be elected chairman of the Vacancy in See Committee charged with presenting the needs of the diocese to the Crown Appointments' Commission. Most of the remainder of Colin Buchanan's time in Birmingham was dominated by the organisation of Archbishop Desmond Tutu's mission visit to the city in 1989 (see chapter 24); though he also found time to be a nominated suffragan bishop at the 1988 Lambeth Conference. He became secretary of his working group at the conference through having a computer – and being able to bring it and use it!

Following his resignation in the wake of the financial losses sustained by the Tutu mission, Bishop Colin was invited to be an assistant bishop in the diocese of Rochester. In 1991 he became Vicar of St Mark's, Gillingham, and in 1996 was invited to be Area Bishop of Woolwich in the diocese of Southwark. He retired in 2004. In 1990 he was returned to the General Synod having been elected by the suffragans to the House of Bishops. He retained his seat until his recent retirement.

John Michael Austin, 1992-2005

67 *John Austin as Suffragan Bishop of Aston.*

John Austin was born in 1939. He took his BA degree in Politics, Philosophy and Economics at St Edmund Hall, Oxford in 1963 and went for theological training to St Stephen's House, Oxford. He was made deacon in 1964 and priested in 1965. He served his curacy at St John's, Dulwich in Southwark diocese (1964-68). He then spent two years in the USA before returning to south London as Missioner at St Christopher's Walworth and Warden of Pembroke House (1969-76). From 1976 to 1992 he was first Advisor and then Director of the Board for Social Responsibility in the diocese of St Albans. He became a prebendary canon of St Paul's Cathedral in 1989. He was invited to become Suffragan Bishop of Aston by Mark Santer in 1992.

Though there had been a long period of nearly three years without a suffragan bishop, as we have seen, Bishop Michael Whinney was in post as assistant bishop helping to ameliorate the rupture in relationships between Bishop Santer and some of his Evangelical clergy following Colin Buchanan's resignation. Matters were probably not helped by the announcement of a liberal catholic suffragan. However, Bishop Michael was close to retirement and Mark Santer had determined on a three-month sabbatical 'term' in the autumn of 1993, so needed a new suffragan to take charge whilst he was away; a challenging Evangelical was not within his purview! Bishop John's consecration was notable as only the second episcopal consecration to have taken place in Birmingham and, rather than being at the cathedral, it took place in St Martin's-in-the-Bullring since the cathedral was undergoing restoration at the time.

Like many of his predecessors, Bishop John has enjoyed a highly-valued pastoral ministry in the diocese, caring for priests and lay people in equal measure. A particular concern was to get groups of clergy with similar ministry circumstances to share their problems and their good practice. As he says:

When I arrived in the diocese there was in existence, what was then called the 'Urban Priority Areas Group'. At the first meeting I attended it became very clear to me it was a kind of pressure group and interestingly enough did not include any of the clergy in the outer estates. I therefore encouraged the formation of two separate groups, the inner urban parishes and the outer estates parishes. I was anxious that these groups should not be seen as 'my' groups but they should clearly belong to those who attended. The first convener of the inner urban group was Revd (now Canon) Rob Morris, and of the outer estates was Revd Wallace Brown. The purpose of the two groups was to build up trust amongst those with a similar ministry in a mission context and to share good practice. Since establishing those two groups we have also established a third group for those parishes we call the 'middle-ring group'. Basically they are the ones who finance the diocese! I don't run any of the groups, but I recognize the importance of my presence at each of them. I give very high priority to my attendance there.

He has had a linked concern with community regeneration projects in the city and the promotion of social action and justice, particularly in Aston itself, where he chaired the Newtown and South Aston City Challenge, one of the numerous government-financed initiatives to develop new employment opportunities and improve the built environment.

Like his predecessors he, too, oversees post-ordination training and some of the diocesan boards and committees, especially the Pastoral Committee, responsible for the administrative arrangements for 'the cure of souls'. That has meant involvement in the painful process of recent years of reducing the number of parishes in the diocese to better fit the financial resources available. This process began with the diocesan report *Together in Ministry and Mission* (1996), the enquiries for which were chaired by Bishop John, and has continued with the current framework *Called to a New Kingdom*. He also led the annual diocesan pilgrimage of young people to Taizé, seeing the number of participants steadily increase. John Austin will retire in July 2005.

Archdeacons

There have been eight Archdeacons of Birmingham, nine Archdeacons of Aston and one Archdeacon of Coleshill during the century of the life of the diocese. The first Archdeacon of Birmingham was Winfrid Burows. He had been a Tutor at Christ Church College, Oxford (1884-91) before becoming Principal of Leeds Clergy School (1891-1900) and vicar of Holy Trinity, Leeds (1900-03). He wrote *The Mystery of the Cross* in 1896. He came to Birmingham as vicar of St Augustine's, Edgbaston in 1903 and became archdeacon the following year. He became Bishop of Truro in 1912 and was later translated to Chichester. He was succeeded by Charles Owen whose early ministry was in Winchester diocese. He probably came in contact with Lord Calthorpe, who lived at Elvetham Hall, Hampshire, because he was made vicar of St George's, Edgbaston (1883-1903) and, when the living of Edgbaston Old Church became free, he moved along the road. He was a Canon of Worcester (1891-1905), Canon of Birmingham (1905) and Rural Dean of Edgbaston (1905). He was made Archdeacon of Aston in 1906 and moved to be Archdeacon of Birmingham in 1912.

68   *The Venerable Charles E. Hopton, Archdeacon of Birmingham throughout the inter-war period.*

Charles Hopton became Archdeacon of Birmingham in 1915. He spent his whole ministry in the dioceses of Worcester and Birmingham. His curacy was at St Mary's, Selly Oak (1884-87) and he was Rural Dean of East Worcestershire (1906-07). He became vicar of St Mary's, Moseley in 1907, Rural Dean of Kings Norton in 1909 and archdeacon six years later. He was to remain in post for the next 32 years! It was he who purchased the fine Arts and Crafts house at 59 Salisbury Road, Moseley, that was to be known as the Archdeacon's house for the next half century. Hopton's successor, S. Harvie Clark, spent his early ministry in the North East and Scotland. In 1947 he came to Birmingham to be Archdeacon, and Vicar of Wishaw in the countryside south east of Sutton Coldfield. The following year he became Vicar of St Peter's, Harborne (1948-67). He represented Birmingham clergy in Convocation and left Birmingham diocese for Lincoln, where he was Archdeacon of Stow.

Vernon Nicholls was ordained in the early years of the Second World War and spent his early ministry in the South West, before becoming a services' chaplain in 1944. After some years in Surrey, he came to the Midlands to be vicar of Walsall (1956-67), where he was also Rural Dean (1956-67), hospital chaplain (1956-67), and Prebendary Canon of Lichfield (1964-67). He was made Archdeacon of Birmingham in 1967. He was consecrated Bishop of Sodor and Man in June 1974 and Dean of St German's Cathedral, Peel. His successor as archdeacon was Gerald Hollis. Hollis's curacy was in Stepney, south London (1947-50) but he then went to Yorkshire where he was Rector of Armsthorpe (1954-60), and Vicar of Rotherham (1960-74). He was a member of General Synod and archdeacon from 1974. He was the last Archdeacon of Birmingham to live at 59, Salisbury Road. Hollis was succeeded by John Duncan who, after a curacy at St Peter's, Birmingham (1962-65), was chaplain to the University of Birmingham for more than ten years (1965-76) (see chapter 18). He became Vicar of All Saints', Kings Heath in 1976 and archdeacon from 1985. He retired to live in Banbury in 2001. He was succeeded by Hayward Osborne who spent much of his early ministry as a team vicar or rector in team ministries in Worcestershire before moving to Birmingham as Vicar of St Mary's, Moseley in 1988. In 2001 he became the second vicar of St Mary's to become Archdeacon of Birmingham.

The first Archdeacon of Aston was Charles Owen who later moved to the Birmingham Archdeaconry (see above). He was succeeded by George Gardner in 1913, whose service neatly coincided with the First World War. John Richards, who became Archdeacon of Aston in 1918, had been Vicar of St Andrew's, Bordesley since 1900, an unfashionably working-class parish from which to become archdeacon. He was noticeable earlier in his career for his temperance work, having been secretary of the Church of England Temperance Society first for Ely diocese (1895-98) and then for Worcester diocese (1898-1900). Richards was archdeacon for 20 years. He was succeeded by Henry McGowan (1938-46), and then by Clement Parker (1946-54) who became Bishop of Aston. The archdeaconry was not filled thereafter until 1965 when Francis Warman was instituted. After early ministry in Coventry diocese, he had been vicar of St Margaret's, Ward End (1943-46) and then Vicar of Aston-juxta-Birmingham (1946-65). He retired to Lewes in Chichester diocese in 1977. Next came Donald Tytler who had spent his whole

69 *The Venerable Hayward Osborne and the Venerable John Barton, Archdeacons of Birmingham and Aston respectively.*

ministry in Birmingham. He was curate of St Edburga's, Yardley (1949-52); Secretary of Student Christian Movement (SCM) at the University of Birmingham (1952-55), Precentor of Birmingham Cathedral (1955-57), Director of Religious Education in the diocese (1957-63), and Vicar of St Mark's, Londonderry (1963-72). He became a residentiary canon in the cathedral in 1972 and Archdeacon in 1977. In 1982 he was consecrated Suffragan Bishop of Middleton in the diocese of Manchester.

John Cooper, who succeeded him as archdeacon, spent his early ministry as a prison chaplain. He came to St Paul's, Balsall Heath in 1973 on the opening of the new church-centre, shared with the United Reformed Church. He was made Archdeacon of Aston in 1982 and in 1990 volunteered to become the first, and so far only, Archdeacon of Coleshill when the diocese was briefly divided into three archdeaconries. When he retired it was agreed that there was insufficient work for three archdeacons. He was succeeded as Archdeacon of Aston by John Barton in 1989. Barton had worked in Canterbury diocese and then the Diocese of London where he was Vicar of St Luke's, South Kensington (1975-83) and Rural Dean of Chelsea. In 1983 he became the Chief Broadcasting Officer for the Church of England and it was from that position that he was appointed by Bishop Santer with a remit, amongst other things, to improve the diocesan communications organisation (see chapter 23). He retired in 2003, to Canterbury, and the archdeaconry is currently vacant.

15

THE CATHEDRAL CHURCH OF ST PHILIP

Birmingham Cathedral has a history almost twice as long as that of the diocese. At the beginning of the 18th century the town was beginning to grow rapidly and the population was too great to be accommodated in St Martin's parish church. It was therefore decided to build a new parish church in the 'High Town'. This was a complicated business requiring a private Act of Parliament. In 1708 the townspeople presented a Bill to Parliament, which was passed in the same year. It required the Bishop of Coventry and Lichfield, within whose diocese Birmingham was then situated, to appoint 20 Commissioners to take possession of the land called the 'horse close', about four acres in size, which had been offered by the Philips family as the site of the new church. There they were to build a new church, dedicated to St Philip, a house for the rector 'with a backside, garden and orchard', lay out a new churchyard, and establish a new parish, the boundaries of which were carefully specified, from the parish of St Martin's.

The bishop proceeded to appoint the Commissioners. Warwickshire landowners and Birmingham businessmen were prominent and amongst them was Andrew Archer of Umberslade, grandson of Sir Simon Archer, whose collection of historical manuscripts had done much to enable Sir William Dugdale to complete his famous book *The Antiquities of Warwickshire Illustrated*. Also appointed was Andrew Archer's younger brother, Thomas, who was a pupil of Sir Thomas Vanbrugh and therefore able to act as architect of the new church. Thomas designed only three churches and St Philip's was his first. The others were St Paul's, Deptford (1730) and St John's, Smith Square (1721) both in London. The latter is now a successful small concert hall. What makes St Philip's such an important church architecturally is that Archer had spent four years travelling in Italy in 1689-93. He therefore had first-hand experience of Italian neo-Classical churches such as those designed by Bernini and Borromini. Thomas Archer had a much more lucrative government appointment as the Groom-Porter to the royal household of Queen Anne and the first two Georges; as such he controlled gambling in the Court and the rest of the kingdom. When he died in 1743 'he was possess'd of a very great estate and has given above £100,000 to his youngest nephew, Henry Archer Esq.' Then, as now, gambling was a lucrative industry.

A public appeal was undertaken by the Commissioners for the funds to build the church and St Philip's began building in 1709. Many of the details of the building operation were recorded in William Hill's memorandum book. Hill was the Commissioners' clerk. Thus we know that the stone came from the quarries of William Shakespear of Rowington, Warwickshire; a bad choice as successor churchwardens were

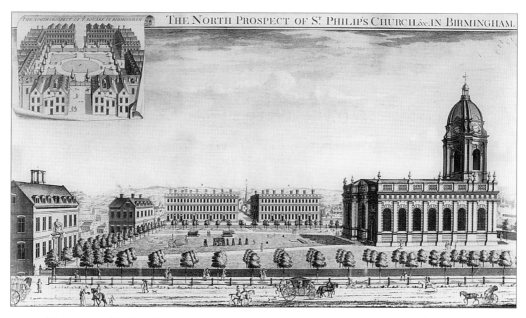

70 *The prospect of St Philip's Church, Birmingham from Colmore Row. The Rectory and the Blue Coat School stand on the eastern side of the churchyard in this mid-18th-century view.*

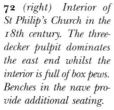

71 *(left)   The East Prospect of St Philip's as illustrated in* Vitruvius Britannicus *in 1715. The tower was not in fact completed until 1725.*

72 *(right)   Interior of St Philip's Church in the 18th century. The three-decker pulpit dominates the east end whilst the interior is full of box pews. Benches in the nave provide additional seating.*

to find, since the stone weathered badly. There were 200 loads of stone transported to Birmingham by road, all cut according to the sizes specified by Mr Smith, the clerk of the works. This man, Francis Smith of Warwick, was the man who actually built the church. There is no evidence that Archer had anything more to do with it once he had delivered his plans. Joseph Pedley was the stonemason for the plain stone. The bricks needed were supplied at eight shillings per thousand and the bricklayers were paid £3 per rod (16.5 feet). William Westley and three others undertook to find the scaffolding for the church for £35 and to supply the galleries for 5s. 6d. 'per square'. The interior plasterwork was done by Richard Haas. He agreed, in May 1711, by which time the church must have been nearing completion, to plaster 'for fourteen pence a yard; the architrave, frieze and cornice for 2s. 6d. per foot and the 'pilaster and Corinthian capitals, fluted, for one pound ten shillings a piece'. 'Wall plastering 6d per

ST PHILIP'S CHURCH, BIRMINGHAM.

73   *St Philip's churchyard with burial party. This early 19th-century engraving shows that the churchyard was already uncomfortably full of burials.*

yard. Whitewash the whole work into the bargain.' Finally, John Hadley and Robert Perks agreed to provide the ironwork for the large windows at 'five farthings by the pound', the Commissioners providing the iron for them. This did not include the fine altar rails, for which no details as to who the designer was survives.

Consecration, Tower and Churchyard

By 1715 the Commissioners seem to have run out of money, though the tower had not yet been constructed, so a consecration service was held on 4 October 1715. The church was able to accommodate 1,750 worshippers (considerably more than its present capacity) and, of these, 500 of the sittings were free of pew rents. The Commissioners had laid down that if there should be any dispute about who sat in which pew, 'ye person who subscribes most to ye said Church shall be preferred'!

The church as built consisted of nave, north and south aisles, a west tower and a slightly projecting chancel at the east end. Its style is a restrained and very English Baroque, well shown on the exterior by the florid oval windows that add interest to the ends of the aisles, and by the design of the west doorways. The outside of the church has Doric pilasters along its length. The large stone urns on the top of the balustrade around the roof, which were to cause so much trouble to later generations, were added in 1756 when John Baskerville, the famous Birmingham printer, was churchwarden.

The tower remained unbuilt for a decade. It was only when in 1723 Sir Richard Gough persuaded Prime Minister Sir Robert Walpole to make a donation of £600 from the King's purse that the tower was constructed. It was finished in 1725 as a plaque over the south-west door records. The first bells were as poor as the stone and lasted only 25 years. In 1750 they were replaced by ten new bells. The tower is a powerful and original design, much admired then and now. The lower stage, square in plan with canted angles and concave sides, contains the bells and the upper stage is an octagon with a clock prominent on the outside. On top is a lead dome and open lantern and originally there was to have been a large cross on top. However, the current ball and weather vane, incorporating the boar's head crest of the Gough family of Edgbaston, was substituted in recognition of Sir Richard Gough's help in obtaining the money towards the costs of building the tower. The interior of the church was whitewashed and the east window had two painted glass panels described by William Hawkes Smith in 1825 as consisting 'of a gay and flowery carpet pattern, with gorgeous borders of foliage, as unsatisfactory to the eye as they are discrepant from every other object within the august edifice which they disfigure'. I don't think he liked them!

There are a number of descriptions of St Philip's in the 18th century. William Hutton, Birmingham's historian, writing in 1780 says, ' When I first saw St Philip's in the year 1741, at a proper distance, uncrowded with houses, ... untarnished with smoke and illuminated by a western sun, I was delighted with its appearance, and I thought it then, what I do now, and what others will in future, the pride of the place'; the churchyard was 'ornamented with walks in great perfection shaded with trees in double and treble ranks, and surrounded with buildings in elegant taste; perhaps its equal cannot be found in the British dominions'. Another writer, the traveller William Toldervy, describes how he 'entered the Town on the Side where stands St Philip's, or, as 'tis commonly called, the New Church.

74 *Churchyard and Rectory. This rare damaged print shows the fine Rectory of St Philip's with its tree-filled garden. The glazed roof of the Great Western Arcade, built in 1876, towers behind.*

This is a very beautiful, modern Building of Free-Stone; ... It stands in the Middle of a large Church-Yard the Buildings are as lofty, elegant and uniform as those of Bedford Row, and are inhabited by People of Fortune. These Building have the Appellation of Tory Row; and this is the highest and genteelest Part of the Town of Birmingham' (Toldervy 1762).

Almost as important as the new church was the new churchyard, since the tiny churchyard around St Martin's was already very full indeed with the deceased remains of Birmingham's citizens. Given the rapid increase in the population of the town in the 18th century, it was not long before St Philip's churchyard also began to fill up. It may be difficult to believe but something over 60,000 bodies were interred before the churchyard was closed. Since a normal burial cost 2s. 6d. (or 1s. for paupers) and interment in the vaults cost £1 1s. 6d., the office of Sexton of St Philip's was a very lucrative one and there were many disputes as to who had the right to appoint/ elect him. A number of simple classical monuments adorn the pillars of the nave, the most interesting probably being that to the Hon. Peter Oliver, the Chief Justice of the 'Massachusetts Bay' colony around Boston. He refused to give up his allegiance to the Crown and was evacuated from Boston when the British troops left in 1776. He died in Birmingham in 1791.

Restorations

In 1837, Temple Row, on the south side of the churchyard, was widened, taking in some of the original ground. In 1844 the path along the south side of the church had to be closed temporarily as there was a fear that the great stone vases on the balustrade might fall on to passers-by below. This was one of the consequences of the poor quality stone originally supplied from the quarry at Rowington and in 1859-69 the whole of the church began to be refaced with better Hollington stone. Earlier, in 1850, the Georgian high box pews had been removed and new oak pews, pulpit and reading desk were installed. This was part of a major long-term refurbishment by one of Birmingham's most notable Victorian church architects, J.A. Chatwin. It included the removal of the west gallery, together with the organ (which was moved to its present position) and increasing the size of the arch into the tower to make a baptistery. In 1880 new windows were inserted in the aisles by Messrs Hardman at

75 *J.A. Chatwin's restoration of St Philip's in the 1870s and 1880s with Corinthian pillars, Gothic pulpit and reredos, and Burne-Jones's stained-glass windows are well shown in this inter-war photograph.*

76 *The conversion of St Philip's to the cathedral of the new diocese included the construction of the bishop's throne.*

a cost of £200. The biggest change was the construction of a new three-bay chancel with large Corinthian columns on each side and a coffered ceiling; this would have been anathema to Archer with his restrained neo-Classical design, but it suited both the more exuberant Victorian age and the more Catholic celebration of the Eucharist that characterised St Philip's. A major donation by Miss Villiers Wilkes paid for much of this work. The original painted windows of Archer's chancel were disposed of in 1884, and in 1885-87 the glory of the church was installed, the three wonderfully rich stained-glass windows by William Morris to designs by Edward Burne-Jones, leading light of the Pre-Raphaelite Brotherhood, who had been born nearby in a house in Bennett's Hill. The fourth window, in the baptistery, representing the Last Judgement, was added 12 years later in 1897 as a memorial to Bishop Bowlby after Burne-Jones had revisited the church where he had been baptised.

Its next restoration was in 1904-05 in preparation for its transformation into the cathedral church of the new diocese. The entire floor of the nave, aisles and chancel was replaced, the pews were removed and replaced with chairs to increase the flexibility of layout, vestries were extended under the galleries on both sides, the grey and brown paint on the walls was removed and white and gold took its place, the old gas lamps were removed and the wonder of the age, electricity, installed and the layout of the chancel was altered to incorporate a grand episcopal throne and the canons' stalls. In 1911 the churchyard was laid out as an ornamental garden for the enjoyment of city-centre workers.

77 *The churchyard was laid out as an ornamental garden for Birmingham's office workers in 1911. The effect of smoke pollution on the stonework is also well shown.*

78 *Second World War damage to the cathedral was extensive.*

The cathedral was badly damaged by incendiary bombs in the Second World War (the Burne-Jones windows had been removed for safe-keeping). It was restored in 1947-48 and a major restoration appeal for £10,000 was launched. New oak doors to the clergy vestry were added as a memorial to Bishop Barnes in the 1950s and the stonework of the tower was refaced in Hollington stone in 1958-59, by P.B. and A.B. Chatwin. The Victorian reredos was replaced by new work in 1963, centred on a modern cross in silver gilt and crystal by John Donald. The cathedral was extensively

79 *Bishop Hugh with Princess Alexandra at the reopening of the Cathedral on 1 November 1980 after its restoration (Peart-Binns 1990).*

restored again in 1980 for the 75th anniversary of the diocese by Michael Reardon. The vaults below the church were cleared and a new undercroft constructed with kitchen, toilets and choir vestry/meeting room. The church was redecorated, the most notable change being the marble painting of the great Corinthian columns of the chancel giving the whole interior a much more Baroque feel. Bishop Montefiore had fixed the date for reopening before the work had begun, but all was well and the building was formally reopened by Princess Alexandra on 1 November 1980, in

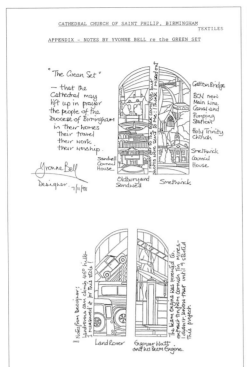
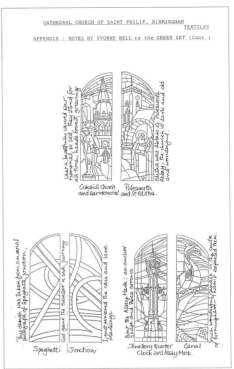

80   *Designs for the cathedral vestments 'green' stoles and notes by designer Yvonne Bell, 1998.*

time for it to be part of the 75th anniversary celebrations. In 1989, as part of the centenary celebrations of the City of Birmingham, the cathedral was chosen for the distribution of the Royal Maundy by Her Majesty Queen Elizabeth II.

In 2001-3 a Heritage Lottery grant enabled the churchyard to be completely

81   *The first Honorary Lay Canons (Mrs Claire Laland and Dr Terry Slater) with Bishop Sentamu at their Installation, Easter Day 2005.*

refurbished with new York stone paving; the railings, which had been removed during the war, to be replaced by modern equivalents; new trees to be planted to recreate the formal layout of the churchyard 300 years previously, and new soil, turf and seating to be established. A few years previously two new memorials had been added to the churchyard, one deliberately and one accidentally. The 25th anniversary of the Birmingham pub bombings of 1974 was the occasion for a proper memorial to the victims to be established for the first time, whilst a tree planted by Diana, Princess of Wales, became the centre of the city's outpouring of mourning on her death, with a huge carpet of flowers surrounding the tree for weeks afterwards.

16

ORGANS, CHOIRS AND ORGANISTS

In the early years of the Diocese of Birmingham the finest organs in the area were to be found in the large nonconformist churches – the Church of the Messiah, Broad Street (Hill 1882), the Old Meeting Church, Bristol Street (Harrison & Harrison 1909), Carrs Lane Chapel (Norman & Beard 1907) and the Methodist Central Hall (Walcker of Ludwigsburg 1898/1903). However, as the 20th century progressed Anglican churches began to catch up with their nonconformist brethren in the provision of good instruments, and many of these were of splendid quality.

Of particular significance to the Midlands was the work of organ-builders Norman & Beard of Norwich, who supplied at least 12 organs to Birmingham's Anglican churches in the early years of the century. The largest were built in the three Handsworth churches – St Mary's in 1905, St Michael's in 1908 and St James's in 1909 – all beautifully voiced and solidly constructed. The work of Nicholson of Worcester also appears regularly in the diocese, their most important instrument being the four-manual organ in the cathedral, rebuilt most beautifully in 1993. Their work in the 1920s was distinguished by reed voicing of the highest quality since W.C. Jones, the legendary expert on reeds, was their voicer, and superb examples of his work can be heard in the Solo orchestral registers of the cathedral organ and in the Swell reeds of All Saints, Kings Heath. In 1906, the firm of Harrison & Harrison of Durham installed a new organ in St Martin's-in-the-Bullring to an ambitious specification based on their epoch-making 1904 scheme at St Nicholas' Whitehaven. Sadly, 16 of St Martin's 61 speaking stops were never inserted, so the organ never achieved its full size and glory. A rebuild in 1955 by the John Compton organ company completed the specification but unfortunately the instrument was moved from its original site to the back of the north transept where the Harrison tonal distinction was compromised. Harrisons also built a beautiful little 12-stop instrument in St Basil's, Deritend, which was lost to the diocese when the church closed some years ago. Other interesting organs have been lost through church closure or city redevelopment and sadly this includes the only 'Father Willis' organ (1850) in the diocese at St Paul's Balsall Heath. I am not sure of the fate of the three-manual 1889 Casson with five manual departments at St Paul's Lozells. The fine 1904 organ by J.J. Binns of Leeds still survives in Bishop Latimer Church, Handsworth, as does the 1926 Conacher of Huddersfield at Castle Bromwich. To redress the balance of losses caused by church redundancy, some new organs have been built including a fine Harrison at St Michael's Boldmere, an effective *multum in parvo* installation by Nicholson at Castle Vale, a pleasant little organ in classical style by R.H. Walker at Perry Beeches, and a fine instrument, originally built by Henry Willis III in 1932 for the Seventh Church

82 *The cathedral organ contains pipes from the 1715 instrument built by Schwarbrick.*

of Christ Scientist, London, and installed at Emanuel Wylde Green in 2002.

Unfortunately the diocese does not boast many historic organs but several instruments do contain old pipework, chief among these being the cathedral organ with pipework by Schwarbrick (1715), Snetzler (1777), George Pike England (1804) and Nicholson of Worcester (1894, 1929, 1948 and 1993). St Paul's in the Jewellery Quarter and St Alphege's, Solihull also contain old pipes from various periods. Merevale has a splendid little Snetzler of 1777, while Baddesley Clinton has an instrument of 1797 almost certainly built by Benjamin Blyth of Isleworth on behalf of Sarah Green, widow of the organ builder Samuel Green. St Margaret's, Ward End has a Bishop organ of 1845 and St Mary's, Moseley possesses an instrument built by Henry Jones of South Kensington for the 1886 National Art Treasures Exhibition in Folkestone. Moseley acquired this organ in 1887 and it remained in its original condition until a rebuild and electrification by Nicholson in 1966. Finally, St Agnes', Moseley acquired a fine Hill organ from the redundant church of St Mark's, Leicester in 1987 and rebuilt it on a new west gallery in 1993-96.

Organ Cases and Organ Builders

The diocese is home to a few fine organ cases, chief among these being the 1715 chancel front by Schwarbrick in the cathedral. In 1972 St Philip's acquired another 18th-century case of *circa* 1730. This started life in Barnet parish church (Hertfordshire) before being moved to St Neots (Huntingdon) in 1749 where it remained until 1855; it was then sold to the organ builder G.M.Holdich in part exchange for a new organ. It was next installed in St Matthew's, Westminster from whence it migrated in 1879 to Forest School, Walthamstow. In 1897 it was purchased by St Chrysostom's, Hockley, where it remained until 1972 when, to prevent imminent vandalism, it was removed by the Diocesan Organ Adviser to the cathedral gallery where it was found to fit very happily on to the west-facing front of the cathedral organ.

Solihull also has an attractive 18th-century case, thought to be by Schwarbrick, and possibly built for old St Martin's-in-the-Bullring. More modern cases can be found at Temple Balsall (Gilbert Scott 1850), St Agnes, Moseley (divided case by G.F. Bodley 1885, from St Mark's in Leicester), Tanworth-in-Arden (Horace Bradley 1907), St Peter's, Maney (1925, probably by a local architect), and Emanuel Wylde Green (Stephen Bicknell 2002). A great loss, when both churches were de-consecrated,

83 *The most travelled organ case in the country? Made in 1730 it now faces west on the north gallery of the cathedral.*

was the demise of the wonderfully flamboyant gothic case with turrets, spires, and its own rose window in Holy Trinity, Bordesley (Francis Goodwin *c.*1820) and the large churchwarden gothic example in Emmanuel, Sparkbrook, originally built by Elliott for old St Martin's in 1822.

Rather surprisingly, in view of the wide variety of trades practised in Birmingham, the city has never been home to a leading firm of organ builders. In the 19th century E.J.Bossward settled in Birmingham, as Hill's representative, to look after the Town Hall organ and he set up his own business in Ladywood as E.J. Bossward & Sons. The firm's last apprentice, W.J. Bird, took over at an early age from the Bossward sons and went on to build sound if unadventurous organs until the Second World War. Solid work by Banfield, Halmshaw and F.W. Ebrall of Camp Hill can still be found in some churches, as can latter-day instruments by Tom Sheffield of Olton. The short-lived firms of Conacher Sheffield of Harborne and their successors, Harris Organs of Sparkhill, were less successful and little of their work now survives.

Organists and Choirmasters

As one would expect, there has been a rich tapestry of Birmingham organists during the last hundred years, many of them excellent amateur musicians who served their churches faithfully and well. Among the professionals, the first organist of the newly-designated cathedral was Edwin Stephenson who, together with Royle Shore the cathedral lecturer, did pioneering work in resurrecting music of the Tudor period at

84 *Appleby Matthews, founder of the City of Birmingham Orchestra.*

the cathedral's daily sung services. One of his successors, Dr Willis Grant, was an enormous influence on the city's music in the years following the Second World War as he also taught at King Edward's School and conducted the Birmingham Bach Society. He moved on to become Professor of Music at Bristol University. The current Director of Music, Marcus Huxley, was appointed in 1986. He was formerly assistant organist at Ripon Cathedral and won the top two prizes at the St Albans International Organ Competition in 1977. He has built a choir of high repute with a number of recordings, overseas concerts and regular appearances on BBC radio to their credit. A separate choir section for girls was established in 1992 by Rosemary Field, the then assistant organist. The choir have given first performances of choral works by a number of notable composers including John Joubert, Alan Ridout, Andrew Downes, John Sanders and Andrew Carter, as well as works composed by Huxley himself.

St Augustine's Edgbaston has had a distinguished succession of organists. Dr (later Sir) William H. Harris was there from 1911 until 1919. Later he became organist of New College Oxford, moving to Christ Church Cathedral and thence to St George's Chapel, Windsor Castle. He was a notable all-round musician and a composer of distinction. He was succeeded by T.W. North, who was also Borough Organist of Walsall and deputy organist at Birmingham Town Hall. He was well known as a brilliant recitalist and a fine choir trainer. His successor was Philip Moore, formerly assistant at St George's. Windsor, who moved on to be Head of BBC Music in Bristol. He, in turn, was succeeded at St Augustine's by Roy Massey who came from St Alban's, Conybere Street. He became Warden of the RSCM at Addington Palace for three years before returning to Birmingham as cathedral organist in 1968. In 1974 he moved to Hereford Cathedral where he served until 2001, and in retirement has become President of the Royal College of Organists. For some years in the latter part of the 20th century St Alban's, Conybere Street enjoyed several brilliant young musicians as organists and directors of music including Raymond Isaacson, Paul Hale (later of Southwell Minster), David Briggs (later of Truro and Gloucester Cathedrals) and John Butt (noted scholar and University Lecturer). Their enthusiasm enabled a 'St Alban's Festival' to be organised from the mid-1980s and, in 1992, when Birmingham was 'UK City of Music', this was transformed into the 'Birmingham Early Music Festival'. The University Liturgical Choir augmented the singers at the festival, which continues to take place annually in the autumn and uses St Alban's as one of its venues.

St Agnes', Moseley was privileged to have Appleby Matthews as its organist and choirmaster in the period 1911-21; he was also assistant organist at the cathedral. Musically precocious, he was giving piano lessons to other children at the age of 10, and by 12 was organist of Alcester Roman Catholic church. Matthews' St Agnes' choir

85 *The choir of St Agnes', Moseley trained by Passfield.*

gained first place in the Birmingham Musical Competition in 1913 and its leading treble, Frank Huggett, was second in the solo competition. He also took pains to try to improve congregational singing by gathering ladies in the congregation to practise the hymns for the following Sunday. Not everyone appreciated his efforts since there was a caustic letter to the *Church Times* in 1914 suggesting that Sunday services at St Agnes 'were practically a Music Hall'. During the First World War Matthews became a musical entrepreneur: he started his own choir, he was local chorus master for the Beecham Opera Company, and he conducted weekly concerts at the Birmingham Repertory Theatre. In 1918 he became Professor of Piano at the Midland Institute, conducted the extremely popular City Police Band, and moved rapidly to conducting nationally famous orchestras including the London Symphony, the Hallé, and the Berlin Philharmonic. In 1920 he became the first conductor of the newly-formed City of Birmingham Orchestra, the predecessor of today's CBSO. Harold Gray OBE, the CBSO's associate conductor for some 50 years from 1932, was organist and choirmaster at Holy Trinity, Sutton Coldfield for an equivalent length of time. At St Agnes, a second well-known organist and choirmaster was appointed in 1931. W. Reginald Passfield was an outstanding organist and teacher, and a composer of note. He left Birmingham in 1938, gained a Doctor of Music degree and went on to be senior music master at King's School, Canterbury and then to the London College of Music.

From 1920 to 1943 the music at St Martin's was under the direction of Dr Richard Wassell, a colourful character and renowned Birmingham musician who was awarded the Lambeth degree of D.Mus in recognition of his many achievements. His successor after the war was Geoffrey Fletcher who, working with two sympathetic rectors, maintained a superb choir of 30 boys and 18 men for almost 30 years. Also after the war, St Peter's Harborne was served by George Miles, an outstanding teacher and performer who was widely known as a recitalist thanks to his numerous broadcasts for the BBC. A modest, shy, scholarly man who had studied in Germany, he was revered by his students and became an immense influence for good in the musical life of the Midlands and at the School of Music where he was Professor of Organ.

Performance

Besides their use for liturgical purposes a number of Birmingham's Anglican churches are valued performance venues. The use of St Alban's has already been noted whilst both the cathedral and St Paul's in the Jewellery Quarter have superb acoustics for choral liturgical music and for small musical ensembles. Choirs and orchestras such as the English Symphony Orchestra, the Birmingham Bach Choir and, most notably, Ex Cathedra, use both churches for concert performances, whilst the weekly lunchtime organ recitals by the City Organist, Thomas Trotter, now take place on the cathedral organ since Birmingham Town Hall is undergoing a lengthy restoration project.

Performance use is not just a feature of the recent past, however. In 1768, St Philip's was the location for Birmingham's first music festival for the benefit of the General Hospital. In the 19th century this evolved into the famous Birmingham Triennial Music Festival with performances in the newly-constructed Town Hall, but in the late 18th century an oratorio was sung in the church in the morning and a play performed in the theatre in the evening, repeated over four weekdays. By the early 1800s, when other churches were also being used in rotation, a Sunday performance was included but, since this interfered with the morning service, the Rector of St Philip's withdrew his permission for it to continue in his church. In about 1880 St Philip's musical tradition was still being maintained since the Sunday service is described as 'lively and attractive, the music being rendered by a choir of well-trained voices, the solos and anthems being given in the most perfect manner'.

Part Three

PARISHES AND PEOPLE

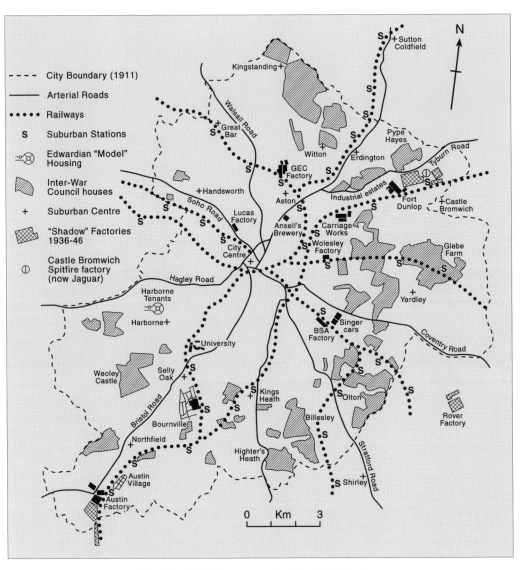

86 *Municipal inter-war council estates in Birmingham.*

17

NEW CHURCHES FOR NEW ESTATES

The City of Birmingham expanded enormously in physical extent in the 1920s and '30s. First the city council built new planned housing estates for the industrial workers who were crowding into the city, and then speculative building firms constructed miles of tree-lined streets of dwellings for those who could afford their own houses. More of both types of dwellings were constructed in Birmingham than in any other provincial city: 50,000 council houses and more than 54,000 speculative dwellings by 1939. Although some slum dwellings in the densely built-up inner areas of back-to-back courtyards were demolished, the vast majority of these areas were not cleared until the late 1950s onwards. The planning of the new council house estates was done with the lessons of Bournville and the Garden Cities movement to the forefront. Low housing densities (no more than 12 per acre), tree-lined cul-de-sac roads linked to radial highways, industrial land uses separated from housing, and careful provision of social and community facilities such as shopping parades, libraries, pubs, schools and churches were the by-words of planning.

By the end of the 1930s vast municipal housing estates ringed the city on all sides but the west. Fifteen of these estates had more than 1,000 houses and the largest, Kingstanding, had 4,802 (Cherry 1994). Unfortunately the social provisions lagged well behind the house building, factory employment was some distance away, and even the schools were slow to be built. The long distances of these estates from the city centre meant that bus and tram journeys were expensive and food in local shops was more costly than in inner-city shops. The churches provided on these estates were by some of Birmingham's most distinguished Arts and Crafts architects. Edwin Reynolds designed the huge St Mary's, Pype Hayes as a red-brick basilica with narrow aisles and a high clerestorey; St Luke's, Kingstanding was also Romanesque in style, by P.J. Hunt, but remained unfinished at the outbreak of war. Holy Cross, Billesley is by H.W. Hobbiss (the architect of King Edward's School) and is again a brick basilica designed in 1937; again the chancel and vestries had to be left for completion in the mid-1960s. Hobbiss was also the architect of St Edmund's, Tyseley, built in 1939-40 as war broke out. Others were much simpler buildings such as St Gabriel's, Shenley Lane built in 1933-4, or St Bartholomew's Allen's Cross, built in 1938.

Private housing estates in the inter-war period tended to occupy areas with good rail access to the city centre where there were already small, established communities of long standing with churches already in place. Examples include Hall Green, where the Ascension found itself with a large new congregation; St Margaret's, Olton, and St James', Shirley where churches were already in place by the late 19th century. There was a similar picture on the outer fringes of Sutton Coldfield where St Peter's, Maney

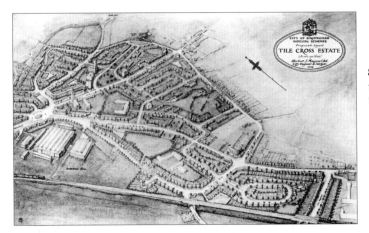

87 *Plans for the Tile Cross estate with new schools and churches incorporated.*

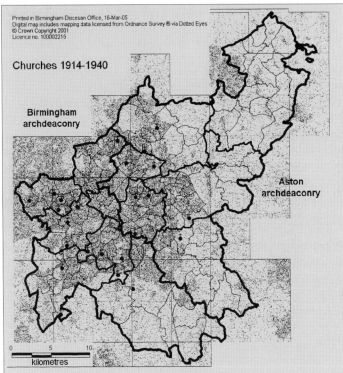

Churches 1914-1940

Birmingham archdeaconry

Aston archdeaconry

Printed in Birmingham Diocesan Office, 18-Mar-05
Digital map includes mapping data licensed from Ordnance Survey ® via Dotted Eyes
© Crown Copyright 2001
Licence no. 100002215

0   5   10.
kilometres

88 *New churches of the inter-war period in the diocese.*

was the last to be consecrated, in 1905, and therefore celebrates its centenary with the diocese. However, there were new churches too, notably St Francis, Bournville, completed in 1925 to designs by W.A. Harvey; and St Faith and St Laurence, Harborne, begun in 1937 to designs by Philip Chatwin, but not completed until 1958-60.

Responding to Growth

The diocesan response to the rapid outward growth of Birmingham began in 1926 with an appeal to raise £30,000 for 'church extension', the intention being to build church halls that could be used for worship and social activities. Nearly all this sum was raised within a year. A second appeal was launched by Bishop Barnes in 1935

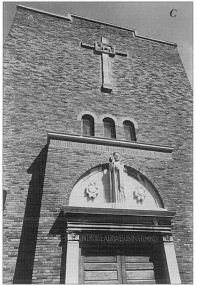

89 *A. St Luke's, Kingstanding. The dramatic Art Deco sculpture of a bull (the symbol of St Luke) over the entrance door. B. St Edmund, Tyseley by architect H.W. Hobbiss. C. Christ Church, Burney Lane (1935) also by Hobbiss. D. St Catherine's, Blackwell.*

for £105,000 (100,000 guineas!). Again, it was successful, thanks to Canon J.C. Lucas who became the full-time secretary of the appeal. Barnes was particularly concerned that the young families moving out to the housing estates on the fringe of the city might become totally secularised if the Church had to rely on older buildings miles from where people lived. In all 15 new church premises were built between 1928 and 1939, the majority brick-built basilicas of one kind or another.

The Second World War led to extensive bomb damage of both housing and industrial premises thanks to the industrial prowess of Birmingham and the Black Country and the region's contribution to wartime production of everything from armaments to aircraft. Churches were given a very low priority by the fire service and many were destroyed or seriously damaged. The loss of city-centre churches was perhaps a blessing in disguise since, by the 1960s, their congregations had been

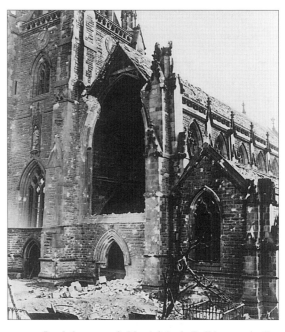

90 *Plan of the new church and hall on the Kingshurst estate designed to cost £24,000.*

91 *Bomb damage at St Martin's-in-the-Bullring, 10 April 1941.*

removed to the new housing estates that were once more ringing Birmingham's outer fringes. Seven of the buildings badly damaged by bombing were quickly listed as not to be replaced, including the vast St Thomas', Bath Row, with seats for more than 2,000 worshippers, St Catherine's, Nechells, St Gabriel's, Deritend and All Saints, Small Heath. In all, 16 churches had been demolished by 1960. Stained glass was even more vulnerable. The glass in St Martin's-in-the-Bullring's Burne-Jones' window, in the south transept, was only taken out and removed for storage elsewhere the day before a bomb hit the church, blowing off the roof and damaging part of the east end. Even churches in the suburbs were not immune: both St Anne's and St Agnes', Moseley were quite badly damaged, the former losing its roof and all its stained glass, whilst St John's, Harborne was destroyed. The other 'benefit' of war-time damage were the payments from the War Damages Commission, some £34,000 in total, much of which could be diverted to new church building.

92 *Watch Night service conducted by Canon Guy Rogers, 31 December 1941, in the Markets air-raid shelter.*

Post-1945 Renewal

The city council had already begun to formulate ambitious plans for slum clearance and new housing estates before the war ended. These plans continued to reserve sites for new churches. Consequently the Diocesan Conference, meeting in May 1945, set up an enquiry as to the needs of the diocese and the provision and financing of new churches. Their plans were based upon more detailed plans submitted by each deanery. Several of these survive and make interesting reading today. In Handsworth Deanery, for example, there were nine out of 16 parishes with populations of more than 10,000 people, the largest, St John's, Perry Barr, having 53,000, since it included the vast Perry Beeches council estate. Only the two central Handsworth parishes had assistant priests. Not surprisingly the needs were identified as: new churches in Perry Beeches and Oscott, new church halls in several parishes, assistant priests in all parishes and six trained women workers. Unfortunately, only one parish could afford the stipends necessary. In Kings Norton Deanery the need for a new parish in the West Heath area and another in Longbridge were

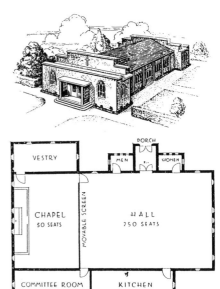

93 *The 'Ten-Year Forward Movement' expected to build nine church halls on this model to provide facilities on municipal estates without churches.*

identified, and a new church at Bartley Green was needed. Even in Solihull Deanery the need for 17 extra clergy was identified since some existing parishes had up to 40,000 inhabitants. It is interesting that the Solihull report expressed a preference for large parishes with 3-4 clergy, rather than single-minister parishes, because that is what came to pass in both Solihull and Shirley where effective team ministries are in place today. Solihull also complained about Bishop Barnes' insistence that clergy in Birmingham had to be university graduates.

In 1946 the diocese inaugurated the 'Ten Year Forward Movement' under the direction of the Ven. Michael Parker, Archdeacon of Aston, to take this work forward. Its terms of reference were as much framed in terms of spiritual renewal and new clergy as for new buildings. The booklet that accompanied the launch of the movement includes a description of the Cherry Orchard church hall sponsored by Handsworth parish church. The two small prefabricated huts were purchased and erected by residents of the Cherry Orchard estate and dedicated by the bishop in 1947. Holy Communion, a family service and an evening service were held weekly, with packed congregations, and an array of men's, women's and youth activities met on weekdays.1948 saw a summer fund-raising campaign which included an open-air service in the cathedral churchyard and a pageant of diocesan life in the Town Hall called 'Lively Stones – Building the Temple of God'. The aim was for £30,000 to build nine church halls, which could be used for services on Sundays until churches could be built. The initial priorities were Rubery, where a small wooden church of 1905 still served the much increased community; Longbridge and Brandwood in Kings Norton parish; Oscott in Perry Barr; Hob's Farm in Castle Bromwich; Garrett's Green in Sheldon parish; and Kitt's Green in Yardley. Shard End, Kingshurst and Hamstead

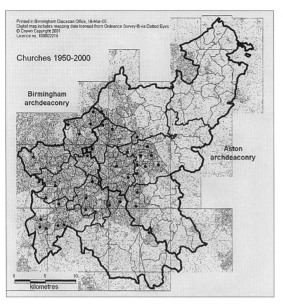

94 *New churches of the second half of the 20th century.*

were to follow once these first priorities had been completed.

Circles without Centres

Large sums of money were raised rapidly and by mid-summer 1949 nearly £37,000 was in hand, almost wholly raised from church people within each deanery. National publicity followed and the national Church Assembly, stimulated by Birmingham's example, initiated new schemes of financial aid for new churches countrywide. The second half of the 'Ten Year Forward Movement', beginning in 1953, had a target of £250,000. Though established in Bishop Barnes' time, it was fully supported by Bishop Wilson and this sum was again substantially exceeded, some £590,000 being raised over the period. In 1956 Bishop Wilson launched a new public appeal with a target of £1,200,000. The 'Circles without Centres' appeal was intended to celebrate the diocesan golden jubilee. Half this huge sum was raised in three years and the first new church, All Saints, Shard End, was completed; 'A very ugly church', says Pevsner! Unfortunately for the future, Bishop Wilson was determined that the new churches should be able to seat 400 people so as to accommodate local schools for their annual services. 'We shall build for the future and for the congregations we are going to attract as time goes on', he said (McKay 1972: 162). Sadly, those congregations have never been attracted.

By 1959, five dual-purpose buildings and six churches were completed or underway. Perhaps the most influential of the new churches of the 1950s and '60s was Hodge Hill. This was planned as a practical academic experiment by the Institute for the Study of Worship and Religious Architecture at the University of Birmingham. The leaders of the Institute, founded in 1961, had approached Bishop Wilson in 1963

95 *All Saints, Shard End was the first church to be completed from the 'Circles without Centres' appeal.*

to ask if they could be commissioned to design and build a church and parsonage to an agreed budget. The Institute contained experts on liturgy, sociology, law, civil engineering, acoustics, heating and lighting, whilst Denys Hinton of the Birmingham School of Architecture was recruited for architectural advice (though the architect of the building was Martin Purdy). A maximum budget of £50,000 was agreed. What was interesting was the community involvement in the design. Some 150 parishioners met fortnightly to listen to the experts and then question and discuss with them the evolving plans

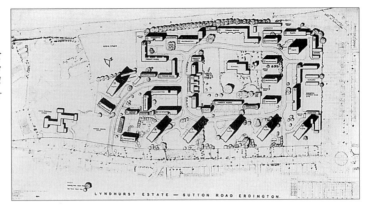

96 *The new municipal housing estates of the 1950s-1970s were high-density with tower blocks and no evidence of sites reserved for churches.*

for the new church centre. Multi-purpose buildings were by then back in fashion and when it was consecrated in 1968 Hodge Hill was community centre as well as church.

Its rector, the Revd Denis Ede, provided an appraisal of the planning, building and life in the church seven years later (Ede 1975). He notes that the parish had a population of 23,000; that the site of the church was donated in 1937 by the Earl of Bradford, and a dual-purpose hall had been built in the same year. It was destroyed by fire in 1966. In the 1950s a congregation of about 100 was built up. In the interesting community meetings planning the new church he says that 'we listened to the things that they wanted to, and discounted the things we judged to be erroneous'; most people wanted a tower with bells for example, but, 'rightly we ignored them'. In retrospect, he says, 'the whole enterprise was amazingly painless and worthwhile'. But despite thousands of visitors from all over the world, few other new church buildings learned the lessons of Hodge Hill. Denis Ede's testimony of his work in the new church is couched not in terms of the buildings but of the way in which new community groups use the buildings; of the need to understand funding to support their work from agencies other than the Church; and of new decision-making processes to enable both worshippers and community to play their full part.

Another church in which the Institute assisted in the planning was the Woodgate Valley church centre, which is again a multi-purpose building with worship area, playgroup space, coffee shop and community hall. It is also shared by Anglicans and Methodists. In this instance it was Bishop Brown who invited the Institute to participate in establishing the needs of the area and how they might be met. The culmination of their work is to be found in St George's, Newtown (1970) and St Andrew's, Chelmsley Wood (1972), where multi-purpose buildings also have worship spaces where the ideals of the 'Liturgical Movement' were given best practical expression. The Liturgical Movement had begun in the 1930s, prompted by A.G. Herbert's book *Liturgy and Society* (1935). It sought to return the Eucharist to the centre of the life of the Church. Its liturgical consequences were a free-standing altar, west-facing celebration of the Eucharist by the minister, and the people gathered 'around' the altar, preferably in a semi-circular arrangement of the seating.

The Institute also had influence in other ways in the diocese. They organised regular tours of European countries to examine new churches there. Revd David Pendleton was one of the participants and what he saw was influential in the planning of St David's Shenley Green (1970), another of the architecturally-admired new

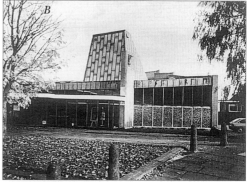
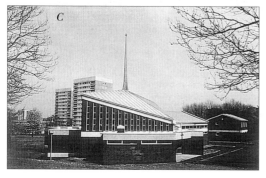

97 *Post-war churches: A. Woodgate Valley Church Centre. B. St David's, Shenley. C. St George's, New Town. D. St Matthew's, Perry Beeches.*

churches of the 1960s in the diocese. St Peter's, Hall Green (1964), built to an octagonal plan in concrete, has fine modern stained-glass by Tristam Rhulman of Strasbourg whom the vicar, Joseph Adlam, met on one of the tours (Gilman 1997). Most spectacular of all was St Matthew's, Perry Beeches (1964) by architects Robert Maguire and Keith Murray, but where surviving correspondence shows that the vicar, Revd Peter Vowles, had a significant impact on the eventual plans.

Retrenchment and Adaptation

The expansionary, serving-the-community, modes of the 1950s through to the 1970s began to give way to retrenchment and adaptation from the 1980s as congregations got smaller and the financial responsibilities of diocese and parishes became more onerous. There were still new churches, most notably, St Bede's, Brandwood, a delightful and practical multi-purpose building replacing a structure destroyed by an arson attack, but adaptation of buildings that were too large became the norm. In many cases this

98   *The Liturgical Movement in action: St George's, Newtown.*

provided multi-purpose spaces similar to new churches such as Hodge Hill. St Luke's, Kingstanding is an example; here the altar was placed in the west apse and one third of the nave and the old chancel separated by a solid wall to provide a community room with offices above. At St Andrew's, Chelmsley Wood a space formerly used for storage, with separate access, was converted for the use of a local undertaker! However, the most notable conversions were those at St Matthew's, Nechells and Christchurch, Oldbury. In both places half the nave, on two floors, has been converted to office space for commercial letting whilst the remaining space provides a modern worship area for the reduced congregation. Finally, there was a need to reduce further the number of church buildings in the inner ring of late 19th-century terraced housing where, by the 1970s, people of other faiths were often in the majority. The reorganisation of parishes in Small Heath was perhaps the most successful. Here three parishes were amalgamated, two churches made redundant and the third refurbished and reordered to form the new parish of All Saints, Small Heath.

Ecumenical Projects

Quite a number of the new churches planned for Birmingham's new estates were ecumenical projects. St Andrew's, Chelmsley Wood was a joint Anglican-Methodist scheme and the Balsall Heath Church Centre brought together Anglicans and the URC in a shared

99   *Stained glass at St Peter's, Hall Green. This is 'The Nativity' by Tristan Ruhlmann. It was dedicated in 1970 by Bishop Brown.*

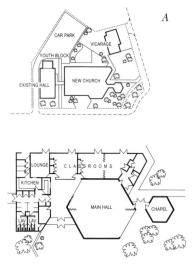

100   *A. Plans of St Michael's, Gospel Lane. B. the new Church Centre in 1971.*

building (see chapter 26). One of the first of these ecumenical projects was St Michael's Gospel Lane, in Hall Green. This was thought to be the first purpose-built Anglican Methodist church centre in the country. It was another of the initiatives advised by the Institute for the Study of Worship and Religious Architecture. The project began in 1965 with dialogue between the ministers and congregations of St Michael's, Hall Green and Gospel Lane Methodist Church. By 1969 the congregations had worked out their commonalities and decided to join together. The new church was designed by Eric Hemsoll with Barrie Hall, still a member of the congregation there, liaising between professional and congregation. It was opened in 1971.

Rather different from these new churches and centres was the reforming of the Church in Cotteridge. There the three churches which stood practically side by side in the suburban shopping centre of Cotteridge came together over the period of a year in 1980-81 and decided that they could do things better if they worked with one another so that buildings, money and people could be used more effectively to serve the local community. They formed a Local Ecumenical Project in 1981. By 1985 they had decided to move into one building, the Methodist church. St Agnes' Anglican church and the United Reformed church were sold and demolished to make way for a supermarket and sheltered housing for the elderly. The large sums of money generated from this redevelopment paid for the extensive rebuilding of the Methodist church to become The Cotteridge Church with a united congregation. After a year 'in the wilderness' in hired school halls, the newly-adapted church was reopened in February 1989 after its £800,000 refurbishment. Two full-time day centres cater for frail elderly people and those with dementia in conjunction with Birmingham Social Services and the South Birmingham Mental Health Trust; the kitchen provides meals for the day centre and for shoppers dropping in each day to the coffee bar; there is a parent and toddler group each morning; extramural classes meet most evenings, together with community groups of all kinds.

A final senten-ce must record the success of Kings Norton parish in winning the second BBC TV *Restoration* series in 2004. This will enable 'The Saracen's Head' and Dr John Hall's school to be restored for parish and community use.

18

EDUCATION

CHURCH SCHOOLS AND CHAPLAINS

Most of the earliest schools of which we have record were those taught by late medieval priests, usually funded by chantries established by landowners and merchants. We have already seen (chapter 3) that King Edward's School in Birmingham had been founded from the estates of the dissolved guild in the town in 1552. However, there was an even earlier school in Birmingham, because a document of 1546 notes that the chapel in Deritend had two chantry priests, one 'teachyng a grammer scole'; similarly, at Kings Norton, where there were three priests in the 16th century 'whereof one hath allweys tought a fre Gramer scole'. In the 1540s the Kings Norton charity paid for an usher 'to ayde the same Scole master, now beyyng charged with the teaching

and insructyng of an hundreth and 20 scollers' but there was insufficient money to sustain a school of this size (Page 1908: 350). The building, with its 15th-century timber-framed upper storey, still stands in the churchyard and was well-known for its library bequeathed by Dr Hall. A similarly early school house stands beside Yardley church. The free grammar school at Sutton Coldfield was established in 1540, by Bishop Vesey of Exeter, a native of the town. The first schoolmaster had to be dismissed, but went on to become Dean of Lichfield! Solihull Grammar School dates from 1560 when the endowments of the chantries in St Alphege's church

101 *Dr John Hall's school, Kings Norton.*

were used to fund a schoolmaster. In 1615 the trustees paid £25 11s. 1d. 'towarde the building of the Scholehous'. Coleshill Grammar School was founded before 1612, probably in the same way, and a Charity School for poor girls was later established in 1720-30.

Charity Schools

Many of the earliest-founded schools in the diocese trace their beginnings in the 17th century to charitable bequests from lay people. One such was Kingsbury School, founded in 1686 by Thomas Coton, who gave land and rents to support a schoolmaster in the village. He was charged with teaching poor boys and girls of Kingsbury, Nether Whitacre and Marston. Coton specified that the master should be 'a religious man and

102 *The 16th-century school building at Yardley.*

protestant, and if convenient, a bachelor, and to exercise the ministry but very seldom'. Another early foundation was Polesworth, which began in 1655 thanks to a bequest from local landowner Sir Francis Nethersole. Two houses were built, one for the schoolmaster and boys and the second for a mistress and girls. Other foundations of this kind include schools at Temple Balsall (1670) for 20 poor boys; Middleton (1672); Castle Bromwich (1703) for boys only; Shustoke (1709), where the schoolmaster was chosen by the vicar and wardens; and Wishaw (1710). The most important in terms of its later significance was the Birmingham Blue Coat School. This was founded thanks to the energies of Elizabeth Phillips, in 1722, using a large sum collected from the inhabitants of Birmingham for the stipends of a master and mistress to teach poor children writing, reading and 'the Christian religion according to the principles of the Church of England'. Further bequests to the school followed through the 18th century and about 160 children were clothed, fed and boarded in the school on the south side of St Philip's churchyard. The children also provided the earliest choir for the congregation of St Philip's.

The 18th century saw the beginning of book clubs in Birmingham, for adult education. The Rector of St Philip's created the first *public* library in 1733 – though only a carefully selected few of the public could borrow the books! In 1779 the first Birmingham library was formed – a subscription library set up by dissenters, whose ambition was that 'it should contain all the most valuable publications in the English Language'.

Sunday Schools

Sunday Schools in Birmingham began with a town meeting in 1784 organised by Charles Curtis and John Riland, rector and vicar of St Martin's and St Mary's respectively. Money was raised, rules established and an advert for teachers followed; the advert notably requested applications from women and men from the beginning. By September 12 Sunday schools for boys and 12 for girls had been opened in different areas of the town with space for at least 720 children – an impressive achievement in three months. To begin with the Sunday Schools were ecumenical, but it was not long before the Nonconformists withdrew to establish their own denominational Sunday Schools. A survey of 1842 showed that the initial 12 schools had increased to 20 Anglican schools and 40 nonconformist schools with more than 19,000 pupils between them.

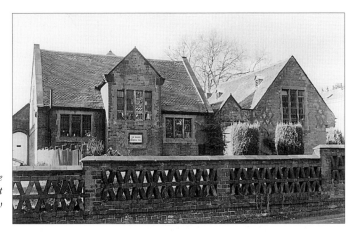

103 *The buildings of the former National School at St Bartholomew's Edgbaston, now the Walker Hall.*

What was taught in the schools was determined primarily by the minister of the church to which most of them were attached, but the General Committee of the Church of England Sunday Schools in Birmingham began to provide advice from the 1820s. So, for example, 'no books should be provided or used but such as are on the catalogue of the SPCK', whilst John Darwall at Deritend explained to parents that writing and accounts would not be taught on Sunday as it would violate the Sabbath. Most of the reading matter, when not the Bible itself, was that provided by the Religious Tract Society and non-religious material was normally forbidden. Many of the teachers had themselves been pupils in the schools by the middle of the 19th century (Jepson 1992).

National Schools

At the beginning of the 19th century the Church began to organise educational provision in its parishes on a more consistent basis. The SPCK (Society for the Propagation of Christian Knowledge) had been founded as early as 1698 to advise on the running of day schools but in 1811 it was superseded, as far as schools were concerned, by the National Society for the Promotion of Education of the Poor in the Principles of the Established Church – if only there had been a communications adviser in those days! Not surprisingly this unwieldy title was usually shortened to The National Society and its aim was to have a school in every parish. As schools came to be funded by the Society they were usually known as National Schools. Nonconformists tried to do something similar with the British and Foreign Schools Society, founded in 1814, but they had less money than the Anglicans so there were fewer British Schools. Even the Church of England, however, still relied on donations from landowners and industrialists to pay part of the cost of National Schools. Consequently, places such as Edgbaston had both more schools and better-resourced schools than did places such as Smethwick before 1870. In Edgbaston, the parishioners financed a church school in 1847; St George's parish provided a second in 1854, and St James's opened a school in 1861.

The parishioners providing the money sent their own children to private preparatory schools, of course – the parish schools were for the poor. Most provided separate facilities for boys and girls and there was still considerable debate as to whether it was worth teaching girls to write! The buildings were small and cramped for the very large numbers of pupils; the schoolroom at St George's accommodated 165 pupils for example (Slater 2002). Once school inspection was instituted by the government in

104 *Hampton-in-Arden Girls' School was privately financed by the lord of the manor.*

1839, they often commented on the cramped conditions. At Polesworth for example, in 1857, the inspector noted 'an undue proportion of children over seven for whom there is no desk accommodation' (Howe 2003: 15). On a rather different scale was St Thomas's National School in Holloway Head, Birmingham. It was founded in 1831 and to begin with had two teachers for 215 children! An inspector noted in 1841 that in a small room that could properly hold 25, 60 are packed. A new school building for infants and a teacher's house were added the following year. Further enlargements followed and by 1894 St Thomas's had 1,220 pupils and was the largest church school in Birmingham. It served the densely-packed courtyards of back-to-back houses on either side of Holloway Head. In 1917 it was reorganised into Senior, Junior and Infant departments and the senior school became one of the diocese's church secondary schools in 1945. The junior and infants school remains one of the diocese's Aided schools today. A large number of the present church schools of the diocese trace their beginnings in a similar manner to the National Society in the first 70 years of the 19th century.

School Boards

In 1870 the state entered education through W.E. Forster's Education Act, which provided for universal compulsory education for the first time. Birmingham men were in the forefront of the campaign for free, universal, non-sectarian education. George Dixon, an Anglican, was joined by George Dawson and Robert Dale, the undisputed leaders of Nonconformity in the town in working towards the 1870 Act. A survey in 1867 found that only 50 per cent of Birmingham's children went to school. The Act was effected through the establishment of district School Boards. These Boards were directly elected by the ratepayers and they provided schools where previously there had been none, or where provision was insufficient. Church schools continued in parallel with the new Board schools. Coleshill and Polesworth were amongst the rural communities which established Boards but they administered only two or three schools each. Much more significant was Aston, with 20, and Birmingham with 109 schools. The Birmingham School Board was dominated by Nonconformists from 1873. They were intent on taking over all the schools in the city so did not provide funds for Church schools to be improved. By 1895 the plight of most of the

Church schools in the city was desperate. Fourteen of the 28 remaining were facing mounting debts and were in danger of closure. The Birmingham School Board had tried to make the Board's schools the finest in England and the high quality of both teaching and facilities in the Board schools contrasted sharply with the ailing fortunes of the Church schools. Bishop Edmund Knox, who had come to the city in 1891 as vicar of Aston, saw improving Church schools as one of the ways to inject new confidence into the clergy of Birmingham. He therefore set up a Church Schools' Board, which had the aim not merely of defending Church schools but, more importantly, of improving them. The rescue of these schools was a long-term business and Knox therefore decided that his immediate task was to carry the attack to the 'enemy' by restoring non-denominational religious

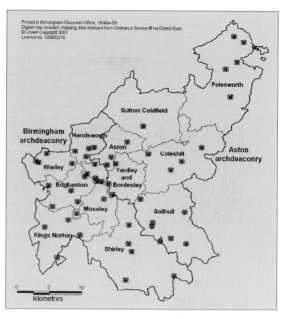

105 *Birmingham diocesan Church schools.*

education in all schools. This might not sound too controversial, but its elimination had been the first victory of the Nonconformist radicals in 1873. In order to succeed, Knox knew that the Church of England had to capture the School Board.

The first attempt came in 1897. The 'Liberal Eight' with all their experience of election campaigns, and helped by the influential *Birmingham Daily Post*, found little difficulty in fending off the 'Church Seven'. Only four Churchmen were elected, and this included Knox who had to stand in at very short notice when one of his candidates dropped out. Over the next three years Knox organised his 'party', using the example of the radicals themselves. His superb use of the transferable vote in the city's wards bore fruit in the famous victory of the 'Church Seven' in the election of 1900. Knox became Chairman of the School Board, and restored religious education in the city's schools, permanently as it turned out, as the Boards were all abolished by the 1902 Education Act. The significance of the victory was basically a matter of morale, for it showed that an organised Church could take on the Dissenters in the city and win. In Knox's words, 'The long age of Church despondency was over'.

From 1902 education was in the hands of local authorities, though Church schools continued to run alongside the local authority system until 1944. The majority of Church of England schools in the inter-war period remained small, overcrowded and occupied buildings that badly needed replacing. So much so that, in 1930, the Archdeacon of Birmingham launched a diocesan appeal to 'save' Church schools. However, Church schools were also predominantly in inner-city districts and were valued by the close-knit communities that they served. Canon Norman Power wrote movingly in the 1960s, as inner-city redevelopment proceeded apace, of the way in which the teachers in his Church schools in Ladywood provided the only stability and love on offer to young children. St Barnabas' School was in Ryland Street and was opened in 1862. It was enlarged and improved in 1924 and had become a Voluntary Controlled school in 1950. Power wrote that the children were 'bright, relaxed and

106 *St Michael & All Angels JI School, Bartley Green was one of the first new schools to be completed after the Second World War.*

eager to be taught, ... they respond warmly with questions after my lesson'. Their teacher, Mr Hewitt, was ' a fatherly type of man and a superb teacher; ... he knows the children and he loves them. Most of the children have known him for several years. ...They bask in the security it brings' (Power 1965: 65-6). St Barnabas was closed as redevelopment advanced across the parish.

By contrast, In St John's, Ladywood School, Power wrote that the insecurities of children involved in moving house and school several times in rapid succession were manifest. In three years nearly 500 children were admitted against a normal intake of 55 per year, whilst more than 400 left the school. Such children 'built a "wall" against any relationships. They had been "bereaved" too often. It took many school terms before they believed in a teacher enough to make any response.' Planning 'removed from the school in one evil sweep the entire choir, the football XI, and the swimming team ... which had been our pride for so long' (Power 1965: 67-8). St John's School was eventually rebuilt on a new site and still serves the community today.

Today there are 51 Church of England schools in the diocese, almost equally divided between Voluntary Aided schools and Voluntary Controlled ones. In Voluntary Aided schools the governors have to build and maintain the buildings and the religious education curriculum is that of the Church of England; in Voluntary Controlled schools the LEA (Local Education Authority) pays for the buildings and the religious education curriculum is that approved by the LEA. Only two of these school are secondary schools: St Alban's, in Highgate and St Michael's, in Sandwell. Periodically there are campaigns for additional secondary schools to be built, especially in Sutton Coldfield, but building a new Voluntary Aided school is a very expensive business and the Diocesan Education Committee has preferred to use its resources to enhance the schools it has. Many schools were rebuilt to modern standards in the 1960s and '70s and some are used for public worship on Sundays. One of the most notable of recent new buildings is St John's C of E School, Sparkhill, where the hall/worship space has been much admired.

Church schools aim to reflect their Christian ethos in a number of ways: they affirm faith in both their staff and students and celebrate the spiritual dimension of life, especially in regular worship; they usually have close relationships with their parish church; they explore religious issues openly and their Christian basis means that pastoral care is strengthened by the conviction that all are children of God. The particular challenge of the post-Second World War years has been the fact that in inner

107 *Pupils at one of the diocesan junior schools.*

Birmingham, and in Warley and Smethwick, the majority of pupils in some schools have been increasingly adherents of other faiths. It is a testament to their staff that Moslem, Sikh and Hindu families often make positive choices to send their children to Church schools and that children learn to respect each other's differences.

University Chaplaincies

The University of Birmingham's charter established an avowedly 'secular' institution and St Francis Hall, the university chaplaincy centre, was built in the 1930s with money provided from the Cadbury charities. They also provided the money to employ the St Francis Hall chaplains who were then 'recognised' but not employed by the university. Some of these chaplains were Anglican, but by no means all. One such was Donald Tytler, subsequently Archdeacon of Aston and then Suffragan Bishop of Middleton, in Manchester diocese. With the dramatic expansion of university education in the 1960s the number of chaplains was increased. Geoffrey Templeman, a keen churchman, had become registrar of the university in 1955, and helped to develop the recognised chaplain's committee in conjunction with Canon Ronald Allen, the Vicar of Edgbaston. Allen's curate, Bob Turnbull, should probably be regarded as the first Anglican, as against St Francis Hall, chaplain to the university. He lived with a group of Anglican students in Chad Hill cottage which stood opposite the *White Swan* on the Edgbaston/Harborne border and which became, *de facto*, the Anglican chaplaincy.

Quite quickly the chaplaincy moved to a large villa, nearer the university, on the corner of Richmond Hill Road and Farquar Road where 25-30 students could be accommodated together with a common room, dining room, bar and chapel. Turnbull was succeeded by lay worker Helen Holman and Arthur Mace, an ordained member of the Chemistry Department, who subsequently married. John Duncan, later Archdeacon of Birmingham, was appointed in 1965 to be chaplain, but not warden

108 *Children of St John's C of E School, Sparkhill at Bishop Sentamu's Installation.*

of the chaplaincy. His brief was to do pastoral work on Birmingham's campus and in the new halls of residence complex at The Vale. The chaplaincy expanded into another house so that it could accommodate 50 students and a succession of resident wardens provided meals and organisation; folk evenings in the bar were in vogue for a time and there was a regular mid-week Eucharist. Sometimes there were services elsewhere, including university departments; John Duncan remembers a memorable one in the Medical School with a skeleton standing on his right-hand side!

Edgbaston church people, notably Mrs Ann Kenrick, were supportive of the chaplaincy with gifts of both money and their time. For a time it was also supported by the British Council to provide a home for international students; some residents of this period have subsequently continued to serve the Church, including the present Bishop of Exeter. However, it was always a financially and logistically fragile operation and the chaplaincy closed in the early 1990s.

Sunday services for students began in St Monica's, the mission chapel of Edgbaston Old Church, but when it was demolished they moved to the chapel of Queen's College, the ecumenical theological training college. Ecumenism was very much in mind in the late 1960s and by the early 1970s, when St Francis Hall had been expanded, the chaplains of all denominations began to work from the building and increasingly to work as a team. There was a regular 'University Eucharist' for a period and famous theologians (including Hugh Montefiore before he became bishop) were invited to give 'teaching weeks'. Unfortunately, the Cadbury money to employ chaplains ran out and chaplains are now employed by their denomination, whilst the university looks after the building. Today St Francis Hall has become a multi-faith building and there was much complex negotiation in the 1990s to adapt it for Muslim as well as Christian worship.

Chaplaincy at Aston University began in the late 1960s as the Birmingham College of Advanced Technology was in process of becoming a university and, like Birmingham, the chaplains were based at first in the Students' Union. The university provided office accommodation and, eventually a chaplaincy centre called the Martin Luther King Centre. Chaplains were involved in some ethics teaching for the business and engineering courses as well as pastoral work. At the University of Central England (UCE) the diocese began to appoint chaplains from the late 1980s. From the beginning they were welcomed and supported within the Student Services department of the new university, and here, too, the Anglican chaplain has worked with part-time other-faith chaplains in an avowedly pluralist institution.

19

WORK WITH CHILDREN
AND YOUNG PEOPLE

It is extraordinarily difficult to get a fair perspective on work with children and young people across the diocese, and across time, since the vast majority of such work goes on quietly, in individual parishes, according to the enthusiasms of clergy and lay people and the ebb and flow of younger ages in the churches of the diocese. It is still perhaps something of a shock to discover that, until the end of the Second World War, class divisions in society were replicated in church work with younger children. In the majority of middle-class parishes there were therefore two Sunday Schools, one for 'ordinary children' and another for children who attended private schools and who could not therefore be expected to mix with other parish children. In the 19th century, Sunday Schools were seen as a means not only of teaching young people about the faith, but also whereby adults and children could be given a basic education. Reading and writing were taught using the Bible as the basic text so that secular and faith education were one and the same thing. Some of these Sunday Schools were huge undertakings. That at the notable Anglo-Catholic parish of St Jude's, Hill Street, close to the city centre, catered for over 900 children in the 1880s and there were clubs and classes of all kinds. Another notably successful work was the Street Children's Union established by Canon W.H. Carnegie when he came to be Rector of St Philip's in 1913. Staffed by young men from the universities coming to learn something about social work in a big city, it had more than 60 clubs for boys and girls all over the city within a year or two.

Uniformed organisations and football teams

At the beginning of the 20th century Anglican and other churches were in the forefront of providing sponsorship for the uniformed youth organisations which are such a feature of Edwardian Britain. Beginning with the Boys' Brigade, and continuing with Boy Scouts, Girl Guides, Girls' Brigade, Girls Friendly Society and Woodcraft Folk, thousands of youngsters were meeting in church halls and 'tin tabernacles' across the diocese by the 1920s. Indeed, such groups were often one of the stimuli to building a church hall right through to the 1960s. At St John's, Ladywood, for example, the parish built a new hall in the 1960s even as much of the housing in the parish was being demolished, so as to be ready for children's and youth activities once new housing and new families were established (Power 1965: 39). Quite frequently it was the clergy and their wives who were dragooned into leading these organisations, but in other places lay people came forward to take up the training that was on offer. In some places these organisations grew very rapidly indeed; brass bands were formed and the march to the monthly church parade formed a recruiting platform in its

109 *Brownies meeting at St Agnes' church hall in 1928.*

own right. That was certainly the case at St Germain's, Edgbaston where the 74th Birmingham Scout Group was formed in 1912 and, by the 1920s, had their own 'hut' and a band that long-time residents still remember today (Slater 2002).

Another basis for work with young people to encourage their faith development was through church choirs and altar serving teams (almost entirely boys until the 1960s, of course). Some churches encouraged football teams: at Highter's Heath in the late 1940s, Norman Power started a local league of football clubs all over his extensive parish and the first 'cup final' attracted some 4-500 spectators (Power 1965: 21). Church football teams were often derived from choir members and the largest choirs usually enjoyed a summer holiday week away together in a rural or seaside location. St Agnes', Moseley was certainly one such choir in the 1930s that had both a football team and an annual camp. In 1936 they stayed in a large flour mill beside the River Wye, near Brecon. They 'slept on hay bags in the top storey of the mill and Mr Passfield (the choirmaster) joined the boys in all their sports, hiking, fishing and even in an exciting rat-hunt of half an hour' (Slater 1984, 70).

In the immediate aftermath of the Second World War all of this continued with little change but, by the 1950s, the 'teenager' had been discovered/invented and life was never quite the same again! Government reports and professional youth work followed but Birmingham was rather looked down upon in such professional circles as 'an absolute wilderness' as far as youth work was concerned. Nonetheless, things were happening in some Birmingham churches. At St Martin's-in-the-Bullring the junior church rapidly began to flourish from the 1950s onwards. Anything from 60-100 children under twelve met each Sunday morning during the time of the church service, being taught in age-specific groups, whilst some older teenagers joined with local Pentecostalists to use St Martin's Hall for a Sunday evening coffee bar. This enabled them to talk to their fellow teens about Jesus and for about a year anything up to 120 14 to 20-year-olds met in this way (Green 1994).

Children's Work from the 1970s

By the time Marjorie Freeman began work as Diocesan Children's Officer in 1969 a major shift in the way Sunday schools operated was already well under way. Most parishes had moved to a morning Parish Communion service where the whole family

110   *Children at St Mary's, Hobs Moat pre-school group learning about Baptism and Marriage with Revd Bill More.*

arrived at church together. There were already lots of other things to do on Sunday as the growth in personal wealth and car ownership encouraged recreational pursuits of all kinds. Afternoon Sunday schools therefore ceased as both teachers and children's families had many other things to do. In some churches, if they failed to adapt to the new circumstances quickly enough, almost no children came to church. Most churches moved their children's groups to coincide with the Parish Communion and children were allowed to join the adults for the early and later parts of the service.

At the same time learning was changing. Children no longer sat in neat rows absorbing what their school or Sunday school teachers told them. Experiential methods were being encouraged together with thematic approaches which linked exploration of children's everyday experiences with Biblical and theological teaching. Jeanne Shaw of St Cyprian's, Hay Mills, remembers: 'We would upturn a table and all sit in it; that would be Noah's Ark … When we sang songs we did actions; one of our favourites was "With Jesus in the boat we shall smile at the storm"'; there seems to have been a distinct nautical flavour there! Magnificent nativity plays with fully-costumed performers, or with life-size puppets, are remembered by many Sunday school teachers and Christingle services attracted hundreds of children and their parents to many churches on Christmas Eve. Training, and the production of new materials to resource these new methods, was an important part of the Children's Officer's work. Many of these developments were assisted by strong ecumenical links. The Birmingham Council of Christian Education's training team organised courses for children's workers in parishes and all-age events for church members of all denominations. Cooperative working in ecumenical or

111   *Harvest Festival is easily made participative for youngsters.*

112   *Zap Club activities at St George's, Newtown.*

deanery groups was strongly encouraged and some parishes began to experiment with mid-week children's groups. Even more effective were mother-and-toddler mid-week groups, which provided the opportunity for young mothers to share time with each other and discuss faith issues with the leaders of such groups.

All-age worship began to develop rapidly in the 1980s with informal family-based worship services taking place as part of a broader more varied monthly pattern. Such services ideally include a range of creative activities, discussion, teaching and worship. This was very demanding on clergy who had not been trained for this role and therefore lay leaders, often trained teachers, increasingly helped to plan and lead all-age worship as part of parish teams. Again, training materials, courses and support was provided by the diocesan team. Marjorie Freeman gained a national reputation and went, in 1984, to be Children's Officer to the Church of England Board of Education.

Currently, there is a shift away from seeing children's work as solely educational. Research has shown that it is important to enhance children's spiritual capacities in prayer and worship, though teachers from the 1960s and '70s, such as Jeanne Shaw from St Cyprian's, report: 'It always amazed me how the children often came out with spiritual truths, and I often felt that I learned a lot more from them than I ever taught.' Some churches have found that outreach work with children on weeknights through after-school clubs and holiday events is the way forward in today's very different society. Churches as different in outlook as St Mary's, Moseley and Christchurch, Sparkbrook operated extremely popular summer holiday activity programmes in the 1980s and '90s. The latter, under the guidance of Revd Simon Holloway, undertaking particularly challenging work in a parish dominated by families whose faith was Islam, not Christianity. Again much of this work needed to be done co-operatively since statistics show that around one third of churches have no children whatsoever in their congregations and about a quarter have fewer than ten. It also continues to require training support, now delivered through the Bishop's Certificate in Children's Ministry, and some parishes now employ full- or part-time children's workers. Child Protection policies in every parish where children's or youth work takes place were a necessary and important development in the 1990s too.

Teens, Mods and Rockers

At least some of the new curates being trained in the early 1960s were determined to change the way that the Church related to young people. One such was David Collyer who arrived fresh from Cambridge at St Matthew's, Perry Beeches and the vast sprawl of inter-war local-authority housing which it served. Before long he was running a youth club, and then introducing new styles of worship for the young people who came along. There was jazz, a folk group, jiving in the aisles; quickly followed by complaining letters upbraiding him for 'bringing the scruffs of the Earth into the Church of England' and the inevitable reports in the local press about the

'Rolling Stone Curate' (Collyer 1973). It proved a stimulus for other such attempts to relate worship to popular music styles, however.

The Church of England in Birmingham quickly leapt from the wilderness to the forefront of new styles of pastoral work with young people when Bishop Wilson invited David Collyer to become 'Chaplain to the Unattached'. His brief was to develop pastoral work and a caring ministry to those who went to discotheques, folk clubs, pop concerts, dance halls, pubs and bowling alleys in the city and for whom neither the Church nor the youth service seemed to have any relevance. He began his work by using the media to announce to the world what he was supposed to be doing. That was new too. The Church of England had no local experience of getting the media on its side. More postbags of letters to Collyer followed including: 'The Church of England is in decline because of people like you who spend all their time with the dregs of society', and 'You are driving nice respectable people away.' For six months he got to know his 'flock' in the coffee-bars, pubs and clubs of the town, always wearing his dog-collar so that they knew he was a clergyman. Then he found the Rockers at Alex's pie stall in Sutton Coldfield. 'Dave the Vic', as he became known, joined the motorcycle fraternity and found his flock.

Soon afterwards they began to use the nearly redundant church premises of St Basil's, Deritend, with the permission of the bishop. The church hall was redecorated and a coffee bar opened in November 1965 under the benevolent dictatorship of a committee of seven of the Rockers; *Double Zero* was in being. By March 1966 well over 300 young people were using the coffee bar regularly. Local students were recruited to work behind the counter so that David Collyer could concentrate on the pastoral needs of the customers but, since David insisted that the Rockers were the bosses, many found the work difficult. They felt that the lack of evangelism and the focus on simply caring was not 'proper' youth work, or 'proper' work for a minister.

The group got involved with one of Birmingham's first Christmas 'Don't Drink and Drive' campaigns by delivering posters to pubs and clubs and they had their first religious service, Midnight Mass at St Basil's church, after a Christmas Eve dance. In the coffee bar a juke box was added, never playing at less than maximum volume, and good relations were established with the local police who got used to having 'a quiet word' with members whose exhaust was too loud or whose licence needed renewing, rather than booking them; one young police-woman even became a helper at the club. More community work was undertaken by members, including an emergency dispatch rider service and collecting tins for the Lord Mayor's Appeal. By the end of its first year nearly a thousand young motorcyclists were being attracted to the club, which was open four nights a week from 7pm until midnight.

The bishop decided to appoint Collyer priest-in-charge of St Basil's and thereafter a regular Sunday half-hour service was held in the church at 9pm with folk music, no vestments, and a talk and discussion. Bishop Wilson attended the first anniversary celebrations, quickly becoming 'Len the Bish' after reminiscing about his own motor-cycling days, and a party was held for more than a hundred local old people. Soon afterwards the club started opening for seven nights a week, 12 hours a day in response to the perceived needs of the young people they were serving; trained social workers were employed thanks to Local Authority grants, whilst others came on youth training placements as part of their course.

By early 1967 it was increasingly common for people turning up at the club to be without a bed for the night and so Collyer began to compile an emergency bed list of people who were willing to provide a few nights' accommodation for youngsters

113   *Bishop Mark Santer with diocesan youth representatives.*

often going through some temporary emotional crisis. So began St Basil's long and continuing association with young homeless people (see chapter 20). It was from these years too that David Collyer began to acquire his expertise in fund-raising and major appeals since more equipment was needed, the buildings needed improving and expanding, and staff needed to be employed.

By the middle of 1970 the club had become a fully licensed for the sale of alcohol and had made inroads into serving the even more difficult Hell's Angels motorcyclists; some members had met their deaths in motorcycle accidents; one was in prison for murder; babies had been born, marriages celebrated; the club premises had been 'trashed' by rival youth on one occasion, and pastoral problems continued to come thick and fast as St Basil's began to become a centre for a much broader spectrum of youth-oriented activities. Collyer was increasingly becoming a coordinator and administrator of activities and, given this, Bishop Brown asked him to become the Diocesan Youth Officer. He accepted.

Youth work from the 1970s

His successor, Juli Wills, was in post for the 75th anniversary celebrations of the diocese and one of her most vivid memories is of the 'mitre-making workshop' in the cathedral churchyard in the pouring rain of the celebratory day! The other event was an action-packed six-week visit to Malawi with a small party of young people from across the diocese. More regular activities included the annual youth vigil in Holy Week, usually at St Martin's, when large numbers offered their worship in creative music, drama and art. Juli particularly remembers walking into the church with six flaming torches one year thinking she really ought to have checked the insurance details before proceeding!

By 1980 the priority for the Youth Officer was training support for parish youth workers and the provision of programme materials for successful youth activities in the parishes and this was carefully developed over the next 20 years. By the early 1990s there was a network of funded full- and part-time youth workers in the diocese. The other characterising feature of youth work in this period was ecumenical cooperation. RC, Baptist, Methodist, URC and Anglican youth leaders got together to run 'Spectrum', an inter-denominational 10-week youth leaders' training course.

Juli Wills was succeeded in 1986 by Chris Feak, now vicar of Aston. For him the period was dominated by the outcomes of *Faith in the City*, which led to a major review of youth work in the diocese. One outcome was 'Beacon Break', a regular residential gathering at a school in Malvern for 100 young people from UPA parishes. This evolved later into 'Act One', a diocesan youth camp for young people in parishes where there are only small numbers of young people in church. The report also spawned a number of youth work projects funded by the Church Urban Fund (CUF). The first of these were detached youth worker projects at St Boniface Quinton (Martin Thompson) and Christ Church Summerfield (Kevin Chandra).

An example of more conventional parish work with early teens comes from St Philip's, Dorridge where the Revd Trevor Maines began 'The Seekers' in 1973 for all young people in the church as they moved from junior church and school at age eleven. Activity days and fortnightly Bible classes led, after a year, to their becoming 'probationary communicants' with the bishop's permission (General Synod did not adopt this policy nationally until 1996). A further year of Confirmation classes and helping to lead children's groups resulted in some 20 or more young people being Confirmed each year.

The Malachi Trust worked in Birmingham schools from 1986 to create musicals sung and partly written by the children and youth. All this was the vision of the founders Gordon and Lyn Lee, who were members of St Mary's Wythall and then St Boniface Quinton Road West. They were encouraged in their work by Chris Feak, Diocesan Youth Officer, and the Diocesan Mission Committee, though they had to raise all their own financial support. Sadly, the diocese failed to take more of a risk and stand with them more fully with commitment and money. 'It was the one piece of genuinely ground-breaking missionary work into the secular schools sector being undertaken by the Christian Church in Birmingham at that time', says Bishop Michael Whinney, 'and they have continued to reach out with the message of God's love in Christ through these musicals to the hundreds of families from all ethnic backgrounds. As with all single-minded and slightly offbeat prophets Gordon and Lyn have not found it easy to work alongside the structures of the established churches nor have those churches always understood or properly supported their work. I for one thank God for their perseverance, at times against overwhelming odds, and for the transformation that has happened as a result to so many young people's lives.'

Bishop Michael Whinney was involved in youth outreach in the 1990s from his base in the cathedral. He particularly remembers November 1995 when the cathedral was:

> stripped of pews, stalls and much else ready for a Friday all-nighter entitled 8-2-8. During the first three hours from 8 to 11pm we had two Christian music groups playing, with interviews in between songs; some of these were local celebrities and some were by phone-link from abroad including Archbishop Desmond Tutu. This was followed by food for the 600 who had come, and a soft drinks bar was open throughout in the Undercroft. At 11pm some of the younger ones went home and about 300 stayed on for the rest of the night. The programme moved into a different gear starting with a dozen workshops around the building. After this there was quieter music for a time followed by an hour of quiet prayer, which ran from 2 till 3am in the morning. It was a remarkable time of seeing all these young people in groups praying together both out loud and in silence. The 'dawn closing service' took place outside in the churchyard with candles; a hot breakfast quickly followed in the increasing light. What a fitting way it was to have an 'agape' meal, within which we 'broke bread', to finish our time together. Warmed inside, there were lots of hugs as these young Christian disciples exchanged the Peace and said goodbye – with a hopeful 'See you next time!'.

Robin Rolls, the current Bishop's Adviser for Youth Ministry, came to the diocese at the very end of 1999 and thinks that youth work appeared to be suffering from a

114 *Young people at the 'Bish-Bash', Bishop's Croft, summer 2004.*

low priority in the eyes of many parishes. Today, the diocese is acutely aware of the haemorrhaging of young people from the Church. It seeks to support and resource the work parishes are doing with their own young people. Over the last five years the diocese has moved to become one of the leaders of Anglican youth work in this country. First, the number of full-time workers in the diocese has increased to 20, from only eight in 1999, whilst there are many more part-time workers. New projects have been started in every deanery with full-time workers being established from inner-city Handsworth to suburban Solihull. Bishop Sentamu established the Bishop's Youth Council in 2003 to ensure that young people were represented at every level in diocesan decision-making. They have already been involved in presentations at Diocesan Synod, job interviews for youth workers, deanery presentations, and a huge youth event in 2004 in the garden of Bishop's Croft entitled 'Bish Bash'. The Diocesan Synod have agreed that every parish in the diocese must have at least two young people on its Parochial Church Council and have a dedicated budget for youth work. From September 2004 the spirit of '8-2-8' has been wonderfully resurrected with the Saturday night youth gatherings every other month called 'Reunited' at St Martin's-in-the-Bullring where anything up to 1,000 young people are in attendance each month.

Under the title 'b-cent', a huge city-wide mission and resourcing initiative has been launched to celebrate the centenary of the diocese. The 'b-cent' web site takes hundreds of 'hits' a day as young people network with each other; 'b-cent' so far includes a youth-work training course leading to the Bishop's Certificate in Youth Ministry; a Young Leaders conference; a city-wide social action programme for young people; and a music-based 'gathering' in the city-centre Victoria Square in July 2005. The diocese has seen some exciting growth in youth work over the last five years, but the work is far from over. It is still important for us to convince those who see young people as 'the church of tomorrow', that they are in fact the church of today, and that pushing them into tomorrow might keep us as the church of yesterday.

20

Providing Housing for the Elderly and the Poor

The Church of England has had a concern with housing since its formation in the 16th century. From the later medieval period onwards Christian folk had been leaving money in trust to clergy and churchwardens to provide charitable alms, food and drink, clothing, and especially accommodation, most often for widows. Following the Dissolution of the Monasteries in the 1530s, and still more the dissolution of hospitals and chantries a decade later, a part of the rental income of these institutions was diverted into the building of charitable housing, to the extent that there were few settlements of any size in Elizabethan and Stuart England that did not possess a row of almshouses. They are a very distinctive part of the English landscape, though the majority of them were repaired, or more often totally rebuilt, in the 19th century. Charitable bequests of this kind continued to be made through the 18th and 19th centuries.

Charities and Almshouses

Yardley parish provides an interesting example of such bequests in all their variety. In 1671, Humphrey Greswolde provided money for 'four gowns for four poor aged men', one from each of the four quarters of the parish; in 1701, Job Marston gave a bequest for bread and coats 'for the poor attending church'; John Cottrell left two cottages to be used as almshouses in 1715; and Joseph Fox provided money for coals for poor widows in 1721. By the end of the 19th century, these and many other bequests were under the administration of The Yardley Charity Estates and, in the first decade of the 20th century, six new almshouses were built in Church Road for six women, together with a resident nurse to look after them. Today, Yardley Great Trust has developed into a modern almshouse trust providing sheltered housing and nursing-home care for several hundred people.

Perhaps the best known almshouse trust in the diocese today is The Foundation of Lady Katherine Leveson, at Temple Balsall. It was established under the 1674 will of one of the granddaughters of Robert Dudley, Earl of Leicester. Lady Katherine left instructions for almshouses for 20 poor women (as well as a school for 20 poor boys). The almshouses were 'to reflect the Christian virtues of loving care and concern, whilst representing freedom for all' in the words of her will. The courtyard of houses was constructed in 1679. Additional houses were added for incapacitated residents in 1771, and a matron employed to care for them, and the Master's house was rebuilt in 1835. The Foundation now houses 48 older people in modernised self-contained units.

The largest of the Birmingham almshouse trusts was Lench's Trust, founded originally in 1526 for the repair of roads and bridges in the parish under the will of

115   *Lench's Trust housing at Camp Hill.*

William Lench; only the residue of the funds was to be applied to the poor. Further charities of the 17th and 18th centuries were added to Lench's Trust and their first purpose-built almshouses (a courtyard with two terraces and a master's house) were constructed in 1688, in Steelhouse Lane. A second set was constructed in Dudley Street in 1801, and other groups in Park Street in 1815 and 1820, and in Hospital Street in 1824-27 as the value of the charity's lands increased with the development of Birmingham. By 1947 Lench's Trust had 180 housing units, most in Ridgeacre Road, Selly Oak. In the second half of the 20th century more sheltered housing was provided for the elderly including developments in Moseley and Sutton Coldfield.

Housing Associations

In 1914, there were more than 40,000 back-to-back houses in Birmingham, most arranged around more than 2,000 courtyards in a dense ring around the city centre with as many as 80 houses to the acre. They had been built in the first half of the 19th century and by the 1920s were deteriorating rapidly since they had been 'jerry' built in the first place. Many had no running water or water closets and so they were difficult to keep clean. These conditions led to a number of efforts on the part of church people to improve the housing lot of the poor. The most dramatic intervention came with the establishment of Copec.

The Copec House Improvement Society was founded in 1925, its founders being drawn from the churches and leading citizens of Birmingham. They were delegates at the Christian Conference on Politics, Economics and Citizenship (COPEC), which took place in Birmingham's Methodist Central Hall in April 1924. It brought together delegates from every Christian denomination from all over Britain to generate 'a response by Christians to the needs of the material world'. It was chaired by William Temple, at that time Bishop of Manchester, but later Archbishop of Canterbury. After the conference four groups of delegates, including one from Birmingham, founded housing associations. The key individuals were Anne Robinson, a local factory inspector, who became the Secretary, Professor Frank Tillyard, head of the Commerce Faculty at the university, who became Chairman, Bishop Hamilton Baynes, Provost of Birmingham Cathedral, and Florence Barrow, a Quaker who worked for the Birmingham Settlement (Gulliver 2000). They had a keen sense that campaigning on housing issues and publicising the scandal of slum housing was part of their Christian duty. They concentrated on trying to improve poor housing in the central slum areas of the city. Their

116 *An early Copec refurbishment in Tower Street, Summer Lane. Mosse houses were named after Canon W.G. Mosse, Vicar of St Anne's, Moseley, whose parish raised the funds to buy and refurbish them (Gulliver 2000).*

approach was a managerial one: first improve the physical condition of the houses, then help tenants to look after the houses, and third work actively to reduce disputes between tenants. Weekly visits by sympathetic rent-collectors who, very quickly, were almost entirely female, meant that problems were dealt with immediately they arose. This was a style of management pioneered by Octavia Hill in the late 19th century, in London. The first improvement scheme in Birmingham was in Pope Street and 19 houses were re-roofed and re-plastered, their stairs were repaired, new fireplaces built, and gas and cold water supplies installed. In the courtyards the wash-houses were rebuilt and each house was provided with a WC. Despite continuous financial problems Copec expanded its operations to include cooperation with the local authority, converting commercial properties (including pubs), building new houses and blocks of flats, and providing social facilities such as gardens and children's play areas. Some 300 properties were owned by 1939 (Gulliver 2000).

During the Second World War more than 12,000 houses were destroyed by enemy bombing, and thousands more badly damaged. Copec's houses were mainly in the Summer Lane area of the city which was particularly badly affected by bomb damage because of its proximity to munitions factories. One tenth of its housing stock was destroyed. Copec's staff made contributions to the Bournville Village Trust's famous report *When We Build Again*, which provided ideas for Birmingham's post-war development, but in the event it was to be the plans of the city council that dominated post-war rebuilding and redevelopment. These plans, based on the compulsory purchase of slum properties for comprehensive redevelopment, meant

117 *Tree-planting by Clare Short MP to mark the refurbishment in 1990 of a group of houses in George Street West which are Grade II listed buildings. The Ven. John Duncan, Archdeacon of Birmingham and Chair of Copec, stands behind (Gulliver 2000).*

that four-fifths of Copec's housing was demolished in the 1950s and early 1960s. However, in these decades it moved into the provision of living accommodation for single women, for refugees, and housing for older people.

In 1966 concern about housing was re-ignited by the formation of 'Shelter', the campaigning group for homeless people, and the BBC documentary 'Cathy Come Home' about homelessness, much of which was filmed in Birmingham, though this was not mentioned in the film. Shelter's national launch was in St Martin-in-the Fields, in London, but there were regional launches in other cities, including Birmingham, in the cathedral. The public were shocked and large sums of money were raised by Shelter, much of which was redirected into Housing Associations in the major cities. Once more Christians were in the forefront of founding new organisations to provide housing for those who had slipped through the net. In Birmingham, further publicity for the plight of the homeless was stimulated by Canon Norman Power, vicar of St John's, Ladywood, who wrote a book, called *Forgotten People*, on the plight of people living in the city's redevelopment areas as the redevelopment process was on-going, for which the Focus Housing Association provided sponsorship (Power, 1965).

A number of new Housing Associations were formed in the later 1960s in response to the Shelter campaign, some of them by churches working ecumenically within specific areas. An example is the Moseley and District Churches Housing Association (MDCHA), founded in 1966, with the vicar of St Mary's, Moseley, Freddie Carpenter, as its chairman. It is still flourishing today though the specific Church focus is no longer present in the organisation. Another was the Birmingham Housing Trust (BHT), established in 1965 by a group from the University of Birmingham led by its Anglican chaplain, John Duncan, who was elected chairman, and including students in the Student Christian Movement (SCM). The city council and Shelter lent BHT sufficient money to organise and buy its first properties. It concentrated on buying large properties and converting them into flats. By 1970, when it merged with Copec, it had some 260 properties.

In the 1970s and 1980s Housing Associations developed into major providers of social housing and specialist housing, for example for the disabled. They therefore became large organisations employing large numbers of professional people, not voluntary organisations run by church people in their spare time. Today, for example, Focus, the successor to Copec and BHT, manages some 12,000 homes across the West Midlands. Like many such organisations it began as a charitable undertaking, with a substantial Christian input, but since 1974 it has been part of state housing provision with substantial public funding. Nonetheless, its chairman continued to be John Duncan, Archdeacon of Birmingham, until his recent retirement.

St Basil's

Another major contribution to housing by the Church in Birmingham is St Basil's. Again this grew out of concern for the homeless, in this case homeless young people. The Revd Les Milner was Birmingham-born and was educated at King Edward VI Camp Hill grammar school and Birmingham University. He went to Peshawar in Pakistan to teach chemistry and English. It was while he was in Pakistan that he felt his call to Christian ministry and so he returned home for training. He was ordained in 1963 and became curate at St Edburga's, Yardley. It was here that he began working with young people, running the church youth club, and he continued with this work at his next church in Leeds. He became really concerned with what was provided for difficult and disturbed young people. He was drawn more and more to this work and returned to Birmingham in 1971 to work with the team of detached youth workers at St Basil's church in Digbeth.

In October, 1972, Revd Les Milner opened the church hall in Heath Mill Lane as the first night shelter in the West Midlands for homeless young men. There were beds, a coffee bar, an advice centre and two-and-a-half staff. Les and his volunteers opened the doors and waited for their first clients. Les used to recollect how naïve they were, how they believed that they could solve the problems brought about by homelessness in a couple of days. Over the next few years they learned differently. They discovered that young people who came to the centre brought a whole range of problems with them. There were no typical customers, just individuals with their own problems, all of which took time to follow up. The hostel for young men became known as The Boot, mainly because everybody that went there had been 'booted out' of their previous accommodation. It quickly became full every night and more accommodation was needed. Over the years that were to follow the St Basil's family grew and changed the face of youth homelessness in Birmingham.

The Boot Night Shelter provided up to three weeks' accommodation for young men; Tennyson House provided up to a year's accommodation for the youngest homeless young men; whilst the first new accommodation to open was Yardley House, an emergency project to cater for the growing number of young women that came to St Basil's. Trentham House provided space for vulnerable mothers and their babies and a number of other houses around Birmingham provided further places. By the time Les Milner retired in 2000, the agency offered almost 300 accommodation units across the city, together with a resettlement centre, an employment, education and training division, and the first 'Foyer' housing development in the city. The Kiosk offered advice and information to more than 12,000 young people a year and The Link acts as a referral centre to other agencies providing accommodation. It has grown to be the largest regional organisation working with young people who were homeless or in severe housing need. More than 3,000 young people are referred to St Basil's each year, of whom some 1,000 are accommodated in St Basil's housing. Sadly Les Milner died in 2003. Always the motivation for expansion was the same: what can we do to improve the life chances of the young people who come to us? This has led to new projects begun by new director, Jean Templeton. This has moved the organisation into the field of family mediation and prevention work. After three decades of dealing with the results of homelessness they are now trying to prevent it wherever they can.

The heart and the headquarters of St Basil's, the organisation, are still at St Basil's, the church. This Grade I listed building houses all the administration and management, finance and fundraising offices, and the extensive training facilities. It is still owned by the Anglican Church, and is rented to St Basil's at a peppercorn rent, and stands as testament to what the Church can do working through other agencies. It is also not a bad legacy for a redundant church in an industrial setting.

21

THE MOTHERS' UNION
AND WOMEN'S MINISTRY

The Mothers' Union had been founded in 1876, by Mary Sumner, in her husband's parish in Winchester diocese. She was a philanthropist who believed that an organisation which brought 'lady mothers' and 'cottage mothers' together to discuss how children might be brought up in the Christian faith would prove beneficial. Her beliefs were typically Victorian in that she believed it was the Christian duty of women born fortunately into the upper classes to help working-class women in their duties as wives and mothers. However, it quickly became apparent to Mary Sumner and her helpers that mothers from all walks of life meeting together for prayer and instructional talks was of value in breaking down social prejudice and personal barriers.

The Bishop of Winchester commended Sumner's methods to all the parishes in his diocese and within a decade it had begun to spread to other dioceses, often through friendships between the wives of diocesan bishops or as clergy moved from one diocese to another. In 1888, Mrs Perowne, wife of the Bishop of Worcester, had formed a Mothers' Union for Worcester diocese and in January 1892 she organised a meeting in the Temperance Institute for more than 80 clergy wives, to encourage them to form branches in Birmingham archdeaconry. The meeting resolved to form a Birmingham branch of the Worcester Diocesan Mothers' Union with Mrs Perowne as president, and Mrs Bowlby and Mrs Wilkinson, wives of the rectors of St Philip's and St Martin's respectively, as vice-presidents. Mrs Philip, wife of the vicar of Edgbaston, was secretary. A month later an executive committee was formed and by the summer the ladies were working hard at forming new branches in the parishes of the archdeaconry. By March 1893 there were 25 parish branches with nearly 1,200 members and within five years membership had doubled to more than 2,500. The largest branch in 1898, St Paul's, Balsall Heath had an amazing 267 members. Another eight branches had over 100 members. These were evenly spread between inner-city parishes like Christ Church, Sparkbrook, outer suburban parishes like Kings Norton and Selly Oak, and respectable large parish centres such as Solihull and Sutton Coldfield. Northfield Rural Deanery had the most members with 939 mothers in nine branches.

Annual services helped bring members together and, naturally, these were held in the cathedral. To begin with they were held on the Monday nearest to Lady Day (25 March). On several occasions the small size of the cathedral posed problems and members had to be turned away. In 1913 advertising was kept to a minimum so as not to encourage excessive numbers to come! In the 1920s there was a move to St Martin's-in-the-Bullring, which was rather larger, but in 1928 it was agreed that two services should be held at 3 pm and 7.30 pm with the same speaker. The date was also changed to sometime in May, when the weather was better.

155

118 *Mothers' Union members learn drumming with Bishop Sentamu.*

By the 1940s the two services had evolved to one for each of the two archdeaconries into which Birmingham was divided and had returned to the cathedral. The noise of the ladies chattering before the service began was causing concern to the committee in the 1950s, but there was no satisfactory solution. In 1955 a central MU choir was formed on the occasion of a visit from the national president and it continued in being for many years after, giving fund-raising concerts as well as singing at the annual services. It was directed by Revd E.F.S. Wilmot, the vicar of St Cyprian's, Hay Mills. Perhaps the most spectacular of all these annual services was in 1981 when the first cathedral Flower Festival was largely undertaken by Mothers' Union members.

Meetings and social concerns

The executive committee arranged public meetings as well as the annual service. In 1893 Mary Sumner herself visited Birmingham, speaking in the Methodist Central Hall. Her theme was the 'four great rivers wrecking the lives of young people'. These were defined as: the low moral tone of the country; intemperance; irreligion and divorce; and teaching denying the truth of Christianity. An 1895 meeting at King Edward's School tackled 'Some principles of training children', whilst smaller branch meetings, such as those at Christ Church, Summerfield, often with husbands encouraged to be present, tackled subjects ranging from: 'older children'; 'punishments'; 'girls when they leave school', to 'information on difficult subjects' (I think they meant sex) where only mothers were to be present! Rallies were frequently held in the Town Hall in Birmingham – in 1923 on the theme of 'Christian citizenship', and in 1959 there was a two-day meeting on the sanctity of marriage called 'Their life in your hands' which included a pageant, a film, and a procession of witness through the city centre by some 900 members with branch banners flying. The centenary of the Mothers'

119   *Celebrating 125 years of the Mothers' Union at SS Philip & James, Dorridge.*

Union was celebrated with a garden party at St Peter's College, Saltley in 1976 and another pageant at the cathedral. The 75th anniversary of the diocesan branch in 1980 was marked by an exhibition called 'Steps in Faith' and a festival service on a very cold wet Saturday in June.

Social concerns of the Birmingham central council in the early 20th century focused on the care and protection of girls in domestic service; homes for unmarried mothers; the increasing amount of 'cheap objectionable literature becoming available' to children; and temperance campaigns. In 1914 even Bishop Wakefield wrote to them asking what the MU was doing to stop 'the increase of drinking among women in this city?'. There were calls to the licensing justices that pubs should be closed at 10pm. In 1915 there were protests at indecent adverts of cinema films and theatre plays. However, these paragons of virtue were unanimously in favour of the retention of flogging for first offences in the Criminal Law Amendment Act of 1912! By the 1920s, like many other Christian women's groups, there were calls for legal control of the sale and advertising of contraceptives and the first concern to warn children 'against accepting the invitation of well-dressed strangers ... to drive with them in motor cars'. In the 1970s there was a well-received scheme to allow runaway children to leave messages for parents called 'Midland Message Home'. Support for overseas work really began in 1920 when an Armenian nurse, Deaconess Parentzem, was funded for her work with Persian, Armenian and Jewish women in Persia and this continued with support for the Isfahan maternity hospital. In the 1950s Birmingham MU was linked with the MU in Natal, South Africa.

By the 1950s there was much concern that the Mothers' Union had grown old with its initial membership. There was therefore some activity to try to encourage new young members with children. It was always unlikely that they would be able

120   *Mothers' Union group at the 'Make Poverty History' rally, Birmingham Cathedral 2005.*

to mix easily with elderly ladies and so, in many parishes, 'Young Wives' groups were begun, sometimes under the aegis of the MU and sometimes not. Without an organisational framework, of course, these groups depended on the enthusiasm of their leaders; that tended to last through the child-rearing years or, if the leader was the vicar's wife, as long as his incumbency. Nonetheless, between the 1950s and the 1970s young wives' groups were an important element of the social activities of many parishes. Even more destructive of relationships from the 1950s through to their new constitution in 1974 was the Mothers' Union's attitude to divorced and illegitimate women. The vicar of Kings Norton was not alone in his action in closing two branches because of their insensitive treatment of women in his congregations. The Mothers' Union is still active in the diocese in many parishes but it is put to shame by the enthusiastic support that is seen for the organisation in our link diocese of Malawi, where the pale blue 'uniforms' of Mothers' Union members dominate every great church occasion.

Women's Ministry

One of Bishop Hugh's last episcopal ministries as Bishop of Birmingham had been to ordain the first group of women as deacons in the diocese. He had been a long-time supporter of ordaining women and had been chosen to give the proposing speech in General Synod in 1978 when it was first up for debate. The motion was lost and, with others, he helped to establish the Movement for the Ordination of Women (MOW). In the same year he edited a book, *Yes to Women Priests* (1978). It was to be nearly a decade later before the Women's Ordination Measure passed through General Synod. On 21 March 1987, Bishop Hugh had the satisfaction of ordaining in his

121   *The first women ordained deacon by Bishop Hugh. The later Dean of Women's Ministry and Diocesan Director of Ordinands, Canon Marlene Parsons, is second from the right in the front row.*

cathedral some 20 women, who had previously practised a ministry as a deaconess, as deacons in the Church. For some this ordination into the threefold order of ministry came after years of patient waiting and debate, for others it occurred as their initial ministerial appointment.

Following Hugh Montefiore's retirement, the appointment of a new Bishop of Birmingham was eagerly awaited. Hopes were high that he would continue with a similar approach and encouragement to the women, as had been known in Bishop Hugh's time, but Bishop Mark Santer's style, and the way in which he showed his support, was quite different. Nonetheless, his support for the women clergy of the diocese was considered and consistent. He took seriously the role of the Dean of Women, ensuring that her voice was one which contributed to considerations regarding the pastoral care, deployment and continuing ministerial education of the clergy. In January 1989, Bishop Mark had appointed the Dean of Women, as the first woman to be an honorary canon of Birmingham Cathedral, thereby affirming the developing ministry in parish and chaplaincy posts that women deacons were undertaking.

During his time as bishop, the diocese, and indeed the Church of England continued with the debate regarding women and priesthood. Bishop Mark spent much of his time listening to the concerns, theological and ecclesial, expressed within the whole Church from those with fundamentally different understandings of these matters. He kept his own counsel, and to this debate he brought a clear theological insight, and wide experience of the hopes and fears of our ecumenical partners Catholic and Reformed. Indeed, it is probably fair to say that no-one knew, when he went to the General Synod on 10 November 1992, how he would vote. When the vote was declared he saw himself as having a responsibility to speak immediately with those who were most deeply affected by the decisions, those who desired it and those who opposed it.

Over the weekend of the 20-21 May 1994, Bishop Mark ordained some 33 women priests in the Diocese of Birmingham. It was a momentous weekend in the life of the diocese, and since that time the number of women serving as deacon and priest has increased, the breadth of the ministry they undertake has developed, and has included parish priests, theological educators, city-centre and cathedral chaplains, chaplains in higher education and hospital and hospice appointments. It has been a time of exploration and review as, under Bishop Mark, the diocese sought to be creative over the contribution women were encouraged to make, whilst trying to ensure appropriate support available for this 'new wine' in the Church.

22

THE LINK WITH MALAWI

When Bishop Wilson arrived in the diocese in 1953, he regarded its churches and church people as too inward-looking. They seemed to have no understanding of the wider world in which he had spent his ministry. Whilst he had been Dean of Manchester he had organised a meeting about the Central African Federation and Dr Hastings Banda had been one of the speakers. Banda was to become Prime Minister of the Nyasaland Protectorate in 1961, and then President when it gained independence as the new nation of Malawi in 1964. As a result of Bishop Wilson's meeting with Banda, his daughter, Dr Susan Cole-King, went to work in Malawi at the Blantyre Children's Hospital, and so, when Bishop Wilson looked for a mission partner for the diocese, Malawi seemed an obvious choice.

The Anglican Church in Malawi was very much subsidiary to the Roman Catholic and Presbyterian Churches. President Banda himself was an elder of the Presbyterian Church. The Anglican diocese in the 1960s covered the whole country and was staffed by the celibate missionary society called the Universities Mission to Central Africa (UMCA). Birmingham's first mission partner was Canon John Parslow, a Birmingham-born priest who had gone to St Paul's church in Blantyre in 1960 and was to serve the people of Malawi for 35 years.

The international gathering of Anglicans in Toronto in 1963 began to work out a more reciprocal way of linking churches and dioceses in what was called 'Mutual Responsibility and Interdependence' (MRI). It was at this conference that Bishop Wilson met Bishop Donald Arden from Central Africa. The UMCA churches were in crisis when Arden became Bishop of Nyasaland in 1961; the number of missionaries was declining and, apart from the three churches for Europeans, most Malawian Anglican churches were in poor repair and African clergy were poorly trained and paid a pittance. Arden broke the

122   *Mothers' Union members provide famine relief in 1981.*

161

123 *Canon Bob Jenkins with a map of Malawi. Canon Jenkins was the Malawi Link coordinator for many years.*

mould by marrying in 1962 and, together with his wife, Jane, set about reorganising the Church by training African clergy and building modern churches, schools and hospitals. MRI seemed a Godsend and links were established first with the diocese of Texas and then, in June 1966, with Birmingham. Bishop Wilson met again with Donald Arden in 1965 when visiting his daughter.

The Birmingham diocesan conference that approved the link in 1966 agreed to send £5,000 per year to help the diocese of Malawi. It continued to do this until 1974. The money was used for specific projects in Malawi including clergy housing, pensions and new churches such as St Mary's in the Biwi district of Lilongwe, Malawi's capital city. Besides the main link there were a number of parish projects, the most notable being that of St Leonard's, Marston Green who had an active link with St Anne's Maternity Hospital at Nkota Kota, on the shores of Lake Malawi. In Birmingham the link was publicised through the *Compass* church newspaper and by visits by Birmingham clergy to undertake voluntary work; David Porter, the Bishop of Aston, also visited the link diocese. Another link was with three sisters from the Nursing Order of St John the Divine, who went to work in St Anne's Hospital for four years in 1970. In the opposite direction Donald Arden, who became Archbishop of Central Africa in 1971, visited Birmingham and, in 1972, spoke in every deanery of the diocese to enthuse people to give generously to the link. Bishop Josiah Mtekateka also visited Birmingham. He was the first Bishop of the new diocese of Lake Malawi, created in 1971 to serve the northern and central parts of the country.

Renewing the Link

By the mid-1970s the link seemed to have lost its initial impetus but a new group of clergy began to go from Birmingham to Malawi for short visits or longer periods of

124 *Malawian villagers gathered to greet visitors from Birmingham.*

service encouraged by Bishop Brown. In 1975, Revd Tony Cox and his wife Helen, a doctor, left Warley for Malawi where they were to live and work for the next 12 years; Bishop Brown went himself; he then sent Revd Bob Jenkins and Colin and Sylvia Bishop to make a more extensive visit and collect experiences to enthuse Birmingham congregations. They visited more than 50 churches, schools and colleges on their return and provided more material for the annual newspaper that was distributed around the parishes: *Malawi on the Move*, which became *Mirror on Malawi* in 1978. From Malawi a number of priests came to Birmingham's Selly Oak Colleges, or the University of Birmingham, for theological training, some of whom were subsequently to become bishops or archdeacons in Malawi, including Bishop Peter Nyanja of the Lake Malawi diocese.

Bishop Montefiore went to Malawi in 1983 and made a great impact. He had learnt to speak some sentences in Chichewa, the local language, which caused great excitement. He was impressed with the way in which the Church ran clinics and hospitals and he was impressed with the way that these practical expressions of love for neighbour brought about conversions. He conducted confirmations in several of the churches and he was moved by the worship; 'people like to be blessed' he told his flock back in Birmingham.

In response to soaring inflation caused by the oil crisis of the early 1970s, Birmingham's financial contribution to Malawi was increasing steadily. By 1986 it totalled £16,000. A number of new mission partners were recruited including John Workman, an accountant who worshipped at St Agnes, Moseley, who went in 1980 to work as treasurer and auditor for the Malawi dioceses. He died there four years later. Another clergy-doctor couple, Revd Keith and Dr Jill Gale, went from St Martin's-in-the-Bullring in 1981 and worked there for the next 13 years. In 1981, the Diocesan

125 *Bishop Hugh Montefiore exchanging gifts with Malawian hosts.*

Youth Officer, Juli Wills, took a party of young people to Malawi and a reciprocal visit was paid by a party of not-quite-so-young Malawians!

Inflation and refugees

The 1980s saw a reorganisation of the missionary societies and of the way overseas mission was portrayed in Britain. The societies became mission societies and a number of them amalgamated, as did their training colleges, many of which were located in the Birmingham suburb of Selly Oak. One of the students from the College of the Ascension in 1990, James Tengatenga, was consecrated Bishop of Southern Malawi in 1998. In Birmingham, a world mission resource centre was opened in Carrs Lane church in the city centre for all denominations in 1987, though it relocated to the Anglican diocesan offices in Harborne in 1994. The end of the 1980s was an especially difficult time for the people of Malawi. The government of now 'President-for-life' Hastings Banda had become more and more autocratic and political repression was endemic; the repayment of international debts acquired in the early days of independence was beginning to cripple the country's economy; in 1988 a vicious civil war erupted in neighbouring Mozambique, thanks to the work of the South African secret service, and something like one million refugees fled across the border into Malawi; whilst the following year a series of natural disasters, including earth tremors and floods affected the country. A special appeal in Birmingham diocese, where the reception of so many refugees without violence made a deep impression on Christians, raised large sums to enable additional funds to be sent.

126   *Brick-making in Malawi. Help is given by Birmingham visitors including Rachel Jepson (centre) now a Lay Member of General Synod for Birmingham.*

127   *The Birmingham-Malawi youth exchange of 1999.*

128   *One of the Birmingham lorries at work in Malawi. The Venerable John Cooper and Canon David Lee (centre) went with the lorries to hand over the gift.*

1991 marked the 25th anniversary of the link with Malawi and Bishop Mark Santer led a group of ten diocesan representatives on a celebratory visit to Malawi, whilst in 1994, after three difficult years during which clergy lives were in danger, elections were held and power passed peacefully from President Banda. In 1995, a third diocese, Northern Malawi, was created and Jack Biggers, an American, was elected its first bishop. He was succeeded by Canon Christopher Boyle, the Rector of Castle Bromwich, in 2001. The link continues to evolve: a Trust Fund has been established in Birmingham to provide scholarships for Malawians training for the ministry in Birmingham; two lorries were sent as gifts to the southern diocese; and in 2004 the Bishop's Lent Appeal raised funds for motor-bikes for Malawian priests with large parishes to get around their churches. All this against the background of continuous annual financial support which now approaches £50,000 per year.

23

COMMUNICATIONS

The Church is often reckoned to be behind the times when it comes to communicating with the outside world. That may be so, but Birmingham diocese has been in the vanguard of trying to make best use of modern communications technologies. Radio broadcasts were an important feature of the ministry of Guy Rogers at St Martin's with services being broadcast from 1927 onwards. These included children's services, Christmas carols over several years, and a service for the Birmingham Cooperative Society. The 1933 carol service included an appeal for holiday play centres and the address was given by Mrs Rogers. Radio programmes from St Martin's continued during the war years. Rogers' successor, Bryan Green, was already a well-known broadcaster before he came to Birmingham. He appeared frequently in the 'Lift up your hearts' series for the BBC. He also wrote for national magazines, most notably the 'God spot' in *Woman* where he reflected on typical human situations. He went on writing for *Woman* magazine until he was nearly 80 years old. Canon Norman Power, of St John's, Ladywood, was another long-serving writer of this kind, writing for the *Birmingham Post* and *Evening Mail* newspapers for nearly half a century.

The printed word

The Revd Nick Stacey, when he was Bishop Wilson's chaplain, started an eight-page tabloid newspaper in 1958. *National Christian News* was syndicated around the country and was used as an insert for parish newspapers. It was written and produced in a tabloid style and had a circulation of 50,000. In the 1950s and '60s parish newspapers were 'flavour of the month' as far as local parish communication was concerned and were an alternative to the traditional church magazine. It continued to be produced in Birmingham, later becoming becoming 'Compass Newspapers' edited by Geoffrey Brown (Rector of St George's, Newtown) with Michael Dodd and John Duncan (later Archdeacon of Birmingham). Revd Michael Blood came to Birmingham in 1969 as curate at St Agnes', Moseley (a Compass parish) and joined Compass editorial board in 1971. He took over as editor in 1973 with Stephen Lowe (later suffragan Bishop of Hulme) and John Cox (later Archdeacon of Stowe) This was also the team who produced *March Together*, the newspaper of the 'New Initiative' (chapter 25)! The newspaper closed in 1975. Its success sparked a number of local district community newspapers, often ecumenical, and with a Christian slant, including, not surprisingly, *birmingham 13*, in Moseley. This ran for many years with the byline 'By Moseley churches for the community' and is still in production more than 30 years later.

129 *Midlands communications group meet at the cathedral. From left to right: Ms Sue Primmer (Diocesan Communications Officer); The Provost, The Very Revd Peter Berry; Mrs Claire Laland (Editor, MAP Bulletin); Nigel Gibbons (Head of Religious Broadcasting Central TV) and Colin Morris (former Head of Religious Broadcasting BBC*

Radio and TV

Michael Blood became involved in religious broadcasting at BBC Radio Birmingham, and was eventually appointed producer of religious broadcasting. Radio Birmingham had a small audience then, and religious broadcasting was farmed out to local church groups of volunteers with limited effectiveness. In 1980 'A Word in Advance' was born on what had become BBC Radio WM. It consisted of a ten-minute recorded programme, featuring an interview with someone who was preaching later in the day, with a Bible reading and suitable music. It was extraordinarily successful and people visited the churches featured to hear more. Over the years the programme was lengthened, and then was broadcast live in 1988 as a 90-minute programme. It was finally expanded to two hours in 1992. By then it consisted of a mix of interviews, events, reflections and music. It built strong links not only across the Christian community but also across and between faiths as well. Since the 1990s it has been consistently amongst the programmes with the highest weekly audience – a weekly 'congregation' of 160,000, with three people needing to be employed to answer the phones to cope with all the calls.

Michael Blood retired from the programme after 30 years at the beginning of 2005. A listener's letter sums up its appeal:

> My partner of 24 years has never understood why I – an Atheist for the last 44 years, since the age of 14, would want to get up early on a Sunday morning to listen to a religious programme rather than stay in bed with her. I can only say that this is a tribute to how you as a Christian respond, not only to your own beliefs, but also to those of other beliefs or none. Anyway, the best of luck in your retirement, and as Dave Allen would have said, 'may your God go with you!'.

Michael Blood continues to contribute to national broadcasting on the 'Pause for Thought' programme on Radio 2 and 'Prayer for the Day' on Radio 4.

Contact with local television companies began even earlier than radio since the activities of Revd David Collyer with the 'Double Zero' club had attracted widespread media interest. Collyer looked on the media as friends rather than enemies, and he both valued the support that media personnel offered him in his difficult job, and realised that media outlets could promote the Church if given a supply of interesting stories. The opening of the Double Zero club was widely covered in the media and the BBC later filmed at the club for a programme on youth. In 1967

David Collyer began to appear regularly on the Epilogue programme for ATV, the Midlands' independent company, and he notes that he often found it an effective way of communicating Christian ideas back to the young people in his youth club, who watched the programme avidly (Collyer 1983:128-31). Within a year he was appearing on another ATV late-night discussion programme called 'Pulse' and a weekly Sunday night debate on London Weekend TV's 'Roundhouse' programme. Though tempted by the lure of television, he later cut down on such work, but remained convinced of the good that it can do.

Film and video

Not all of this media work was by the clergy. In 1966, George Tuck, an Evangelical lay person, heard the Lord clearly speak to him from Ephesians (Ch. 4:15-16) that the work that he should attend to from then on, as long as he lived, and wherever he was living, would be to knit together parts of the global Christian Church. Concurrently, he felt compelled to reflect on St Paul's words 'if by any means I may win some' to try to understand what Paul would have meant by 'by any means' in the later 20th century. When he and his family moved to Wolverhampton he set up a 16mm film ministry to serve the Church in six Midland counties. He built up a well-trained team with top quality projectors and films that enabled them to show Christian films in prisons, hospitals, schools and colleges, army units, and in parish churches for use in their outreach. Each year more than 400 showings of these films reached some 25,000 unchurched people a year.

Tuck designed and built an open-air back-projection film trailer, with its own Honda Generator, which he took annually to the Llangollen Music Festival, to Manchester and Glasgow Flower Festivals, and to the Malvern Show. Later, the suppliers of his films made 35mm films suitable for projection in cinemas. On moving to Birmingham he obtained the agreement of the Cannon Cinema chain to screen 'The Jesus Film' in all their 16 West Midlands' cinemas, and in 15 other towns within 50 miles of Birmingham via other cinema groups. In the Classic cinema at Quinton the team had every seat booked for the evening showings for two weeks. There were also early morning shows for schools, and on more than one occasion schools where the majority of pupils were Moslem attended.

Tuck was also involved with Christian Radio, attending the inaugural meeting of European Christian radio station directors and was instrumental in the formation of the 'European Christian Broadcasters' network'. A third initiative was to develop ministry resources for video. He purchased two large-screen video projectors which were used by 'Mission England' for relays from Villa Park to other Midland towns and he joined the Birmingham Mission England team giving nearly 100 showings of the Sydney (Australia) Crusade film, to let Christians know what a Billy Graham crusade was like. Each church that took part received a video version of the film, which could be used to encourage Christians to lend the video to their friends and then invite them to a crusade meeting.

By the 1970s most people claimed that television was now their main source of information for what was going on in the world. Intense competition between and within the various branches of the media, coupled with the growth of investigative journalism, meant that established institutions and authorities lost any protection they might have enjoyed hitherto. Religious reporting was no longer the province of members of the clergy with a journalistic bent, who were largely sympathetic to their subject. If the Church had any hope of balanced reporting, it had to catch up with the changes, learn how to swim in shark-infested seas and provide a professional service to the media.

Communications Officers

Bishop Laurence Brown was one of the first in the country to appoint a Diocesan Communications Officer, in 1976. The Revd (now Canon) Alan Priestley, vicar of St Mary's, Hazelwell, was the pioneer. Self-taught and with the assistance of a competent secretary, he combined this new post with his parochial duties. He had his work cut out, for successive bishops – and especially the polymath Hugh Montefiore – enjoyed national and international status as spokespeople for the Church of England and were in constant demand by press, radio and television. Priestley established very strong links with all sections of the media, which was considerably helped by the fact that Canon David McInnes was one of the Religious Advisers at ITV and Canon Michael Blood at BBC Radio WM. Bishop Michael Whinney remembers from this time that: 'Nick Meanwell at BRMB welcomed me warmly and, together with John Austin, then Chaplain at Aston University, I had frequent opportunities to broadcast with regular phone-ins and their main religious slots. I enjoyed it enormously and still wear the BRMB lambswool sweater they presented to me – the Radio WM one is now relegated to garden wear as somehow it got paint on it!'.

In the meantime, the development of desktop publishing and the Internet required a sophisticated presentation of information beyond the everyday capacity of the Church; by the mid-1990s it became clear that a major diocese like Birmingham needed a full-time Director of Communications. Sue Primmer was the first holder of this title. Sue arrived with a great deal of experience in the presentation of printed matter and quickly became media savvy. At times it was frustrating for her and the Communications Advisory Group, which had been formed to support her, to encounter resistance to a co-ordinated approach to publishing and it took her some years to gain acceptance for even a modified version of a national house style for the Church of England. She gained the respect, not only of local and national media, but also of her colleagues throughout the country, who nominated her to assist with some of the first national poster advertising campaigns. These proved controversial, especially with Christians – who were not the intended audience – and became media events in their own right.

When Sue moved on to the University of Birmingham in 2000, she was succeeded by Arun Arora. Arun, a Birmingham-born lawyer, had a shrewd understanding of what was needed and quickly established himself as a professional with the media. He was a loyal and perceptive adviser to two bishops and developed a personal talent for journalism and broadcasting. Arun left to train for the ordained ministry in 2004. Jessica Foster became the third full-time Director of Communications later that year. She arrived knowing that Bishop Sentamu, like his predecessors, was greatly in demand by journalists and broadcasters.

The Christian Faith centres on the belief that God has communicated good news to the human race and it is the calling of all Christians to communicate this news, by word and deed, to the rest of the world. The media are gifts of God and, like all gifts, can be abused or used rightly. When the Church grasps the opportunity to collaborate constructively with the men and women who produce articles and programmes, it is fulfilling part of its worthy calling. In the Diocese of Birmingham, this missionary task is taken seriously.

24

EVANGELISTS

Birmingham's own Evangelist

This chapter must begin with Birmingham's own evangelist, Canon Bryan Green, Rector of Birmingham from 1948 until 1970. Before coming to Birmingham he had been a curate at New Malden, Surrey where, every Sunday, he had 250 boys at Sunday youth meetings – many were ordained in later life and a number became bishops. He quickly began to travel throughout the country addressing young people's organisations, pupils at public schools, and university students. He came to Birmingham from being vicar of Holy Trinity, Brompton, in London, where he had already built a formidable reputation as preacher and evangelist including lecturing and preaching tours to Canada and the US. Unusually, he was instituted as Rector of Birmingham by Bishop Barnes, privately, in the chapel at Bishop's Croft on 4 October 1948. The reason was that evangelism took first place from the beginning. He had previously accepted an invitation to lead a gospel preaching mission in the Cathedral of St John the Divine, New York in November 1948. He filled the enormous cathedral's 6,000 seats every evening for a week with the young Billy Graham amongst his congregation. He was inducted to St Martin's more publicly, when he returned in January 1949.

The following Sunday morning, the church was full and in the evening it was packed again with over 1,200 people present at each service. Very quickly everyone in Birmingham wanted to hear Bryan Green preach. There could be 1,600 people present on Sunday evenings. If you were not in the queue outside St Martin's by 5.30 pm, you probably wouldn't get in! The pews were filled to capacity, extra chairs were put in the aisles, people sat on the pulpit steps and on hassocks from the pews.

Bryan Green explained that he wanted people to worship at their local churches, if they belonged to one, but that they could also help bear witness in the city centre by coming to St Martin's at least once a month. He described himself as being liberal evangelical, thoroughly Anglican, believing in the gospel of God's grace in Jesus Christ as the heart of the Christian faith. Bryan Green believed that the beginning of any man's career as an evangelist, beyond his parish or local church, happens when he finds himself drawn into it; but response depended on the parish as much as the man. He often said that he was fortunate in Birmingham to have a church which understood his calling and was willing to release him each year for three months, in month-long blocks, to go to different parts of the world in response to the invitations which he received to share the gospel which he was preaching at St Martin's (Green 1994).

130 *Bryan Green preaching in the circus ring at Bingley Hall, Birmingham.*

Bryan quickly introduced lay ministry to St Martin's through a Monday fellowship meeting. Attended by 80-90 members of the congregation, they prayed, read their Bibles together and discussed parish spiritual policy. He started a half-hour 'Epilogue' service on Sundays at 9 pm for cyclists, and those who had been out walking for the day; for National Service men who had been home for the weekend and who were waiting in the Bull Ring for their coaches back to barracks, and anyone else who wanted to come. Members of the earlier evening congregation were asked to go out with leaflets inviting people in. One Saturday afternoon in 1950, Win Green, the rector's wife, returned home from shopping in the Bull Ring. She told Bryan that there were so many people in the Bull Ring and suggested that he start a shoppers' service. It began that October: a brief 15-minute service at 4 pm which has continued ever since. Win was the youngest of ten children. Her father was a vicar; she had seven brothers and six of them became clergymen, two of them bishops!

Bryan Green also restored the church, after substantial war-time damage, and built the church hall. This building was opened in May 1957 after £100,000 had been raised in six months. He didn't need a fundraiser, he had great powers of administration and he was extremely persuasive. You just couldn't say 'no' to anything he asked you to do. He raised a further £50,000 in 1966 to build the St Martin's Youth Centre in Gooch Street. Bryan Green retired from St Martin's in 1970, but not from preaching or world tours which he continued until 18 months before he died on 6 March 1993 aged 92. Lord Coggan, former Archbishop of Canterbury, said:

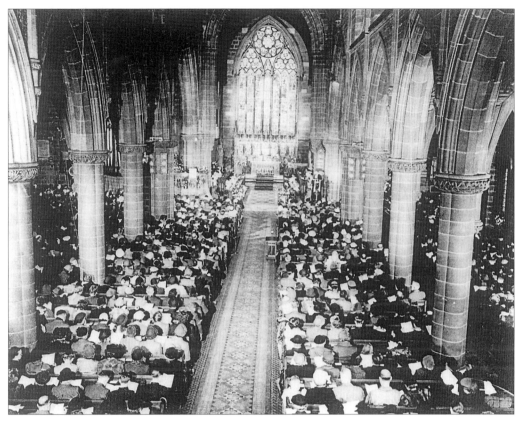

131 *A packed congregation at St Martin's-in-the-Bullring waiting to hear Canon Bryan Green preach.*

On any reckoning Bryan Green was an unusual man. You don't meet many of them in a lifetime. He was glad that God made us individuals and in his own individuality he rejoiced. By God's good grace there would be, as years went by, a process of refining going on, but that did not mean a process of taming – God forbid! Bryan Green liked to surprise us, sometimes to shock us, often to shake us out of our indifference. His restless energy put us to shame (Green 1994).

Billy Graham described Bryan as one of the world's greatest evangelists. Thousands of people throughout the world have reason to be thankful to him for their faith. In St Martin's, there is a memorial plaque inscribed with the words: 'I press forward that I may lay hold of that for which Christ Jesus laid hold of me.'

Even this year, in 2005, J Salmon Ltd produced a calendar 'with reflections by Canon Bryan Green', so, 12 years after his death, Bryan is still communicating the Gospel!

Evangelists to Birmingham

Birmingham Churches organised a number of high-profile visits from evangelists in the second half of the 20th century, frequently on an ecumenical basis. First was the American 'hippy' street preaching evangelist, Arthur Blessitt, from Los Angeles. Quite a number of folk from Birmingham had gone to the 'Festival of Light' in London in

132 *Bryan Green standing beside the foundations of the new hall at St Martin's for which he raised some £100,000.*

September 1971, and Revd David McInnes got the opportunity to invite Arthur Blessitt (who had 'turned up' at the Festival, and carried the huge crowd with his preaching at the climax of a rally in Hyde Park) to come to Birmingham in November. McInnes got together a small group to organise the event. He remembers that:

> We acquired 500 torches which could be lit and carried through the streets; circulated leaflets and stickers around the city; arranged for a Christian pop group to play on the back of a lorry; and set up a preaching site in the Bull Ring market area. On a cold but dry November night, an estimated 2-3000 people, predominantly young, gathered at the cathedral, and marched with torches blazing (we hadn't got nearly enough!) down New Street to the Bull Ring. Following the pop group, Arthur spoke with a delightful combination of humour and challenge, and then made an appeal for personal commitment. We hadn't prepared for the kind of response that came, and had to hastily get cards and pencils from St Martin's to take down 300 names and addresses of those, mostly teenagers, who wanted to make a commitment.

He returned the following year, in May 1972, and held evening meetings in the Bull Ring on the Friday, Saturday and Monday evenings and had 1,000 people praying on their knees. Mary Jepson of St Martin's congregation remembers it as a very moving occasion. On the Sunday afternoon, he spoke in Handsworth Park and, since he was particularly gifted for the open-air ministry, many people responded.

133 *Billy Graham on an early visit to St Martin's in 1961 with Canon Bryan Green.*

In October 1981, 'Birmingham Alive' was led by the charismatic evangelist David Watson from St Michael le Belfry, York. It was based in Birmingham Town Hall and over 130 church congregations, comprising widely differing denominations, joined in. The Town Hall was packed for five days. It was professionally organised with pre-mission training for church members, a monthly news-sheet, counsellors in attendance, follow-up teams and good financial support from the participating churches. There was a special day at the Great Hall of the University at which Bishop Hugh Montefiore spoke and Bryan Green gave the keynote address. David Watson returned to the Town Hall in March for a celebratory service, followed by training workshops next morning. In the afternoon there was active evangelism in the city centre, which included a big procession. The traffic stopped and it was silent, so the Christians sang songs and hymns – unrehearsed! There was an inspiring rally in the cathedral churchyard at the end. David Watson continued over the weekend with evangelistic meetings for young people at the Methodist Central Hall on Saturday night and again on Sunday.

Billy Graham

Billy Graham first came to preach at St Martin's in 1954 for the British Industries Fair annual service. He came several times after that but is best remembered for the huge week-long 'Mission England' campaign in July 1984, held at Villa Park, the 40,000-capacity football stadium of Aston Villa football club. Once more this was a carefully choreographed event. Birmingham's National Exhibition Centre was the place at which training was provided for a large proportion of the regional centres

134 *'Mission England' poster.*

that summer: 12,000 people one cold January day were provided with song books, literature and a packed lunch, together with an opportunity to listen and be inspired by what Billy Graham told them of the plans for the summer.

The Birmingham campaign began in June with teams from local churches trying to visit every house in their parishes to invite people to go to Villa Park and tell them about transport arrangements; most areas arranged special buses to the stadium. The crowds went, filling the stadium on most evenings; other evangelists joined Billy Graham on the platform; Bryan Green on the Saturday evening; Cliff Richard gave his testimony at the youth-oriented evening when some 5,000 young people were present. Again, this was an ecumenical event, with a large choir drawn from all the churches of Birmingham, trained counsellors, literature and follow-up procedures for all those who went forward across the emerald turf as they were invited to affirm, renew, or begin their journey in faith at the end of each evening. The intention was always to connect them with their local church. This national event also produced 'Mission Praise', the song/hymn book still used in some parish churches today.

The Moseley community newspaper, *birmingham 13*, carried a report on people's reactions. These were some of them:

'It was quite an experience to go to something with so many people. It was all very low key and unemotional but very moving to see people going forward and realise how much they needed God';

'I found he spoke in a direct way. It was sophisticated preaching but it spoke to me directly. I was moved by it to go forward and affirm my faith';

'I got nothing out of it; simplistic theology, no atmosphere and a TV camera that kept pointing at me';

'I shall be interested to see how many of the thousands are part of the Church in a year's time. That will be the real test';

'It was something the Holy Spirit used to reach the many people who need a focus. I felt the whole of God's love focusing on the stadium, holding it'.

135 *A packed Villa Park football ground for 'Mission England'.*

'God loves … You!': Archbishop Tutu

In 1989, Birmingham celebrated the centenary of the granting of its city charter but there were few events which commanded the enthusiasm of a broad spectrum of the population. Birmingham Churches, with the relative success of 'Mission England' still fresh in their memory, decided to organise a week-long mission. The idea had originated early in 1987 in the diocesan evangelism committee. Colin Bevington, its chairman, had suggested Festo Kivengere as missioner but Colin Buchanan, Suffragan Bishop of Aston, said 'What about Tutu?' It was agreed that the bishop would make contact with Archbishop Desmond Tutu. He responded, 'Yes: 18-23 April 1989'. It took some time to get an organisational structure in place, but in February 1988 the archbishop was officially invited by 55 Christian leaders of Birmingham to come and lead the mission. The invitation, which they signed individually, included the words, 'We accept full financial responsibility.' Lesslie Newbigin was chairman of the Council but the real work was in the hands of an executive led by Colin Buchanan. The Birmingham Diocesan Synod was asked to endorse the invitation and vote £30,000 towards its cost, which they did unanimously.

The ambitious plans were intended to allow as broad a cross-section of the population as possible to make contact with Tutu. There was a deeply moving visit to Winson Green Prison; a disco at the Black-owned 'Humming Bird' nightclub where young people from all Birmingham's ethnic communities danced together; meetings with leaders of the other faith communities in the diocese; rallies at the National Exhibition Centre and a final celebration at Villa Park. Archbishop Tutu's infectious personality, apparent even in the huge spaces of the NEC, and his memorable catchphrase 'God loves … you!' meant that many went away with their faith renewed,

136 *Archbishop Desmond Tutu at the cathedral.*

or with a new faith beginning. Certainly many of the comments recorded from participants thought so:

- It is the best thing Birmingham has ever done.

- I took a friend who was going through a messy divorce and when she had to say 'God loves me', she just began to cry.

- It was the most wonderful week I've ever had. The Hummingbird was amazing, and brilliant to take one of my non-Christian friends to – she loved it and stayed right to the end.

- One friend who plays heavy metal now just wants to give his whole life and his music to God.

- There is a wonderful new prayer spirit amongst our people.

- Thank you for the vision which enabled so many people to experience the passion and faith of one of the great Christian leaders of the world.

At the beginning of the following week *The Birmingham Post* and *Birmingham Evening Mail* newspapers were ecstatic in their praise of the event and of the Christian Churches of Birmingham for organising it. Unfortunately, the enormous costs of

137 *Poster for one of Archbishop Tutu's mission rallies.*

staging the major events were not sufficiently met by the donations from participating churches, institutions and individuals, and the numbers attending the events. There were liabilities of £179,000.

Many factors led to this state of affairs. First, international and local politics intruded because Archbishop Tutu was a political as well as a religious leader. There was thus an insidious campaign from South Africa to the effect that Tutu was a communist; an unbeliever; that he was coming only to ask for sanctions against South Africa to be intensified. The Tory minority on the city council were totally opposed to the visit and turned down a request that Tutu be given the Freedom of the City – an award which by convention needs bipartisan agreement. The final Villa Park rally was on St George's Day, which led to the newspaper headline: 'Black archbishop replaces England's patron saint' (Newbigin 1995).

All this meant constant niggling reports and letters in the local press undermining the confidence of some people in the event, especially in the white, middle-class, conservative congregations of the outer suburbs. Consequently, attendances at the NEC, though large, were insufficient to cover the costs. Secondly, the final rally at Villa Park filled only a tiny portion of the seats. 23 April 1989 was eight days after the Hillsborough football stadium disaster when scores of fans had been crushed to death, and it was the coldest April day of the 20th century. Neither fact was conducive to encouraging large numbers of people to go to another open air stadium! Finally, the organisational structures of other Churches, and their different geographical bases, meant that it was extraordinarily difficult to get participative leadership, administration, or financial control properly in place and there was little help forthcoming from the Diocesan Office. Most of the hard work and decision-making therefore fell on the shoulders of Bishop Colin Buchanan. Despite his enormous capacity for hard work, with hindsight there can be little surprise that the financial control of the mission went awry. He felt compelled immediately to offer his resignation to Bishop Mark Santer, who accepted it by return of post. There was no attempt to discuss with other Church leaders what might be done; Anglicans took the burden upon themselves and a highly-regarded suffragan bishop became the scapegoat. In fact more than half the deficit, £91,000, was covered over the next few weeks by donations, including many from individuals living in inner-city communities with few personal resources, and others from friends and colleagues of Bishop Colin. A year later the deficit was down to less than £60,000, but none of this was ever communicated to the Diocesan Synod. From the perspective of today it is clear that an appropriate management team for such a major event was never established by the 55 representatives of the participant Churches and other organisations; that proper financial control was missing; that Church representatives, other than Anglicans, did not live up to the promises made at the beginning, and that one man suffered disproportionately as a consequence.

The trauma of the weeks following Archbishop Tutu's visit has continued to reverberate, both in the Church of England, where unemployed bishops are not an everyday occurrence (Bishop Buchanan eventually became Area Bishop of Woolwich in the diocese of Southwark, but never the diocesan that might have been expected); and in Birmingham, where every large-scale event subsequently organised has operated in the shadow of the 'Tutu affair'. Since the largest event of the diocesan centenary in 2005 is to be a mission by the evangelist J. John, preaching his famed 'Just 10' interpretations on the Ten Commandments, over ten weeks in a tent in Aston Park, the prophesiers of doom have been heard again recently. Bishop Sentamu felt compelled to tell his Diocesan Synod in November 2004 that, after 15 years, the diocese needed to move on and put the 'Tutu affair' behind it.

25

FORTY YEARS OF RENEWAL
AND EVANGELISM

Towards the end of the 1960s a new world-wide movement was gathering force in the Churches. Individual Christians began speaking of rediscovering the love and power of God in their lives; people began to pray in small groups for the Holy Spirit to renew their lives; larger gatherings began to experience the miracles of Pentecost happening today: vivid personal testimony; speaking in tongues; spiritual and physical healing; 'Baptism in the Spirit' was seen as the key phrase. Others were wary of the emotionalism of this new Pentecostalism as it was sometimes called. It affected all Churches from Roman Catholic to Nonconformist, but it was particularly powerful in some Anglican parishes which began to network with each other and then to network ecumenically across the denominations. It was 'renewal' rather than denomination that was important. Some of the new work that got underway is illustrated in the following paragraphs.

Tuesday lunchtime talks

In 1966 Tim Royle, a business executive of Hogg Robinson Insurance brokers, who was based in Birmingham temporarily, saw the possibility of starting a work similar to that which was flourishing at St Helen's Bishopsgate, in London. He persuaded the Provost to invite Revd Dick Lucas, the Rector of St Helen's, to do some Tuesday talks for businessmen in the cathedral. Revd David McInnes had been with Lucas as his associate from the outset of the St Helen's ministry. Some time in the spring of that year, they began travelling up each week alternately to Birmingham to give the talks, while Tim Royle, and a friend called Sandy Landale, working for the Engineering and Employers Association, invited a number of their business friends to come. There was a sandwich lunch immediately after the half-hour address, and the numbers gradually grew from an initial 50 or so at the beginning.

A year later, the Provost approached David McInnes to ask whether he would consider the post of Precentor at the cathedral, with a view to running the Tuesday talks on a full-time basis, and doing evangelism in the city centre. He moved to Birmingham in late 1967. At the same time, Tom Walker (later Vicar of St John's, Harborne) was appointed Succentor. A year or two later, Guy Hordern, who had trained for the ministry but not been ordained, joined them.

Things were not easy to begin with. Although the talks on Tuesday were well attended, spiritual development was slow. A prayer fellowship formed out of some of the lay leaders from the Tuesday gathering proved significant, both as a support for what was going on, but also as a cell for worship, use of spiritual gifts, and deepening commitment. Out of the prayer times a number of significant events emerged. First,

138   *A Praise Service with Roger Jones at St Stephen's, Selly Park.*

was the start of a lunchtime gathering for young people in the cathedral, called 'Cat Time', organised by Tom Walker, with visiting celebrities such as James Fox. Then there were events in the St Philip's churchyard such as a testimony by Derek Nimmo, the film and TV star. There was a debate with a notorious academic, Dr Cole, from Aston University, known as the sex doctor, who was advocating 'modern' ethics. From this prayer group, there also arose the vision of inviting Gordon Bailey to establish work in the schools of the city, particularly to reach youngsters who were outside the church framework. They prayed about housing, and thanks to the help of Michael Calthorpe (of the Calthorpe Estate family) a delightful Regency house was provided at a 'peppercorn' rent, and Gordon Bailey moved in, and the work of schools outreach began. A trust fund, the Birmingham Businessmen's Christian Trust, was conceived to fund some of these developing initiatives.

Other evangelistic activities at this time included a significant visit from Jean Darnall, a gifted person with a prophetic and healing ministry and a three-day 'Keswick' conference at Carrs Lane URC church, with Revd David Watson as leader, followed a year or two later by David Pawson, speaking on 'Turning the Church inside out'. These meetings proved valuable rallying points for many churches. In late 1970 David McInnes remembers being involved in planning for the 'Festival of Light', which took place in London in September 1971. About two weeks before the festival there were rallies held at beacon sites around the country, symbolic of the beacons lit at the time of the Armada. In Birmingham there was one held at Barr Beacon at which he spoke and, rather to his surprise, a crowd of somewhere between 500-1000 came.

Work with young people

Following Arthur Blessitt's first visit to Birmingham (see chapter 24) and the unexpected response of so many young people, a follow-on meeting at the cathedral was hastily announced. To the amazement of the organising group, 300 young people turned up the following Thursday, only half of whom had been at the Bull Ring, but had heard of Christ from those who had been present. Almost spontaneously, according to McInnes, they announced a regular Saturday evening meeting to be held fortnightly in the cathedral, with an invitation to any young people to come. They decided to give it the name 'Youthquake' (which had been used by Mary Quant for a fashion sales drive), and from the outset it was packed to the doors.

Nick Cuthbert (recently graduated from the Christian Life College and who had joined the team) was given the role of leading 'Youthquake', Anthony Rose (who later got ordained) led the worship with a guitar, and David McInnes did the teaching. The format was simple, and included testimonies, prayer for healing, and opportunities for exercising spiritual gifts. McInnes remembers how on one occasion:

> A girl told of how God had spoken to her through a song that we were singing, and she found an injured knee simultaneously instantly healed. She was followed by a young spastic lad, who had difficulty getting to the microphone, describing the love shown to him by another teenage lad. The friend had offered to pray for him, and he reluctantly agreed. To his amazement, although his physical condition remained unchanged, he found all the bitterness of years vanishing, and an overwhelming peace filling him. There were regular stories from those who had come to the meeting to give their lives to Christ.

The Jesus Centre and new music

The leadership team began to sense the need for a place which could be an alternative to the night clubs in the city centre, and began praying that God would show them suitable premises. There were a number of derelict buildings in the city centre which were explored with local estate agents. The building which seemed most appropriate turned out to be a recently closed club over a cinema in New Street. The lease was £60,000, a very large sum in those days, but the group had already had some experience of divine provision and so, with £30 in the bank account, they decided to go ahead! The initial deposit asked for was £10,000. David McInnes happened to be speaking at a yachtsmen's service at Cowes a week or two later, and Sir Maurice Laing was in the congregation. A little diffidently he told him of the project, and a few days afterwards a cheque for £5,000 from his Trust arrived in the post. Michael Calthorpe was also interested in all that was going on, having himself come to a living faith a few years previously in London, and sent a further £5,000 from his family trust. There were many small and sacrificial gifts. Two elderly ladies, who told them that they had been praying for just such a work to come into being, sent a silver tea service, and a carriage clock, for them to sell for more funds. So the Jesus Centre came into existence, providing a base for an enlarged team. Volunteers helped re-furbish the

139   *The New English Orchestra rehearsing in the cathedral.*

building, and lunch was served there, besides evening openings. The Jesus Centre became the base for the Renewal Group and also provided the administrative facilities for the large evangelistic events of the next few years, including 'Mission England' (see chapter 24).

One member of the enlarged leadership team was Nigel Swinford, a gifted musician. He had a vision for combining Classical music with worship songs, and collected together young Christian musicians from around the country to form an orchestra, which became known as the New English Orchestra. Its first concert, a sell-out, was in February 1976 in Birmingham Town Hall with a gale raging outside. It was entitled 'Feast of Praise'; the songwriter Graham Kendrick was one of the soloists, and it was later recorded by Word, the music publishers. One of the early ventures was to take the orchestra and singers to Salzburg for the Music Festival there, which has since become a regular event. The comment of folk in Salzburg was to the effect that while other groups had more skill, this orchestra was restoring the soul of music.

It was in the early '70s that Jean Darnall brought news of a musical called 'Come Together' by an American composer, Jimmy Owens. The renewal team put on the highly participatory event in the cathedral, Nigel Swinford having gathered a choir together, and then took a group round some 40 or 50 venues in the city and around the Midlands, which was led by Nick Cuthbert and members of the Jesus Centre. It introduced a large number of churches to the possibilities of a fresh form of worship, with a combination of form and informality, as well as contributing to a renewal of life and faith. Another musical followed, less successfully, and a later series of concerts in 1977, entitled 'The Trumpets are Sounding', starting in the Town Hall once more, was designed as a wake-up call to the churches to take seriously the urgency of the times. The singers and orchestra also provided musical input at the lunchtime talks at the cathedral for a period. The NEO dispersed for 18 months but then reformed and has been performing concerts under Nigel Swinford's direction in venues across Europe ever since.

Birmingham has been richly blessed with musicians since at much the same time Roger Jones began to develop his Christian Music Ministries from Christ Church, Burney Lane. It was his group that provided the music at great diocesan events such as the Bishop Hugh farewell service and the 'Mission England' and Archbishop Tutu missions. He is especially renowned for his Bible-story-based musicals that can be produced on a grand scale to fill theatres, but which can also be produced with parish resources in local churches or by schools. His latest production, 'Jailbreak', has been commissioned to celebrate the diocesan centenary and will be premiered in October 2005.

Some time around 1974, the team ran their first summer camp in a field near Tamworth owned by John Cheatle, a Birmingham businessman. Although it bucketed with rain throughout, it was a huge blessing said David McInnes, with some 500 or more people taking part. It involved running water pipes and electricity into the field and, to avoid this hassle and cater for more people in the following years, they used the Stafford showground, and more than a thousand people came each year. In some ways this was a precursor of the now famous 'Spring Harvest' and 'Dales' weeks.

Black Power

In 1978, there was an exciting evangelistic rally in Handsworth Park to which the team invited the former Black Power leader, Eldridge Cleaver. He had been involved in a shoot-out with the police in Los Angeles in the late '60s and was then given refuge first in Cuba and later France. During this exile he became a Christian. Cliff Richard agreed to come as well, and a splendid black singer called Danniebelle was invited. Bishop Hugh Montefiore had just arrived in Birmingham and came to give his testimony as a Jewish believer. The team had planned a rally in the city centre, outside the cathedral first, but there were great battles with the Police Superintendent responsible, who was clearly very reluctant to allow a meeting there.

In Handsworth Park there was a huge crowd around the platform, and a large but fairly inconspicuous police presence. The climax came with Eldridge Cleaver's presence on the platform was greeted by a gang of Black Power supporters who had got themselves into the middle of the crowd with banners, barracking and cans of urine which they began to throw at him. 'He made a magnificent sight, with his large figure swaying to avoid the missiles, while he eloquently described his renunciation of violence for the love of Christ', remembers David McInnes. Danniebelle then swept onto the platform, seized the microphone and drowned the protesters with a deep-voiced rendering of 'Soon and very soon, we are going to see the King' in which the whole crowd joined in lustily. The police, who had been edging their way towards the trouble-makers, looked immensely relieved.

In 1986, the group hosted a rather different event, this time in the National Exhibition Centre. It was Michael Harper who had the vision for an international conference for Renewal, and delegates from France, Germany, Sweden, Norway, Finland, Yugoslavia, USA, and others were invited, many of whom were put up in the homes of Birmingham church people. John Wimber, the American leader of the Vineyard Christian Fellowship, was the main speaker. The worship and dance was directed by Nigel Swinford, and there was a line up of international speakers, including Michael Green who gave the Bible readings.

Prayer Breakfasts

George Tuck, a layman from St Stephen's, Selly Park, is the person particularly associated with the prayer breakfast ministry in Birmingham from the 1970s. So as to try to develop an effective network of Christian business and professional people in Birmingham, George invited Michael Fenton-Jones, the UK chairman of the International Federation of Christian Chambers of Commerce, to a breakfast to which he had invited 70 Christians in business and professional leadership in Birmingham. The breakfasters found it too early to identify with an International Network, when there was no city-wide network in Birmingham. So he then invited six men in different walks of life to meet him after that first gathering to work together to develop the prayer breakfasts as a means of networking men and women from different church traditions and professions. Between 1986 and 2001 more than 125 breakfast meetings were arranged, where more than 5,000 people attended at least two breakfasts. One of the great needs that Christian businesspeople expressed was that their churches did not support them, nor pray for them, but rather looked to them to part with large sums of money and act as church treasurers and the like.

When people asked to come to a breakfast George Tuck would send them a questionnaire listing all the work roles he could think of, together with a request for a list of their Christian concerns and involvements. Typically between 80 and 200 people booked for each gathering. He would pray over the names, and the information they had given him, sometimes to put people together with a high degree of common interest, and at other times to link those with complementary work or Christian interests. Having held about 20 breakfasts he then persuaded his steering group to widen the net to leaders in any walk of life, including Church leaders, so as to enable clergy to hear people talking together, and thus be in a better position to help and support them back in their parishes.

As he obtained the names of several people in the same area of interest he was able to develop specialist networks who met outside the breakfasts. One of these, for example, was headed by Martin Knox, a partner in Anthony Collins, Solicitors, and comprised people working in the public, private and charitable sectors. They met to give each other encouragement and to introduce one another to good contacts in the city housing department, and in the national Ministry of Housing. There was another group for people in banking, finance and accountancy; another for those engaged in management training and development; another for younger professionals in the early days of their professional life, and another for those with direct involvement in local and national politics. Though the story is little known in Birmingham, George Tuck's effective networking methods for Christian 'movers and shakers' in cities spread to other cities across the world through the international network and his own extensive travels to spread the word.

Renewal in Parish Life

It is impossible to tell the story of every parish affected by the Renewal Movement but Canon Tom Walker's central place in the story means that something must be said about St John's, Harborne. We have already seen that the church had been bombed to destruction in the Second World War but it had a long pedigree of Evangelical Bible-

140   *The Liturgical Dance Group of St John's, Harborne.*

based ministry. Tom Walker tells the story of his arrival at St John's himself (Walker 1982). He was instituted in July 1970 to a declining membership and a tradition of the clergy teaching and the people listening. The very next day people were invited to pray together in church about the future direction of the parish. The prayer meetings continued under the title 'Open to God' and slowly things began to change as those attending learnt to listen to what God was saying to them. More traditional prayer meetings were held on Tuesday evenings, but these too, by 1972, eventually took the pattern of the 'Open to God' meetings. Numbers were eventually so large that they had to be held in church. A little later home groups were introduced on alternate weeks with the prayer meetings, and numbers became more manageable.

Tom Walker talks in some detail about the 'spiritual warfare' that raged in Harborne as he and others in the core group became aware of the large number of witch's covens and Satanists in Birmingham and of how, once prayer was directed to the problem, evangelistic activities became more successful. A mission in the parish was led by Michael Watson in 1972 and by the following summer the use of worship songs and a more flexible structure to services meant that 'staid Anglicans started to clap their hands; tambourines appeared from nowhere, and suddenly there was a new expression of praise' (Walker 1982: 99). The Acts of the Apostles describes the people of God being 'all together in one place'; the sense of God's presence and power 'filled all the house where they were sitting'. In a very small way the corporate body of people at St John's relived just such an experience, said one member of the congregation who lived through those times. The home groups led to mission groups – people went out from the home groups to visit their neighbours in the parish with five simple questions, the last of which was what can St John's do for you? One need was for a playgroup, so staff were employed and St John's began operating and ministering through its playgroup and crèche on its church premises. From 1975 lay elders were commissioned to share in the ministry and leadership of the congregation, and especially of the numerous home groups.

In 1983, the bishop asked St John's to offer help to the neighbouring parish of St Germain's, Edgbaston, which was facing closure as its congregation had shrunk to tiny numbers. With missionary zeal a group of people from the congregation of St John's moved house to live in St Germain's parish. Over a period of four or five years the congregation began to grow and St Germain's is now a flourishing and self-sustaining congregation reflective of its multi-cultural area. More recently an experimental church-plant is underway in the clubs and pubs of the city's entertainment district of Broad Street. There is no church; meetings take place in the pubs and clubs as the young people from St John's who form the core of the 'congregation', under the direction of the Revd Geoff Lanham, befriend and talk with those who frequent the area. St John's Harborne was not alone in its experiences in the 1970s and '80s; St Stephen's, Selly Park, St John's, Walmley, and Knowle parish church were developing in roughly similar ways, so there are other stories that could be told.

The Decade of Evangelism

The 1990s was the nationally designated 'Decade of Evangelism'. Canon Bruce Gillingham was by now Diocesan Missioner. He produced an excellent 'Mission Roadshow' which toured the diocese providing resourses for parishes wanting to improve their evangelistic activities. The Cathedral Chapter were eager to respond to the need for more outreach in mission from the cathedral. It was the Chapter which funded an innovative outreach programme from 1993 to 1995 with lunchtime events in the cathedral grounds and itinerant minstrels and clowns in the streets and shopping arcades. There was a small stage in the churchyard for a music group – different ones from various black-led and city-centre churches each week for a summer month – and the music was interspersed with a speaker, who had five minutes to capture the attention of passers-by and those eating their sandwiches in the sunshine. Clowns, mime artists and helpers handing out leaflets mingled in the crowd. People who responded were invited into the cathedral for prayer and counselling.

Out on the streets in the first summer there were wandering minstrels, Simeon and John with flute and guitar, who toured the main shopping streets on Saturdays together with mime artists, Dave and Ken, all of them people Bishop Michael Whinney had worked with at Lee Abbey. Others spoke to shoppers and handed out leaflets. In the second summer the same team went into the main shopping arcades in the city – the Pallasades, City Plaza, the Pavilions and the Bullring. In the third summer Victoria Square was an ideal venue in good weather for much more of a staged presentation with drama, dance, music and song, together with speaking between items. Though the impact of these events could never be fully known, the numbers of people who stopped to listen grew as they became known.

141   *Open-air drama by St Stephen's, Selly Park at Selly Park Carnival.*

There were plans to have a celebration of Baptism and Confirmation held in the recently-opened National Indoor Arena. A feasibility study was done, costings calculated carefully, the NIA was offered to us at the charitable rate and fund raising began. Twelve out of 14 Deanery Synods agreed enthusiastically to support the event, though the main worry was that people did not want another financial failure like the Archbishop Tutu mission, and the Area Deans would not support the plans.

As a result a smaller event in the cathedral to celebrate Confirmation was organised. Everyone who had been confirmed in the past three years was invited to come to renew their promises at this celebration in 1993. There was a huge response and in order to accommodate the numbers all the pews and clergy stalls were removed and kneelers were provided in the nave for the young to sit on, while keeping some chairs at the back for the not-so-young! It was an inspiring occasion and it has been repeated every three years through to the present.

In 1995 there was a great 'Songs of Praise' celebration in Victoria Square in the city centre led by Pam Rhodes and Don MacLean as the BBC presenters. The square was packed and the music groups, singers and choir were all local. Bishop Michael was interviewed as Patron of the Malachi Trust about their attempt at making a record-breaking knitted scarf! Sue and Don were presented with needles and a ball of wool and invited to knit a length to be joined into the scarf. Rumour had it that Don got one of his family to do it for him! The scarf project involved hundreds of schools, children, parents and friends from the West Midlands all knitting metre-lengths, which were to be joined together for an attempt on the *Guinness Book of Records*. After this the scarf was to be divided up and restitched to make 6,000 cot blankets which were sent out to Bosnia during the conflict. The eventual length of 18,000 metres was declared at a special Malachi production of 'The Prodigal' in the National Indoor Arena. It fell short of the record by 5,000 metres, but was a great attempt.

The Millennium

Organising the celebration of the millennium fell to Canon Dr David Lee. There were two central events: first, was the 'Flame of Hope' lit in Centenary Square, Birmingham by Sir Cliff Richard at the start of the New Year 2000. The Flame was a gift from the Diocese of Birmingham to the City and burned continuously for millennium year. Sponsorship kept it burning for another two years before the money ran out and the Flame was quenched. It was relit in mid-2004 and is burning brightly for the centenary celebrations. The other event was 'Pentecost in the Park'. The birthday of the Church was celebrated at a great ecumenical event at Pentecost in Cannon Hill Park. It was a glorious warm early summer day; there was a huge number of participatory events; an outdoor auditorium with a programme of music and worship, and there were huge numbers of people. Many congregations joined together in pilgrimage walks to the park with banners waving and songs being sung. What is more the event ran to budget! This was important in restoring confidence in the diocese that it could organise successful large-scale events with proper budgetary control. It was a marvellous birthday party.

142 *The Millennium Flame of Hope in Centenary Square, Birmingham.*

143 *Stewards prepare for the influx of Jubilee 2000 demonstrators at Carrs Lane Church.*

Jubilee 2000

This chapter must not close without brief mention of the great 'Drop the Debt' rally that marked the summer of 1998. Birmingham was privileged to host the G8 summit of the leaders of the world's richest nations that summer. A coalition of charities and churches had begun to campaign for 'first world' nations to mark the Millennium by cancelling the indebtedness of 'third world' nations so that they could begin to improve their education and health-care facilities. This 'Jubilee 2000' campaign captured the public's imagination in Birmingham. Jubilee 2000 organisers requested people to ring the city centre of Birmingham, to clasp hands, to pray, and to wave banners and make a noise, whilst the G8 summit was underway on the Saturday afternoon. People came in their thousands, by coach and by train from all over Britain, but they also came from all over Birmingham, and the churches were in the forefront of encouraging the crowds. Again the sun shone and there were rallies in the Bullring, at St Martin's, and in front of the cathedral, with an impressive cohort of speakers. From 3 pm people moved off around the city centre to their allotted station and by 4 pm the chain was complete, in many places with crowds four or five deep. There were at least 100,000 people there, probably more. It was completely peaceful, full of hope, and deeply moving for all who took part. It was when world leaders began to take seriously the problems of the national indebtedness of poor countries.

144 *Speakers inside and out at St Martins-in-the-Bullring drew huge crowds before the chain was formed.*

145 *Even Bishop Charles Gore was drawn into the demonstration outside the cathedral!*

26

FAITH IN THE COMMUNITY:
SOCIAL ACTION

The publication of the Archbishop of Canterbury's Commission on Urban Priority Areas entitled *Faith in the City*, in 1985, prompted a period of reflection on the part of the Church as to how it was engaging with the urban poor in the midst of a period of traumatic economic and social change in many parts of the country. Nowhere was that change more traumatic than in the diocese of Birmingham where, in the space of a few years, Britain's most prosperous industrial region was reduced to penury. The motor-car manufacturing industry, so long the basis of the regional economy, began to disintegrate and, as factories closed in ever-greater numbers, unemployment began to rise in proportion. By 1985 it was the West Midlands, not Merseyside, Tyneside, or the Clyde, which recorded the highest levels of adult unemployment in the country. As the high-wage economy was removed, people could no longer keep up with mortgage payments and growing homelessness also resulted.

Detailed research by the Commission showed that these and other problems were further concentrated in inner-city and outer-fringe housing estates developed only two decades previously by local authorities. They could no longer afford to maintain and manage these estates properly, whilst many were suffering from poor construction, damp, inadequate heating and lack of social infrastructure. There were few opportunities for local employment, and almost none at all for those lacking skills, whilst poor schools were replicating the problems for the next generation who were leaving with no qualifications. The despair for people trapped by their circumstances was then leading to increases in criminal behaviour, and to an escalating drugs-based culture. These were the basic characteristics of 'Urban Priority Areas' (UPAs) and Birmingham diocese had a greater concentration of such areas than any other diocese. Almost a third of the local authority area of Birmingham was included as within the top 10 per cent of 'most deprived' urban districts in the country. Of the diocese's 183 parishes, 77 were considered to be UPAs. In these places the Church often provided the only community building and the minister was often the only professional living in the parish.

Faith in the City of Birmingham

The Commission Chairman, Sir Richard O'Brien, was invited by Bishop Hugh Montefiore to present the findings of the Commission to the Birmingham Diocesan Synod, and was then persuaded to chair another Commission concentrating on Birmingham alone. *Faith in the City of Birmingham* (1988) was extremely well received. In part this was because it paid more attention to theological underpinnings than the national report, thanks to work by Bishop Lesslie Newbigin, whilst its investigations

146 *'Faith in the City of Birmingham' Battle Bus which travelled around the diocese to launch the report.*

were supported by Birmingham City Council, the University of Birmingham, and a number of charitable trusts in the city, who provided the finance. Like the national report, it gave recommendations to the government, the city and the Church. It was especially good in seeking examples of good practice by Christian organisations across the city and revealed, perhaps for the first time to a wide audience, the level of hurt in the Black and Asian communities of the city, emphasising time and again how important good race relations were to a flourishing urban community. The point was well made and it was heard by the leaders of the Christian Churches. It fell to Bishop Mark Santer to receive the report of the Commission's labours and begin to put in place policies that would enable the Church to act effectively in UPA areas.

Fund Raising

Nationally, the most notable and long-lasting consequence of *Faith in the City* was the establishment of the Church Urban Fund (CUF) in 1988. This was funded by an appeal to sympathetic organisations and individuals based in every diocese of the Church of England that succeeded in raising more than £20 million for urban regeneration projects. Despite its poverty, the diocese of Birmingham succeeded in raising not only its proportion of the national Church Urban Fund, but a further substantial sum for a diocesan fund for similar purposes, the Action in the City Fund. Much of this fund-raising work was undertaken under the leadership of Canon David Collyer. The CUF was originally intended to spend all its money through grants over the succeeding 25 years, but the Church has recently decided that it is so effective that a further fund-raising campaign will be undertaken to replenish its resources.

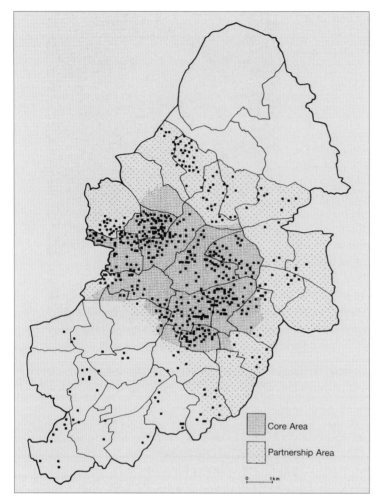

147 *The Birmingham Census Enumeration Districts that fell within the most deprived 10 per cent in England and Wales in 1981.*

☐ Core Area

☐ Partnership Area

0 ___ 1km

Faith in the City of Birmingham is helpful in documenting many of the social action projects being undertaken in the diocese before the 1980s, including those managed ecumenically. One of the oldest such projects is The Birmingham Settlement, founded in 1899 to assist disadvantaged people. In the second half of the 20th century the Settlement became renowned nationally for its financial advice work with poor people. It has a variety of telephone help-lines for money and debt advice and helped found the Newtown/South Aston Credit Union to help people get small loans at low rates of interest. It also runs youth music clubs, holiday play schemes, elderly day centres and an area caretaker for the Newtown estate of high-rise tower blocks. Other Credit Unions were developed by the Summerfield Foundation and Handsworth Forum of Churches. The latter also set up a legal advice centre and training and employment schemes. A number of churches were quickly involved in training schemes for young people or the unemployed, especially in the Handsworth and Lozells districts following the 1985 disturbances there. 'Greenspring' was set up by Bishop Latimer Church in Winson Green to train people in building skills and information technology. Finally, the Birmingham Churches Managing Agency was created in 1986 by the Churches

Industrial Group to manage government-funded community projects in the inner-city and within two years was employing more than 100 community workers, many of them linked to Anglican churches.

Community Projects

We have seen (chapter 17) that many of the new churches established in the diocese in the 1960s and 1970s were planned as multi-purpose buildings where social action projects were recognised from the beginning as an important part of the Church's mission to the district. Many of these new churches were ecumenical too. St Andrew's Church Centre is a joint Methodist and Church of England venture on the largest of the city's post-war housing estates at Chelmsley Wood. The team ministry originally consisted of three clergy and a youth worker, together with the nearby Bishop Wilson Church of

148   *Bishop Lesslie Newbigin.*

England School. A Citizen's Advice Bureau, youth centre, counselling centre, mother and toddlers' group, play group, and literacy and numeracy classes were all in being by the late 1980s. Balsall Heath Church Centre is an inner-city equivalent used by St Paul's Anglican church and the Balsall Heath URC which was opened in 1980. Here the emphasis was on ministry to the elderly with a day-care centre, a visiting service for the elderly, as well as youth work and holiday play schemes. The churches also got involved in the environmental 'Balsall Heath is Beautiful' campaign.

Since 1980 the availability of CUF and diocesan project funding has been instrumental in establishing large numbers of social action projects in the inner-city and outer-estate parishes of the diocese. However, their continuation is often reliant on local authority or government funding since grants from CUF are for only three years. Adapting to the changing national and local funding regimes is therefore an important part of any project management. The current 'buzz phrases' are 'civil renewal', 'community and social cohesion', and the 'regeneration of local urban neighbourhoods'. Increasingly, national government sees faith communities as potential partners in initiatives to regenerate neighbourhoods and communities. By 2002 the diocesan community regeneration department was able to list 40 projects funded through CUF grants to employ a community or youth worker, and 20 other parishes with funding for other types of project. All

149   *Members of the Sparkhill Project.*

150 *'The Hub' at Hazelwell.*

of these projects have additional volunteer workers from their congregations, of course.

A recent independent assessment of a sample of 12 Birmingham projects has been published (CVAR 2004). It provides thoughts from leaders, volunteers and recipients of the perceived value of community projects:

- 'The Centre is very visible, local, and a cheap resource; there's lots going on here, from lace making to work with young people';
- 'We provide much-needed pre-school facilities for the community and if we hadn't done it 55 children wouldn't be getting it';
- 'We work with young families; building relationships among community members; meeting specific needs of single parents, the youth and care for the elderly'. There were also plans for new work;
- 'We want to help refugees and asylum seekers integrate with the local community';
- 'Our future plans focus on health issues – there are many problems on the estate related to poor diet, smoking and coronary heart disease'.

The transformative power for local churches of some of these projects can be illustrated from the example of Holy Cross, Billesley. This parish serves an inter-war council estate in the southern suburbs of the city. Many of the houses were purchased by their occupiers in the 1970s and there are shops, playing fields and schools, but few other community facilities. The congregation of Holy Cross had shrunk to an elderly remnant by the 1980s; there were problems with the church roof and the social cohesion of the community was disintegrating. A new vicar, Revd George Hodgkinson, provided a new vision for a community centre as a base for outreach to local children, youth, and older people; a few people caught the spark despite the seemingly huge sum of money required; the first £5,000 raised by the congregation proved that local people could do things together successfully; CUF and other grants followed, all requiring matching funding to be raised by the now growing congregation and local people; building work began to attach a modern community building to the church, sharing some of its space, but consequently repairing the building faults, and today a now flourishing Holy Cross church is once more a viable and lively congregation at the heart of its local community.

Even more recent is The Hub, the impressive new community centre at St Mary Magdalen, Hazelwell. In the mid-1990s the congregation at Hazelwell were joined by the local Methodist congregation from across the road to form a new Local Ecumenical Project (LEP). It was sitting down together to decide exactly where they were going that inspired their social outreach project. Hazelwell is a mixed parish with older council housing and late 19th-century terraces. As at Holy Cross, the Hub building is attached to the older church building and was funded by the European Regional Development Fund together with smaller grants. It was opened in 2003. There are four funded managerial staff and an enormous variety of users from professional trainers' courses to computer courses run by South Birmingham College, dance groups, martial arts, and the Brownies. A rather different example, both in the community which it serves (inner-city, multi-ethnic), and in that it uses existing buildings more effectively, rather than building new ones, is 'The Springfield Project' at St Christopher's, Springfield. Funding from the CUF and the Tudor Trust allowed for the employment of a project worker from 2000. The project has concentrated on work with children including a parent and toddler group, a boys' club for eight to 12-year-olds, a holiday play scheme and family support work.

27

BLACK AND ASIAN BIRMINGHAM

Slavery and Anti-Slavery

Black people were resident in Birmingham at least from the 18th century. Most were servants in prosperous White households and several are recorded in the burial registers for both St Martin's and St Philip's. Thus 'Ann Pinard, a black, 12 January 1773' is recorded at the latter parish, and 'George Pitt Charry, a batchelor [*sic*], a black, 10 February 1774', at St Martin's, whilst Levi Baldwin 'born 1770 or thereabouts in North America, a man of colour' was baptised on 10 April 1821 at St Martin's, and William Davidson, a Jamaican cabinet-maker lived in Birmingham in the early 19th century (Grosvenor *et al.* 2002). Birmingham businessmen had grown rich in the 18th century as a result of the slave trade and though the connections are less obvious than in Bristol or Liverpool, they are no less real. Birmingham's guns were traded for slaves in West Africa and Birmingham's metal-bashers turned out shackles and chains for the dreadful voyage of the slave ships from West Africa to the Caribbean and the southern states of North America. On arrival, they were set to work on sugar estates where spades and sugar presses had been shipped over from Birmingham manufacturers, and where the estates themselves were often in the ownership of families with close links to Midland entrepreneurs, such as the Adderleys of Hams Hall. There were also early links with the developing Indian Empire and, in the 1860s, an Indian Christian convert, Dada Bhai, was running a lodging house for Asians in Birmingham.

Birmingham Christians were not only helping to perpetuate slavery, however, they were also in the forefront of the campaign to abolish slavery. The best known was Joseph Sturge, political reformer, pacifist, campaigner for workers' rights, as well as abolitionist. His statue still stands proudly in the Five Ways roundabout gardens in Birmingham with the figure of Charity holding a black child. Sturge quickly became involved with the Anti-Slavery Society in Birmingham and was its secretary from 1826. The passing of the Emancipation Act in 1833 was not the end of the matter for him, since he regarded the apprenticeship system, which replaced it, as slavery in all but name. In 1838 Sturge led a march from the Town Hall to found the Emancipation School celebrating the end of the Caribbean apprenticeship system. The famous painting in the National Portrait Gallery of a London meeting of the Anti-Slavery Society shows not only Sturge but also Richard Cadbury, and Birmingham clergy including Revd John Angell James (Minister at Carrs Lane) and Revds. Thomas Morgan and T.M. McDonnel. The Female Society for the Relief of Negro Slaves was founded in 1825. Sturge's wife and his sister were founding members and it continued in being until 1919, helping Black American women and orphan children in the later years of the 19th century (Grosvenor *et al.* 2002). It is also important to note that Birmingham had a West Indian minister as early as the first decades of the 20th century. The Revd A.R. Runnells-Moss was Vicar of St John's, Ladywood at the time of the First World War and was remembered by parishioners with affection and respect long afterwards. He drew large congregations from all over the city with his evangelistic preaching full of Caribbean emotion and fire (Power 1965: 35).

Twentieth-Century Migration Streams

Black, south Asian, Chinese and Yemeni people, amongst many others, continued to come to Birmingham in the inter-war years of the 20th century, but it was the Nationality Act of 1948, which gave British citizenship to residents of former British colonies, which encouraged migrants to set off for the 'Mother country' in pursuit of jobs and economic advancement. The

151 *(right)   The Sturge Memorial, Five Ways, Edgbaston.*

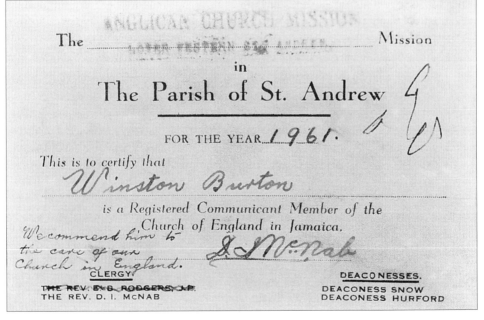

152   *Letter of Commendation from the West Indies to 'our Church in England'.*

most numerous group was from the West Indies who to begin with were predominantly young men, but women and children were soon to follow. Earlier generations of missionary priests had done their job well and these migrants were solidly Christian: Methodists, Baptists, but mostly Anglican. On Sunday they put on their best clothes and went to their local Anglican parish church to worship God. They were met by puzzlement, curiosity, occasionally a warm welcome, but most frequently by hostility and fear from both congregations and ministers. Comments recalled by today's Black Anglicans in Birmingham include:

- 'Do you know there is a church just round the corner where your people, people of your colour, go?'
- 'You are not my type. It would be much better if Black people could speak English.'
- 'You must sit at the back of the church.'
- 'On my first Sunday in Birmingham my friends and I, we put on our best suits and went to church. But after the service the vicar told us not to come again. His congregation wouldn't like it, he said' (Wilkinson, 1993).
- 'The first time I entered a church the minister was very welcoming, because he served in Trinidad for seven years, but the congregation was very reserved thinking what is she doing here? They did not say anything to my face, but action speaks louder than words.' (Barton, 2005)

A longer testimony of early experiences comes from Henry Brotherson. He had worked for the British Government in St Kitts from 1946-55. He came to Britain in August 1955 and went first to Manchester, but moved to Birmingham to be with his brother and sister. I will let him tell a small part of his own story:

> I arrived in Birmingham 1.15pm on 3rd December 1955. I met my brother and sister. We were glad to be together and glad that we did not have to share room with strangers. ... I did not work on Saturdays so I went round to inquire of the vicar of the parish. I found the vicarage. I rang the bell. A lady came to the door. I said Good day, told her my name and asked if I could speak to the vicar. He came and asked, 'What can I do for you young man?' I told him my name, also that I had just moved into his parish. I gave him a letter I brought from my vicar in the West Indies. He asked me to take a seat while he read the letter. When he finished he shook my hand, told me his name, called his wife, introduced her to me and told her that I was a server, Sunday School teacher, Lay Reader, and lay representative to Synod in my parish in St Kitts. She turned to her husband and said, 'Use this man.' Five minutes later she gave me tea and biscuits, and asked me all about St Kitts and my wife and family. She really made me feel welcome, nice lady. The vicar told me where to find the church and he hoped to see me on Sunday. I bid them good day and left.
>
> Sunday I went to church. I met a man as I stepped in the church. He asked if I am Mr Brotherson. I said, 'Yes'. He shook my hand, said he was the warden, and the vicar had asked him to meet me; he gave me service books and showed me where to sit. Just before the sermon the vicar asked me to stand, he then told the congregation all he knew about me and hoped I would be happy in his parish ...

At work sometimes I experienced racism, but I persevered. I worked hard and soon became the highest paid operator on my job. I was also training anyone they wanted to train. Later I was also promoted to chargehand. When I had two years in the UK I saved enough to send for my wife. In St Kitts my mother looked after the kids for us. We lived in rented rooms in Aston the first month. Then moved to Saltley, better living accommodation. My wife was working at the Accident Hospital. … My wife and I are now seniors, still serving God and taking each day as it comes. I know all the problems we Black people have to endure. I do know there are some who dislike the Blacks but not all. Let us pray for each other and be thankful to God for all his mercies. (Barton, 2005)

Pictures from the Census and the Church

There is a long history of academic investigation into the characteristics and distribution of the minority ethnic populations of Birmingham as recorded in successive censuses. Jones's research (1967) using the birthplace data from the 1961 census showed that, of Birmingham's total population of 1,107,187, some 16,290 (1.4 per cent) were immigrants from the West Indies and 10,232 (0.9 per cent) were from the Indian sub-continent; adding children born in the UK he estimated that some 3 per cent (35,000) of the city's population were Black or Asian in 1961. These ethnic groups were highly concentrated into those 'middle-ring' parishes consisting mainly of Victorian and Edwardian bye-law housing. Thus Soho and Handsworth, to the north-west of the city centre, contained more than 27 per cent of the West Indian population, whilst Aston, Sparkbrook and Balsall Heath contained nearly 35 per cent of the south Asian population of the city. In other words, these two ethnic groups were already spatially separated from one another. None of the smallest census tracts (enumeration districts) had a majority Black or Asian population. In the 1960s, Asian migrants were still mainly young men, but West Indian migrants had already established more normal family structures with women and children having followed the young men to Britain. So 24 of the city's primary schools already had 20 per cent of their pupils who were Black or Asian and three had 50 per cent in these categories (*The Times*, January 1965).

The housing conditions in the middle ring quickly deteriorated as landlords discovered that they were ideal for multi-occupation. Large rooms enabled groups of single men or families to be housed in tolerable comfort, though with shared bathrooms and kitchens, giving large profits to often unscrupulous landlords. Overcrowded houses, overgrown gardens, streets choked with parked cars and a general environment of neglect and decay was characteristic of the 1960s in these areas (Slater 1998). Unfortunately, the city council's points system for the allocation of council houses meant that migrant families were effectively excluded from rehousing whatever their need (Rex and Moore 1967). By the middle of the 1960s the Black and south Asian population of the city had almost doubled to nearly 50,000 people (4.7 per cent of Birmingham's total population), the majority of the newcomers being from the Indian sub-continent and therefore living primarily in Sparkbrook, Balsall Heath, and Sparkhill, where they became owner-occupiers of their houses rather than renting as the majority of West Indian families did.

The Church's response was both diocesan and parochial. In a pioneering experiment Bishop Wilson appointed Revd Paul Burrough as Bishop's Chaplain for Overseas Peoples in 1959, with a brief to get beside the Caribbean migrants, provide welfare support, and assist their integration into parishes. Burrough was an old friend from Singapore days who was invalided back to Britain from Korea. To do the job he chose to live in a caravan, which he parked on friendly vicarage drives as he moved about the twenty or so parishes where immigrants were living, and he rode a huge motorbike. He was not a typical Anglican vicar! He had Wilson's blessing who said to him: 'I shall never ask reports or results from you. I merely want you to show something of the love of God to these people in the streets of Birmingham who move my heart with their great need' (McKay 1972: 173).

His ministry, which continued until 1967, is warmly remembered by everyone who came in contact with him. Aubrey Longe writes: 'people met to introduce themselves and shared cultural experiences. We had people-to-people week, an annual event, one of which I attended was in Witton Road.' Henry Brotherson recorded that: 'Canon Burrough came to our home one day and said he heard all about my work in the Church in St Kitts and told me about what he is doing for overseas people in the diocese. I was glad to meet him. I gave him the names of some people I knew. He did a grand job getting people together, and attending and inviting us to various functions. God Bless him.' Bishop Wilson occasionally joined Burrough in his visiting and eventually made him a residentiary canon of the cathedral in order to mark the importance of the work. However, his workload was enormous and, as Canon John Wilkinson remarked, he was 'too hard pressed supporting the ministry of a large number of parishes and too busy sustaining a much-valued pastoral ministry with a formidable caseload, to enable parishes to develop new strategies' (Wilkinson 1993). Paul Burrough is the only person to have been consecrated bishop in Birmingham cathedral when he was made Bishop of Mashonaland.

An inner ring parish in the 1960s

John Wilkinson's published recollection of his time at St James's, Aston (Wilkinson 1993) must stand as one amongst a variety of priestly and parochial workings-out of new theologies, new patterns of ministry, and personal spiritual journeys in response to the increasing Black Christian presence in their midst. He wrote:

> The parish of St James', Aston, had undergone in the post-war years a pattern of social change typical of many inner-ring churches in larger cities in Britain. The pattern consisted of a long period of slow decline, then a rapid acceleration of exodus and decline in response to Black immigration, the failure of the church to understand the significance of social change, increasingly desperate attempts to maintain existing congregational life, lack of resources for the development of new strategies of mission, an overtly racist general atmosphere (though with individual exceptions) and in spite of it all, the 'planting' of a small Black presence in the congregation.

The 1954 St James's Annual Church Meeting was able to report a good number of thriving church organisations; there was a new Envelope Giving Scheme; a new lay reader, and a popular new monthly Parish Communion service. There were 146 Easter communicants, 83 baptisms (including one Black child) and 29 marriages (including six Black couples). Six years later, however, demolition and 'White flight' had brought

153 *The congregation of St James's, Aston, Easter Sunday 1976. The old and the young both seem to have had their 'Resurrection experience'.*

first slow, and then rapid change and decline in church life. Easter communicants had declined by a third and some church organisations had closed.

By 1972 we find a reduction of Easter communicants to only 20 per cent of their 1954 total, inability to manage the church hall, lack of volunteers for the office of churchwarden, and choirboys so unruly that their complete dismissal was proposed at one Parochial Church Council meeting! However, even in these bleak years there were signs of life available to a church that could change – a church with which Black Anglicans could identify. Half of the 900 children baptised between 1962 and 1972 were Black, whilst almost half of the 190 marriages were of Black or mixed-race couples. Within the life of the congregation itself, 17 out of 19 people confirmed in 1972-3 were Black; there were two Black sidespeople, and two Black church council members – at least for one year. Two Black women taught in the Sunday School. It is a sad and moving story, painful and bewildering to live through, and one can only admire the tenacity and devotion of those, both Black and White, who survived it.

A Black Majority Congregation

The new clergy team, John Austen, John Wilkinson, and his wife Renate (an ordained minister of the German Protestant Church), arrived at St James in September 1974, together with three committed lay people. They were unaware of the heritage they were to have the privilege of harvesting. For behind the faithfulness of their predecessor through the years of rapid social change, and the ministry of Paul Burrough in the 1960s, lay the life of the Anglican Church in the Caribbean, and behind that the whole tradition of Black Christianity.

154   *The new youth choir at St James's, Aston.*

At first, came a number of initiatives from both clergy and congregation: the re-forming of the choir by a number of Black youngsters, the introduction of a regular Parish Communion, the starting of a junior church and youth fellowship, as well as the beginnings of social outreach activities. 'It was, however, the tragic death of the single parent of four children, the youngest only eight', says Wilkinson,

> which brought our first vivid encounter with the Black Christian tradition. At the funeral service over 400 of the church's 600 places were filled by mourners who rendered the traditional hymns ... Children and relatives sang and wept. Slowly the entire congregation, resplendent in the dignity of its formal funeral attire, took leave of the deceased as they filed past the open coffin. At the graveside the women again wept as the men filled in the grave and we all sang, "We loved thee well, but Jesus loves thee best, Goodnight, Goodnight, Goodnight". Afterwards crowds gathered at the family home, and the clergy led prayers before the serving of food and drink. It was our first Black funeral, taken because of the circumstances with perhaps especial care. Next Sunday the adult congregation doubled to 70 worshippers.

In the following three years, a new mainly Black congregation rapidly came into being. Organisational and pastoral structures were developed, and the first steps were taken towards the replacement of the ailing church building. A pre-school playgroup and a parish advice centre, the latter mainly serving the Bangladeshi community, opened as church responses to local community need. But the clergy had little conceptual grasp of the history and content of Black Christianity. Naively, they believed that overcoming both the recent rejection of Black people by White, and the mutual fears of Black and White by means of welcome and fellowship would lead to a new congregation whose life would not be particularly different from a White one. And so it seemed for most of those first four years to be a time of growth, consolidation and structuring.

Many things were very positive, says Wilkinson:

> We experienced the power and articulation of the Black tradition of free prayer – especially at prayer meetings, Bible study groups and in times of open intercession and thanksgiving at the daily Morning Prayer. We heard the Black style of singing … and were embraced by the warmth and openness of the Black community at family celebrations and observances such as baptisms, birthdays, times of sickness, or death. We learned more of the sharpness of the unexpected rejection by the 'mother country' and the 'mother Church', the very image of 'mother' showing how deeply that rejection had injured the self-understanding of a people. Young people responded to confirmation preparation and youth work which at least attempted to take their identity and experience seriously. They shared something of the struggles, from home, school and work, of growing up in a society which gave ambiguous and contradictory messages of its expectations. There was from so many people an unforgettable quality of love for me and my family, despite both my mistakes, and the never-ending racism of wider society. Above all, there was the sheer faith, gratitude and openness to God of Afro-Caribbean Christians.

By the end of the 1970s, Wilkinson and other clergy working in Black majority parishes were being forced to reckon with indications of the 'oppressor to victim' difference between Black and White, and even more so with the difference between first and second generation Black Christians. Some young people, apparently settled in church life, left not only church but home as well at the age of 16 to become Rastafarians. Black parents anxiously pressed the clergy to 'do youth work' but their ideas of what that would entail sprang more from the Caribbean past than from an understanding of the difficulties of young Black people growing up in a complex and White-dominated society. At times it was necessary to challenge the apparently conservative, firmly-held theology of older Black members in the interests of responding to problems and questions raised by their children.

The Black-Led Churches

This was the time when 'Black Christianity/Theology' was being brought out of university theology departments and across the Atlantic from the United States. It was clear from early studies that Black-British Christianity was entering a new stage of the Black diaspora. What had been brought from the Caribbean: Afro-Christian heritage; some North American Pentacostalism; a distinctive musical tradition; a living lively faith, had crashed into the White British conservative Christian tradition and had had to sustain the shock of meeting racism, decaying Christianity, and the shattering experience of rejection in British Churches. So Black Christianity developed its own institutions: the Black-led Churches, which were not simply a response to rejection. In these Churches Black Christians found a positive heritage fashioned in suffering and rooted in Africa. It was characterised by a pervasive sense of God as a living force, by attractiveness, joy, liveliness and warmth, and by worship characterised by the 'experiential rise of the human spirit to meet the descending grace of the Divine'. Black British Christians inherited a vision of the church as people rather than building

155 *The Corpus Christi procession of witness, with Father Brian Whatmore of St Benedict's, Bordesley.*

or hierarchy and maintained a universal vision with little division between sacred and secular. Their use of Scripture should not be mistaken for the fundamentalism of White conservative evangelicals; the Bible is rather a storehouse of information about human relationships and God's work of liberating His people, a work in which the Exodus, Exile, Cross and Pentecost were the key and definitive events. This was a rich heritage; it could be offered, but not sacrificed, to the wider Church. First-generation Black Anglicans tried and often failed; their children often did not bother to try; Black-led churches often seemed a more congenial environment or, alternatively, Rastafarianism offered a much freer environment than both.

The 'Handsworth' Riots

The 1980s marked a more serious change than inter-generational conflict, however. First, Birmingham's ethnic 'pot' was being stirred more vigorously as substantial numbers of new migrants from India, Bangladesh, Kashmir, Uganda, and most particularly Pakistan, settled in Birmingham and Smethwick. By 1981 some wards of the city – Handsworth, Soho, Sparkbrook and Sparkhill – had more than 50 per cent of their population who were Black or south Asian, whilst most of the other inner-ring wards had more than 25 per cent of their people in the non-White categories. Perhaps 18 per cent of the city's population were Black or south Asian. Secondly, some 40 per cent of this non-White population were under 16 years of age so inner-city schools, including Church schools, had anything up to 90 per cent of their pupils who were Black or south Asian. Thirdly, this was not just an ethnic 'melting pot' but a religious and cultural one as well. The vast majority of this later migration stream was not Christian. The diocese became home to substantial numbers of Hindus, one of the largest Sikh populations in Europe, and a very large Muslim population, so temples, gurdwaras and mosques began to be a familiar sight in the townscape. With their religions migrants also brought with them other cultural divisions such as caste and Asian social and economic networks. On to this mix of culture, ethnicity, age, class and caste the 1980s poured the petrol of the economic disintegration of the West Midlands economy with unemployment rates reaching 60 per cent in some inner wards of the city.

Civil unrest was first manifested in Britain's larger cities in 1981, including disturbances in Sandwell, Smethwick and Birmingham. However, these paled into insignificance compared with the events of 9-10 September 1985, when, amidst widespread unrest centred on the Lozells Road, two Asian shopkeepers died in the flames of their burning property. The national press 'relocated' the events to better-known Handsworth and 'racialised' them through a dramatic picture of a young Afro-Caribbean man throwing a fire-bomb. A White man was eventually charged with the murder of the shopkeepers and many White and Asian (as well as Afro-Caribbean) men were arrested (Slater 1998). What was clear by the end of the 1980s was that growing numbers of Black and Asian British youth were being severely disadvantaged by the multiple deprivations of poor housing, inadequate education and lack of employment opportunities. The consequence was a growing 'gang' culture of crime and drugs with little connection with the initial migrant cultures or with those of White Britain.

Learning to come alongside one another

White Church structures had to learn some hard lessons – they are still learning – over the next two decades. By the mid-1990s a diocesan survey showed that Black Christians were beginning to make an impact on their local church power structures in those churches where Black and Asian people were a significant minority (some 20 or so parishes). There were nearly 30 churchwardens and more than 180 parochial church council members, but they were failing to impact at higher levels of church government with only 26 Deanery Synod members and six Diocesan Synod members. There were also only five Black or Asian clergy in the diocese and only nine readers. Where these clergy and readers served in predominantly White parishes their isolation and vulnerability was often poorly supported and little understood by diocesan authorities, whilst the small number of Black and Asian lay people at higher levels made them vulnerable to taking on 'representational' roles that they neither sought, nor were necessarily well-equipped to undertake. Consequently there are more stories of pain that need to be heard from this period too, but we also need to note that, compared with other Anglican dioceses, Birmingham had far greater levels of representation than any other.

Where Black and Asian clergy and readers were also women the second rejection of their gifts in the 1990s was doubly painful. Revd Elsada (Elsie) Watson trained as a reader in 1978 and was ordained deacon in 1988 and priested in 1994, one of the first tranche of women to be ordained in the diocese. On her first day as a curate, she remembers her vicar saying: 'I don't know why they sent you here. I am a part-time hospital chaplain. I don't like doing it, so you can take it over.' She told him firmly that she did not come to the parish to do the things he did not like doing but to minister in her own right. Inevitably the partnership failed and she was moved to another parish. There she was asked by the Diocesan Renewal Group to plan a 'renewal' service in her church, 'but the vicar was really angry saying they had never

156 *A Caribbean steel band was part of the 'Blessing of the City' at Bishop Hugh Montefiore's Enthronement (Peart-Binns 1990).*

157 *Children from the Zap Club, St George's, Newtown.*

asked him to do anything like that and I was only a curate. ... He deliberately arranged an outing on the day of the service so that no-one from the parish would go to it; it did not matter, the service was packed out.' Even the then Bishop's Adviser for Black and Asian Affairs, when Elsie was asked to join a diocesan committee, said that 'the diocese are scraping the bottom of the barrel by asking me. I was never so insulted'. Even the second generation Black British Canon Eve Pitts, now the much-loved vicar of Emmanuel, Highter's Heath and for a period one of Birmingham's General Synod representatives, suffered similar experiences of hurt and rejection in a White male-led team ministry, and a period of diocesan helplessness in the face of these problems. Clearly, not everyone's story can be represented here but it is important that the diocesan response to Black and Asian Christians is not represented as a story of steadily increasing acceptance and integration. There is immeasurable love from some individuals and groups; there is great pain and suffering on the part of others. But at its centenary the diocese has a Black (African) bishop, a Black British woman as chair of the house of laity of the Diocesan Synod, and an Asian minister and theologian on the General Synod; it has therefore at least moved to ensure that Black and Asian Christians are in representative visible positions of power and responsibility to a greater extent than elsewhere.

Revd Roger Hooker

It may seem unfair to pay tribute to one man's work in this area of diocesan life, but the Revd Roger Hooker, who died early in 1999, was a pioneer in the field of inter-faith relations which has been so important to the life and well-being of Birmingham and Sandwell in the 1980s and '90s. Roger Hooker often quoted his father-in-law Max Warren, one time Secretary of the Church Missionary Society (CMS), that the question of other faiths was the biggest issue to face the Christian churches since Darwin, and was intellectually tougher than the problems posed by science. After a curacy, he and his wife Pat (they were to remain an inseparable team) went to India and it was there that he was eventually invited to join a group of Hindus discussing their scriptures together. There he learnt a vital lesson: 'I can only understand what another person says if I have first understood what they have not said.' Having already learnt Hindi, he then went to learn Sanskrit for six years at Sampurhanda, one of the major centres of Hindu thought and pilgrimage. He discovered not only something of the faith of others but also a deepening of his own Christian faith.

158 *Canon Roger Hooker talking with residents of Smethwick.*

Roger and Pat returned to Birmingham in 1978, he to teach in Crowther Hall, the CMS college in Selly Oak but then, with CMS funding, to be inter-faith adviser to the Warley Deanery. They became the prime exponents of Christian mission as long-term loving; loving the people of any faith or none whom God gave them to love. In the 1990s he gained a PhD from the Hindi University at Benares, gave the Teape lectures on *Narrating our Nations*, and was appointed Bishop's Adviser on Inter-Faith Relations with a diocesan-wide role. He became a prophet in his own country. He introduced parish clergy to the leaders of their local mosques, gurdwaras and temples. He quickly added Islam, Buddhism, and Judaism to his expertise in the Hindu and Sikh faiths. He encouraged young clergy to expand their understanding of other faith communities, and he led courses for lay people to do the same. His abiding passion was that we need to be able to tell each other's religious story in an inclusive way – from colonialism to the Holocaust – if the story is one of difference and exclusion, of making others less than fully human, then violence and destruction inevitably follow eventually. The Church of England's recent divisions over the ordination of women and the place of gay and lesbian Christians pained him deeply for the same reason. The diocese of Birmingham, and the people of Sandwell and Birmingham, owe him an immense debt for helping us to live with one another more gracefully than we might otherwise have done.

Bibliography

Anon (1905), *Birmingham Bishopric: Brief History of the Movement and Report of the Enthronement of Right Rev. Charles Gore, D.D. as First Bishop of Birmingham* (Diocese of Birmingham, Birmingham)

Anon (1955), *Diocese of Birmingham 1905-1955* (Diocese of Birmingham, Birmingham)

Barnes, John (1979), *Ahead of his Age. Bishop Barnes of Birmingham* (Collins, London)

Barton, Mukti (2005), *Rejection, Resistance and Resurrection* (Darton, Longman and Todd, London)

Bass, T.J. (1898), *Every Day in Blackest Birmingham: Facts not Fiction* (Birmingham)

Bassett, Steven (2000), 'Anglo-Saxon Birmingham', *Midland History* 25, 1-27

Baynes, Hamilton (1915), *Two Centuries of Church Life. St Philip's Birmingham 1715-1915* (Cornish Bros, Birmingham)

Bishop, Steve (2001), 'Bishop Barnes, science and religion', *Quodlibet Online Journal* 3 (http://www.Quodlibet.net)

Briggs, Asa (1952), *History of Birmingham Vol. 2* (University Press, Oxford)

Buchanan, Colin (Ed) (1987), *Bishop Hugh – with Affection. A Retirement Tribute* (Diocesan Board of Finance, Birmingham)

Buteaux, Simon (2003), *Beneath the Bull Ring. The Archaeology of Life and Death in Early Birmingham* (Brewin Books, Studley)

Carpenter, James (1960), *Gore. A Study in Liberal Catholic Thought* (Faith Press, London)

Centre for Voluntary Action Research (2004), *Study on the Role and Contribution of Local Parishes in Local Communities in the Diocese of Birmingham* (Aston Business School, Birmingham)

Chadwick, Owen (1970), *The Victorian Church* (2 vols) (London)

Cherry, Gordon (1994), *Birmingham. A Study in Geography, History and Planning* (Wiley, Chichester)

Collyer, David (1973), *Double Zero. Five Years with Rockers and Hell's Angels in an English City* (Arthur James, Evesham); 2nd (paperback) edition, 1983

Dale, A.W. (1909), *The Life of R.W. Dale* (2nd edn Birmingham)

Dawson (1844), *The Signs of the Times* (a sermon delivered at Mount. Zion, Birmingham)

Diocese of Birmingham (1988), *Faith in the City of Birmingham. An Examination of Problems and Opportunities Facing a City* (Paternoster Press, Exeter)

Driver, Arthur H. (1948), *Carrs Lane 1748-1948* (Birmingham)

Ede, Denis (1975), 'Contemporary Christian presence and ministry. An appraisal of Hodge Hill multipurpose church', *Research Bulletin of Institute for the Study of Worship and Religious Architecture, Birmingham* 50-55

Enraght, R.W. (1881), *Catechism of the Persecution of R.W. Enraght* (Birmingham)

Fisher, Leslie (1954), *The story of Hall Green Parish Church formerly called Job Marston's Chapel* (Birmingham)

General Synod (1985), *Faith in the City. A Call for Action by Church and Nation* (Church of England, London)

Gill, Conrad (1952), *History of Birmingham I. Manor and Borough to 1865* (University Press, Oxford)

Gilman, Michael (1999), 'A study of churches built for the use of congregations of the Church of England between 1945 and 1970 and of their effectiveness in serving the needs of their congregations', Unpubl. PhD thesis, University of Sheffield

Gore, John (1932), *Charles Gore Father and Son. A background to the early years and family life of Bishop Gore* (John Murray, London)

Green, Bryan (1994), *Bryan Green Parson-Evangelist* (Bryan Green Society, Thame)

Grosvenor, Ian, McLean, Rita and Roberts, Siân (2002), *Making Connections. Birmingham's Black International History* (Birmingham Futures Group, Birmingham)

Gulliver, Kevin (2000), *Social Concern and Social Enterprise. The origins and history of Focus Housing* (Brewin Books, Studley)

Hamley, Valerie (1992), *1892-1992 A History* (The Mothers' Union, Birmingham)

Herbert, Arthur G. (1935), *Liturgy and Society* (Faber & Faber, London)

Hodder, Michael (2004), *Birmingham. The Hidden History* (Tempus, Stroud)

Hopkins, Eric (2001), *Birmingham. The Making of the Second City 1850-1939* (Tempus, Stroud)

Howe, David (2003), *Willingly to School. The Story of 900 Years of Education in Warwickshire* (Warwickshire Publications, Warwick)

Ingram, D. and Jones R. (Eds) (2002), *Belfry Life in Birmingham c.1780-1860: the Recollections of John Day* (privately published, Kings Norton)

James J.A. (1990), *One Hundred and Fifty Years* (Carrs Lane Church, Birmingham)

Jenkins, Robert (1996), *In Touch with the Warm Heart of Africa 1966-1996* (privately published, Lichfield)

Jepson, Rachel M.E. (1992), 'The Role of Women in the Evolution of the 19th Century Sunday School Movement with particular reference to Birmingham', unpubl. MA dissertation, Cheltenham & Gloucester College of Higher Education

Jones, Ian (2000), 'The Mainstream Churches in Birmingham c.1945-1998: The Local Church and Generational Change', unpubl. PhD thesis, University of Birmingham

Jones, Philip N. (1967), *The segregation of immigrant communities in the City of Birmingham, 1961* (University of Hull Occasional Publications in Geography 7)

Jones, Philip N. (1976), 'Coloured minorities in Birmingham, England', *Annals of the Association of American Geographers* 66, 89-103

Knox, Edmund A. (1934), *Reminiscences of an Octogenarian 1847-1934* (London)

McKay, Roy (1973), *John Leonard Wilson. Confessor for the Faith* (Hodder & Stoughton, London)

Miller, J.C. (1854), *Home Heathen* (Birmingham)

Mole, David (1975), 'Attitude of Churchmen towards society in early Victorian Birmingham', in *Religion in the Birmingham Area. Essays in the Sociology of Religion,*

Alan Bryman (Ed) (Institute for the Study of Worship and Religious Architecture, Birmingham)

Montefiore, Hugh (1995), *Oh God, What Next?* (Hodder & Stoughton, London)

Morrish, P.S. (1980), 'The struggle to create an Anglican diocese of Birmingham', *Journal of Ecclesiastical History* 31, 59-88

Newbigin, Leslie (1995), *Unfinished Agenda: an Autobiography* (SPCK, London, 2nd Edn)

Owen, C.M. (1894), *Church Extension Work in Birmingham* (Birmingham)

Page, William (1908), *Victoria County History, Warwick Vol.II* (Constable, London)

Peacock, Roy (1975), 'The 1892 Birmingham religious census', in *Religion in the Birmingham Area: Essays in the Sociology of Religion*, Alan Bryman (Ed) (University of Birmingham, Birmingham)

Peart-Binns, John S. (1990), *Bishop Hugh Montefiore* (Quartet Books, London)

Pevsner, Nikolaus and Wedgwood, Alexandra (1966), *The Buildings of England. Warwickshire* (Penguin Books, London)

Power, Norman (1965), *The Forgotten People: A Challenge to a Caring Community* (Arthur James, Evesham)

Prestige, G.L. (1935), *The Life of Charles Gore* (Heinemann, London)

Rex, J. and Moore, R. (1967), *Race, Community and Conflict, a Study of Sparkbrook* (Oxford University Press, London)

Rogers, Guy (1956), *A Rebel at Heart: the Autobiography of a Nonconforming Churchman*

Salzman, L.F. (1947), *Victoria County History, Warwick vol.IV, Hemlingford Hundred* (Oxford University Press, London)

Skipp, Victor (1970), *Medieval Yardley, the origin and growth of a west midland community* (Phillimore, Chichester)

Skipp, Victor (1983), *The Making of Victorian Birmingham* (the author, Birmingham)

Slater, Terry R. (1984), *A Centenary History of St Agnes, Moseley 1884-1984* (St Agnes PCC, Moseley)

Slater, Terry R. (1998), 'Birmingham's Black and South Asian population', in *Managing a Conurbation. Birmingham and its Region* (Eds A.J. Gerrard and T.R. Slater) (Brewin Books, Studley), 140-55

Slater, Terry R. (2002), *Edgbaston. A History* (Phillimore, Chichester)

Stephens, W.B. (1964), *Victoria County History, Warwickshire vol.VII The City of Birmingham* (Oxford University Press, London)

Sutcliffe, Anthony and Smith, Roger (1974), *History of Birmingham III. Birmingham 1939-1970* (Oxford University Press, London)

Toldervy, William (1762), *England and Wales Described in a Series of Letters*

Upton, Chris (2005), *Living Back-to-Back* (Phillimore, Chichester)

Walker, Benjamin (1935), *Saint Philip's Church Birmingham, and its groom-porter architect* (City of Birmingham School of Printing, Birmingham)

Walker, Tom (1982), *Renew us by Your Spirit* (Hodder and Stoughton, London)

Ward, Roger (2005), *City-State and Nation: Birmingham's Political History, 1830-1940* (Phillimore, Chichester)

Willis-Bund, J.W. (1913), *Victoria County History, Worcester III* (Constable, London)

Wilkinson, John (1993), *Church in Black and White: the Black Christian Tradition in 'Mainstream' Churches* (St Andrew's Press, Edinburgh)

INDEX

References which relate to illustrations only are given in **bold**.

215